EUROPEAN CONSENSUS AND THE LEGITIMACY OF THE EUROPEAN COURT OF HUMAN RIGHTS

In order to be effective, international tribunals should be perceived as legitimate adjudicators. *European Consensus and the Legitimacy of the European Court of Human Rights* provides in-depth analyses on whether European consensus is capable of enhancing the legitimacy of the European Court of Human Rights. Focusing on the method and value of European consensus, it examines the practicalities of consensus identification and application and discusses whether State counting is appropriate in human rights adjudication. With over 30 interviews from judges of the European Court of Human Rights and qualitative analyses of the case law, this book gives readers access to first-hand and up-to-date information and provides an understanding of how the European Court of Human Rights in Strasbourg interprets the European Convention on Human Rights.

KANSTANTSIN DZEHTSIAROU is a Senior Lecturer in law at the University of Surrey and Visiting Professor at the European Humanities University in Vilnius, Lithuania.

EUROPEAN CONSENSUS AND THE LEGITIMACY OF THE EUROPEAN COURT OF HUMAN RIGHTS

KANSTANTSIN DZEHTSIAROU
University of Surrey

CAMBRIDGE
UNIVERSITY PRESS

University Printing House, Cambridge CB2 8BS, United Kingdom

Cambridge University Press is part of the University of Cambridge.

It furthers the University's mission by disseminating knowledge in the pursuit of education, learning and research at the highest international levels of excellence.

www.cambridge.org
Information on this title: www.cambridge.org/9781107041035

© Kanstantsin Dzehtsiarou 2015

This publication is in copyright. Subject to statutory exception and to the provisions of relevant collective licensing agreements, no reproduction of any part may take place without the written permission of Cambridge University Press.

First published 2015

A catalogue record for this publication is available from the British Library

Library of Congress Cataloguing in Publication data
Dzehtsiarou, Kanstantsin, author.
European consensus and the legitimacy of the European Court of Human Rights / Kanstantsin Dzehtsiarou.
 pages cm
ISBN 978-1-107-04103-5 (hardback)
1. European Court of Human Rights. 2. International human rights courts – Europe. I. Title.
KJC5138.D94 2015
342.2408′50269–dc23
2015008277

ISBN 978-1-107-04103-5 Hardback

Cambridge University Press has no responsibility for the persistence or accuracy of URLs for external or third-party internet websites referred to in this publication, and does not guarantee that any content on such websites is, or will remain, accurate or appropriate.

For Larisa

CONTENTS

List of figures *page* xi
Foreword xiii
Acknowledgements xvi
Table of cases xviii
Abbreviations xxiv

1 Introduction 1

2 The concept of European consensus 9

   2.1 Introduction 9

   2.2 Definition of European consensus 10
      2.2.1 Terminology 10
      2.2.2 Level of consensus 14
         2.2.2.1 Consensus at the level of rules 15
         2.2.2.2 Consensus at the level of principles 16

   2.3 Spread of European consensus 17
      2.3.1 Importance of consensus 17
      2.3.2 Reasons for limited deployment of consensus 21

   2.4 Application of European consensus 23
      2.4.1 European consensus in action 24
      2.4.2 Limits of application of the European consensus argument 30
         2.4.2.1 Text of the convention and protocols 30
         2.4.2.2 Historical and political justification 32
         2.4.2.3 Moral sensitivity of the matter at issue 34

   2.5 Conclusion 36

3 Types of consensus 38

   3.1 Introduction 38

3.2 Typology of consensus   39
    3.2.1 Consensus based on comparative analysis of the laws and practices of the Contracting Parties   40
    3.2.2 European consensus based on international treaties   45
    3.2.3 Internal consensus within the respondent State   49
    3.2.4 Consensus among experts   55

3.3 Interactions between different types of consensus   56
    3.3.1 Interaction between European consensus based on comparative law and European consensus based on international treaties   57
    3.3.2 Interaction between European consensus and internal consensus   60
    3.3.3 European consensus and international trends   65

3.4 Conclusion   71

4 Behind the scenes: Comparative analysis within the Court   72

4.1 Introduction   72

4.2 Purposes of comparative law   74
    4.2.1 Fit and vision   74
    4.2.2 Information and persuasion   77

4.3. What is wrong with comparison? Criticism of comparative legal research conducted by the Court   78

4.4 Evolution of comparative legal research   82
    4.4.1 Limited factual justification   82
    4.4.2 Recourse to previous findings   84
    4.4.3 Comparative law research prepared by the ECtHR   86
    4.4.4 Comparative research conducted by third parties   97

4.5 Key challenges   101
    4.5.1 Comprehensive comparative research   102
    4.5.2 Legal provisions in context   105
    4.5.3 Subject matter of comparison   109
    4.5.4 Translation of legal terms   111

4.6 Conclusion   114

CONTENTS

5 Criticism of European consensus   115

   5.1 Introduction   115

   5.2 'Anti-majoritarian argument' against consensus   116

   5.3 The minority rights challenge   122

   5.4 Criticism of European consensus as a determinant of evolutive interpretation and the margin of appreciation   129

      5.4.1 Criticism of evolutive interpretation and the margin of appreciation   130

      5.4.2 European consensus: Between margin of appreciation and evolutive interpretation   132

          5.4.2.1 European consensus and the margin of appreciation   132

          5.4.2.2 European consensus and evolutive interpretation   138

   5.5 Conclusion   142

6 Legitimacy of the Court and legitimacy of its judgments   143

   6.1 Introduction   143

   6.2 Lost legitimacy?   144

   6.3 International constitutional challenges   149

      6.3.1 State consent   149

      6.3.2 Dialogue between the ECtHR and the Contracting Parties   155

      6.3.3 Consensus as a source of international law   158

      6.3.4 Subsidiarity   165

   6.4 National constitutional challenges   167

   6.5 Conclusion   175

7 European consensus: Perceptions of the ECtHR judges   177

   7.1 Introduction   177

   7.2 Research design and methodology   178

7.3 Why does the Court use European consensus?   182

7.4 How persuasive is European consensus?   189

7.5 How satisfactory is comparative research that leads to European consensus?   196

7.6 Criticism from within the palace walls   201

7.7 Conclusion   206

8 Conclusion   207

Appendix 1: List of interviewees   212
Appendix 2: List of the Grand Chamber judgments with international or comparative law   215
Index   225

FIGURES

4.1. Judgments of the Grand Chamber in which comparative law materials were deployed (1998–2013). *page* 95
4.2. Judgments of the Grand Chamber in which comparative or international law materials were deployed (1998–2013).   96
4.3. Judgments of the Grand Chamber in which comparative law materials were deployed and where both comparative and international law materials were deployed (1998–2013).   97

FOREWORD

In her introductory remarks to the *Dialogue between Judges*, held on the occasion of the opening of the judicial year 2005, Françoise Tulkens described the 'complementary relationship between the domestic legal order and the international order' as being vital to the defence of fundamental rights. This complementarity is essential in order to maintain the delicate balance in the relationship between the Strasbourg system and the domestic systems. The margin of appreciation doctrine enables the European Court of Human Rights to impose self-restraint on its power of review, accepting that domestic authorities are best placed to settle a dispute. The technique in question remains a topical subject, lying at the heart of a debate opposing judicial activism and restraint, and has given rise to significant consideration in recent years. This has resulted in point 12 (b) of the Brighton Declaration (19–20 April 2012), which calls for the Convention to be amended by the inclusion of a reference to the margin of appreciation in its Preamble and also suggests that the Court should apply this doctrine when examining the admissibility of applications.

Among the factors used in particular to circumscribe the extent of the national margin of appreciation, a major role is played by the existence or absence of European consensus, derived from a comparative analysis. Admittedly it is not always a decisive factor, but it may confer particular legitimacy on the Court's judgments. Having thoroughly discussed the concept of European consensus, Kanstantsin Dzehtsiarou explores the different types of consensus. Based on examples from case law, he identifies four types: consensus identified through comparative analysis of the legislation of Contracting Parties; international consensus identified through international treaties; internal consensus in the respondent State; and, lastly, expert consensus.

In a note to which I contributed for the *Dialogue between Judges* in 2008, the notion of consensus was described as follows: 'Consensus in the context of the European Convention on Human Rights is generally understood as being the basis for the evolution of Convention standards through the case law of the European Court of Human Rights.' The Convention is indeed commonly referred to as 'a living instrument which ... must be interpreted in the light of present-day conditions' and, as stated in its Preamble, it was adopted in particular for the further realisation of human rights and fundamental freedoms. It is clear therefore that the rights and freedoms enumerated in the Convention are not set in stone with regard to their substantive content, which has to evolve along with developments in law, society and science. This evolutive interpretation of the Convention makes it possible to adjust the Convention norms to new challenges generated by the complex development of European societies. While the emergence of European consensus enables the Court to underpin its evolutive interpretation of the Convention, no weakening in the level of protection could be established from any less protective consensus that may be discerned in the future.

An absence of consensus is not necessarily an obstacle to jurisprudential evolution. While the Court generally shows restraint where there is no consensus, the adoption of innovative solutions concerning questions that are not the subject of consensus is sometimes perceived as a sign of judicial activism. Such a conclusion may appear hasty and excessive. It is true that the lack of a common legal approach has not prevented the Court from identifying the existence of a general trend. Thus, in its *Christine Goodwin* judgment of 11 July 2002, concerning a lack of legal recognition of a gender change and the inability for a transsexual having undergone such an operation to marry a person of the opposite sex, the Court attached 'less importance to the lack of evidence of a common European approach to the resolution of the legal and practical problems posed, than to the clear and uncontested evidence of a continuing international trend in favour not only of increased social acceptance of transsexuals but of legal recognition of the new sexual identity of postoperative transsexuals'. However, rather than judicial activism, I would prefer to speak here of a pragmatic progressivism.

European consensus, as has already been said, is sometimes not the decisive factor. This has been shown by recent developments in case law. Even where there is consensus, the Court may impose on itself a degree of restraint. The following example gave rise to a dissenting opinion by Françoise Tulkens and a number of other judges. Despite the existence in a majority of Council of Europe Member States of a consensus towards allowing abortion on broader grounds than those admitted in Irish law, in *A., B. and C. v. Ireland* (judgment of 16 December 2010) the Court nevertheless did 'not consider that this consensus decisively narrow[ed] the broad margin of appreciation of the State'.

Can it therefore be said that the Court's approach to the notion of consensus is becoming increasingly relativised?

Lastly, it is also possible to look at the reasons for the existence or absence of consensus in order to resolve an issue. While it is easier to identify a consensus in the light of State practice (legislation, case law, practice of public authorities), the reasons for an absence of consensus are often difficult to fathom (lack of any official stance on a very new problem, political reasons, lack of interest in questions which are of concern only to minorities, etc.). When faced with an absence of consensus, or even with a comparative legislative vacuum concerning a real question of society, the self-imposition of judicial restraint may not always be the best answer. For a 'negative consensus' may, in extremely rare cases, stem from the deliberate policy of a State not to legislate. But a lack of will to legislate may also be explained by general indifference. Can we still talk of consensus, albeit in a negative sense? In such situations, could a lack of common ground necessarily entail consequences as to the possibility of self-limitation on the part of the Court? This remains rather doubtful.

Kanstantsin Dzehtsiarou's research is based on comparative analysis within the Court. His critique is essential to an appraisal of the legitimacy of the Court and its judgments. Based on a pertinent dialogue with the interviewed judges, Kanstantsin Dzehtsiarou's book is an important contribution to legal scholarship.

Dean Spielmann
President of the European Court of Human Rights

ACKNOWLEDGEMENTS

This book is the result of seven years of research, which was fun most of the time and painful on some rare occasions. I want to thank everyone who helped me during these seven years. They were truly unbelievable.

If anybody told me ten years ago that in ten years I would be a law lecturer in the United Kingdom and that I would publish my book with Cambridge University Press, I would have thought that it was a bad joke. About ten years ago, I was finishing my undergraduate studies in law in Gomel State University in Belarus with the prospect of being a prosecutorial investigator somewhere in rural Belarus. This has not happened.

There have been a few unbelievable turns in my career during the last ten years. In 2005, I won a highly competitive Chevening/Soros Foundation scholarship to do a master's course in contemporary European studies at the University of Sussex. I thank the Soros Foundation and the British Foreign and Commonwealth Office for this. When I came to the United Kingdom, I hardly knew what contemporary European studies was. That said, I did manage to graduate successfully. Then, I received a fantastic Ad Astra Scholarship from University College Dublin, which made some parts of my research project on European consensus possible. I would like to thank UCD School of Law and I would also like to personally thank Colin Scott, John Jackson, Joseph McMahon and Imelda Maher for giving me this chance. My thanks also go to my PhD supervisors, Marie Luce Paris and Graham Finley, for their helpful comments and support. I would also like to address a special thank you to Fiona de Londras, who was one of my supervisors and someone who influenced this book very much. She is a wonderful mentor and a very good friend.

I then moved to the University of Surrey as a law lecturer, and this university has also supported me by funding some of my numerous trips to Strasbourg. The main purpose of these trips was to annoy judges by asking them questions about European consensus. I wish to thank Rob Jago and Indira Carr for their support.

ACKNOWLEDGEMENTS

Throughout these years, I discussed the ideas of the book with nearly all my colleagues irrespective of the area of law they were working in. I would like to thank a few of them – Rudy Baker, Eva Brems, Filippo Fontanelli, Sergey Golubok, Theodore Konstadinides, Luke Mason, Alastair Mowbray, Arman Sarvarian and Vassilis Tzevelekos – for their comments on various chapters of this book.

I would like to thank members of my rather small family who supported me. Skype conversations about my book with my brother Dmitriy were surprisingly helpful. It is sometimes extremely useful to explain your work to someone who is not a lawyer and has very little to do with law. I want to thank my friends in Belarus, Ireland, the UK, France, Ukraine and countries all over the world for tolerating me.

I want to thank my students from UCD, University of Surrey and European Humanities University: some of the ideas in this book originated from the classrooms in these universities. I would like to thank Charlie Eastaugh and Emile McHarsky-Todoroff.

I would like to thank my friends and colleagues in Strasbourg who helped me and supported me in my research. I would also like to thank all the judges who kindly agreed to talk to me on the topic of European consensus. I would also like to sincerely thank Michael O'Boyle and other members of the Court's Registry for the time they spent with me discussing European consensus.

The staff at Cambridge University Press were very helpful and supportive during the preparation of the book. I would like to thank Helen Francis, Sinead Moloney and Elizabeth Spicer for their help.

Thank you very much!

TABLE OF CASES

A., B. and C. v. Ireland, Application No 25579/05, Judgment of 16 December 2010
Ahorugeze v. Sweden, Application No 37075/09, Judgment of 27 October 2011
A.K. and L. v. Croatia, Application No 37956/11, Judgment of 8 January 2013
Al-Adsani v. the United Kingdom, Application No 35763/97, Judgment of 21 November 2001
Aliev v. Ukraine, 7 August 2003, Application No 41220/98, Judgment of 29 April 2003
Allen v. the United Kingdom, Application No 25424/09, Judgment of 12 July 2013
Al-Saadoon and Mufdhi v. the United Kingdom, Application No 61498/08, Judgment of 2 March 2010
Anheuser-Busch Inc. v. Portugal, Application No 73049/01, Judgment of 11 January 2007
Animal Defenders International v. the United Kingdom, Application No 48876/08, Judgment of 22 April 2013
Appleby and others v. the United Kingdom, Application No 44306/98, Judgment of 6 May 2003
B. v. France, Application No 13343/87, Judgment of 25 March 1992
B. and L. v. the United Kingdom, Application No 36536/02, Judgment of 13 September 2005
Babar Ahmad and others v. the United Kingdom, Application No 24027/07, 11949/08, 36742/08, 66911/09 and 67354/09, Judgment of 10 April 2012
Banković and others v. Belgium et al., Application No 52207/99, Decision of 12 December 2001
Bayatyan v. Armenia, Application No 23459/03, Judgment of 7 July 2011
Beard v. the United Kingdom, Application No 24882/94, Judgment of 18 January 2001
Berisha v. Switzerland, Application No 948/12, Judgment of 30 July 2013
Borgers v. Belgium, Application No 12005/86, Judgment of 30 October 1991
Bosphorus Hava Yolları Turizm ve Ticaret Anonim Şirketi v. Ireland, Application No 45036/98, Judgment of 30 June 2005
Broniowski v. Poland, Application No 31443/96, Judgment of 22 June 2004
Burden v. United Kingdom, Application No 13378/05, Judgment of 29 April 2008
Burdov (No 2) v. Russia, Application No 33509/04, Judgment of 15 January 2009
Case 'Relating to Certain Aspects of the Laws on the Use of Languages in Education in Belgium' (Preliminary Objections), Application No 1474/62, 1677/62, 1691/62, 1769/63, 1994/63 and 2126/64, Judgment of 9 February 1967

TABLE OF CASES

Chapman v. *the United Kingdom*, Application No 27238/95, Judgment of 18 January 2001
Christine Goodwin v. *the United Kingdom*, Application No 28957/95, Judgment of 11 July 2002
Cossey v. *the United Kingdom*, Application No 10843/84, Judgment of 27 September 1990
Coster v. *the United Kingdom*, Application No 24876/94, Judgment of 18 January 2001
Cruz Varas and others v. *Sweden*, Application No 15576/89, Judgment of 20 March 1991
Cyprus v. *Turkey*, Application No 25781/94, Judgment of 10 May 2001
D.H. and others v. *the Czech Republic*, Application No 57325/00, Judgment of 13 November 2007
Del Río Prada v. *Spain*, Application No 42750/09, Judgment of 21 October 2013
Demir and Baykara v. *Turkey*, Application No 34503/97, Judgment of 12 November 2008
Dickson v. *the United Kingdom*, Application No 44362/04, Judgment of 4 December 2007
Dudgeon v. *the United Kingdom*, Application No 7525/76, Judgment of 23 September 1981
E.B. v. *France*, Application No 43546/02, Judgment of 22 January 2008
Enea v. *Italy*, Application No 74912/01, Judgment of 17 September 2009
Evans v. *the United Kingdom*, Application No 6339/05, Judgment of 10 April 2007
Fabris v. *France*, Application No 16574/08, Judgment of 7 February 2013
Folgerø and others v. *Norway*, Application No 15472/02, Judgment of 29 June 2007
Fretté v. *France*, Application No 36515/97, Judgment of 26 February 2002
Gäfgen v. *Germany*, Application No 22978/05, Judgment of 1 June 2010
Gas and Dubois v. *France*, Application No 25951/07, Judgment of 15 March 2012
Georgian Labour Party v. *Georgia*, Application No 9103/04, Judgment of 8 July 2008
Golder v. *the United Kingdom*, Application No 4451/70, Judgment of 21 February 1975
Grandrath v. *the Federal Republic of Germany*, Application No 2299/64, Commission report of 12 December 1966
Greece v. *the United Kingdom*, Application No 176/56, Judgment of 26 September 1958
Greens and M. T. v. *the United Kingdom*, Application No 60041/08 and 60054/08, Judgment of 23 November 2010
Gustafsson v. *Sweden*, Application No 18/1995/524/610, Judgment of 25 April 1996
H. v. *Finland*, Application No 37359/09, Judgment of 13 November 2012
Handyside v. *the United Kingdom*, Application No 5493/72, Judgment of 7 December 1976
Harkins and Edwards v. *the United Kingdom*, Application No 9146/07 and 32650/07, Judgment of 17 January 2012
Hirsi Jamaa and others v. *Italy*, Application No 27765/09, Judgment of 23 February 2012
Hirst v. *the United Kingdom (No 2)*, Application No 74025/01, Judgment of 6 October 2005

Horváth and Kiss v. *Hungary*, Application No 11146/11, Judgment of 29 January 2013
Ilaşcu and others v. *Moldova and Russia*, Application No 48787/99, Judgment of 8 July 2004
Issa and others v. *Turkey*, Application No 31821/96, Judgment of 16 November 2004
J.A. Pye (Oxford) Ltd and J.A. Pye (Oxford) Land Ltd v. *the United Kingdom*, Application No 44302/02, Judgment of 30 August 2007
Jane Smith v. *the United Kingdom*, Application No 25154/94, Judgment of 18 January 2001
Janowiec and others v. *Russia*, Application No 55508/07 and 29520/09, Judgment of 16 April 2012
Johnston and others v. *Ireland*, Application No 9697/82, Judgment of 18 December 1986
K.U. v. *Finland*, Application No 2872/02, Judgment of 2 December 2008
Kafkaris v. *Cyprus*, Application No 21906/04, Judgment of 12 February 2008
Karner v. *Austria*, Application No 40016/98, Judgment of 24 July 2003
Kearns v. *France*, Application No 35991/04, Judgment of 10 January 2008
Kimlya and others v. *Russia*, Application No 76836/01 and 32782/03, Judgment of 1 October 2010
Kiyutin v. *Russia*, Application No 2700/10, Judgment of 10 March 2011
Kononov v. *Latvia*, Application No 36376/04, Judgment of 17 May 2010
Konstantin Markin v. *Russia*, Application No 30078/06, Judgment of 22 March 2012
Kurt v. *Turkey*, Application No 24276/94, Judgment of 25 May 1998
L. and V. v. *Austria*, Application No 39392/98 and 39829/98, Judgment of 9 January 2003
Lashin v. *Russia*, Application No 33117/02, Judgment of 22 January 2013
Lautsi and others v. *Italy*, Application No 30814/06, Judgment of 18 March 2011
Lee v. *the United Kingdom*, Application No 25289/94, Judgment of 18 January 2001
Leyla Şahin v. *Turkey*, Application No 44774/98, Judgment of 10 November 2005
Loizidou v. *Turkey (Preliminary Objections)*, Application No 15318/89, Judgment of 23 March 1995
M.C. v. *Bulgaria*, Application No 39272/98, Judgment of 4 December 2003
M.S.S. v. *Belgium and Greece*, Application No 30696/09, Judgment of 21 January 2011
Makaratzis v. *Greece*, Application No 50385/99, Judgment of 20 December 2004
Mamatkulov and Askarov v. *Turkey*, Application No 46827/99 and 46951/99, Judgment of 4 February 2005
Marckx v. *Belgium*, Application No 6833/74, Judgment of 13 June 1979
Matthews v. *the United Kingdom*, Application No 24833/94, Judgment of 18 February 1999
Mazurek v. *France*, Application No 34406/97, Judgment of 1 February 2000
McCann and others v. *the United Kingdom*, Application No 18984/91, Judgment of 27 September 1995
Medvedyev and others v. *France*, Application No 3394/03, Judgment of 29 March 2010
Mehmet Şentürk and Bekir Şentürk v. *Turkey*, Application No 13423/09, Judgment of 9 April 2013
Micallef v. *Malta*, Application No 17056/06, Judgment of 15 October 2009

Murphy v. *Ireland*, Application No 44179/98, Judgment of 10 July 2003
Nachova and others v. *Bulgaria*, Application No 43577/98 and 43579/98, Judgment of 6 July 2005
Nataliya Mikhaylenko v. *Ukraine*, Application No 49069/11, Judgment of 30 May 2013
Neulinger and Shuruk v. *Switzerland*, Application No 41615/07, Judgment of 6 July 2010
Neumeister v. *Austria*, Application No 1936/63, Judgment of 27 June 1968
Norris v. *Ireland*, Application No 10581/83, Judgment of 26 October 1988
Öcalan v. *Turkey*, Application No 46221/99, Judgment of 12 May 2005
Odièvre v. *France*, Application No 42326/98, Judgment of 13 February 2003
Opuz v. *Turkey*, Application No 33401/02, Judgment of 9 June 2009
Oršuš and others v. *Croatia*, Application No 15766/03, Judgment of 16 March 2010
Perdigão v. *Portugal*, Application No 24768/06, Judgment of 16 November 2010
Pretty v. *the United Kingdom*, Application No 2346/02, Judgment of 29 April 2002
Prince Hans-Adam II of Liechtenstein v. *Germany*, Application No 42527/98, Judgment of 12 July 2001
Ramanauskas v. *Lithuania*, Application No 74420/01, Judgment of 5 February 2008
Ramirez Sanchez v. *France*, Application No 59450/00, Judgment of 4 July 2006
Rantsev v. *Cyprus and Russia*, Application No 25965/04, Judgment of 7 January 2010
Republican Party of Russia v. *Russia*, Application No 12976/07, Judgment of 12 April 2011
S. and Marper v. *the United Kingdom*, Application No 30562/04 and 30566/04, Judgment of 4 December 2008
S.H. and others v. *Austria*, Application No 57813/00, Judgment of 3 November 2011
Saadi v. *the United Kingdom*, Application No 13229/03, Judgment of 29 January 2008
Sanoma Uitgevers B.V. v. *the Netherlands*, Application No 38224/03, Judgment of 14 September 2010
Schalk and Kopf v. *Austria*, Application No 30141/04, Judgment of 24 June 2010
Scoppola v. *Italy (No 2)*, Application No 10249/03, Judgment of 17 September 2009
Scordino v. *Italy (No 1)*, Application No 36813/97, Judgment of 29 March 2006
Sejdić and Finci v. *Bosnia and Herzegovina*, Application No 27996/06 and 34836/06, Judgment of 22 December 2009
Sejdovic v. *Italy*, Application No 56581/00, Judgment of 1 March 2006
Selmouni v. *France*, Application No 25803/94, Judgment of 28 July 1999
Sergey Zolotukhin v. *Russia*, Application No 14939/03, Judgment of 10 February 2003
Şerife Yiğit v. *Turkey*, Application No 3976/05, Judgment of 2 November 2011
Sheffield and Horsham v. *the United Kingdom*, Application No 22985/93 and 23390/94, Judgment of 30 July 1998
Shindler v. *the United Kingdom*, Application No 19840/09, Judgment of 7 May 2013
Shofman v. *Russia*, Application No 74826/01, Judgment of 24 November 2005
Siliadin v. *France*, Application No 73316/01, Judgment of 26 July 2005
Sindicatul 'Păstorul cel Bun' v. *Romania*, Application No 2330/09, Judgment of 9 July 2013

Sitaropoulos and Giakoumopoulos v. *Greece*, Application No 42202/07, Judgment of 15 March 2012
Slivenko v. *Latvia*, Application No 48321/99, Judgment of 9 October 2003
Société Colas Est and others v. *France*, Application No 37971/97, Judgment of 16 July 2002
Söderman v. *Sweden*, Application No 5786/08, Judgment of 12 November 2013
Sommerfeld v. *Germany*, Application No 31871/96, Judgment of 8 July 2003
Stafford v. *the United Kingdom*, Application No 46295/99, Judgment of 28 May 2002
Stanev v. *Bulgaria*, Application No 36760/06, Judgment of 17 January 2012
Stec and others v. *the United Kingdom*, Application No 65731/01 and 65900/01, Judgment of 12 April 2006
Stoll v. *Switzerland*, Application No 69698/01, Judgment of 10 December 2007
Stübing v. *Germany*, Application No 43547/08, Judgment of 12 April 2012
Şükran Aydın and others v. *Turkey*, Application No 49197/06, 23196/07, 50242/08, 60912/08 and 14871/09, Judgment of 22 January 2013
Sutherland v. *the United Kingdom*, Application No 25186/94, Decision of 1 July 1997
T. v. *the United Kingdom*, Application No 24724/94, Judgment of 16 December
Tănase v. *Moldova*, Application No 7/08, Judgment of 27 April 2010
Tănase and Chirtoacă v. *Moldova*, Application No 7/08, Judgment of 18 November 2008
TV Vest AS and Rogaland Pensjonistparti v. *Norway*, Application No 21132/05, Judgment of 11 December 2008
Tyrer v. *the United Kingdom*, Application No 5856/72, Judgment of 25 April 1978
Ünal Tekeli v. *Turkey*, Application No 29865/96, Judgment of 16 November 2004
V. v. *the United Kingdom*, Application No 24888/94, Judgment of 16 December 1999
Vallianatos and others v. *Greece*, Application No 29381/09 and 32684/09, Judgment of 7 November 2013
Van der Heijden v. *the Netherlands*, Application No 42857/05, Judgment of 3 April 2012
Vilho Eskelinen and others v. *Finland*, Application No 63235/00, Judgment of 19 April 2007
Vinter and others v. *the United Kingdom*, Application No 66069/09, 130/10 and 3896/10, Judgment of 9 July 2013
Vo v. *France*, Application No 53924/00, Judgment of 8 July 2004
Von Hannover v. *Germany*, Application No 59320/00, Judgment of 24 June 2004
X. v. *Austria*, Application No 5591/72, Commission decision of 2 April 1973
X. and others v. *Austria*, Application No 19010/07, Judgment of 19 February 2013
X., Y. and Z. v. *the United Kingdom*, Application No 21830/93, Judgment of 22 April 1997
Yumak and Sadak v. *Turkey*, Application No 10226/03, Judgment of 8 July 2008
Z. and others v. *the United Kingdom*, Application No 29392/95, Judgment of 10 May 2001
Zaunegger v. *Germany*, Application No 22028/04, Judgment of 3 December 2009

TABLE OF CASES

US Supreme Court

Bowers v. Hardwick, 478 US 186 (1986)
Lawrence v. Texas, 539 US 558 (2003)
Roper v. Simmons, 543 US 551, 617 (2005)

Supreme Court of Ireland

Attorney General v. X [1992] 1 IR 1 (Supreme Court of Ireland, 5 March 1992)

Inter-American Court of Human Rights

Atala Riffo and Daughters v. Chile, Judgment of 24 February 2012

UN Human Rights Committee

Shirin Aumeeruddy-Cziffra and 19 other Mauritian women v. Mauritius, Communication No R.9/35 (2 May 1978), UN Doc. Supp. No 40 (A/36/40) at 134 (1981)

African Commission on Human Rights

Constitutional Rights Project and another v. Nigeria, Communication No 43/95 and 150/96 (1999)

ABBREVIATIONS

ECHR	European Convention on Human Rights
ECtHR	European Court of Human Rights
ECJ	European Court of Justice
EU	European Union
HUDOC	Human Rights Documents (the ECtHR database)
IACtHR	Inter-American Court of Human Rights
ICJ	International Court of Justice
LGBT	lesbians, gays, bisexuals, transsexuals
MP	member of parliament
NGO	non-governmental organisation
UK	United Kingdom of Great Britain and Northern Ireland
UN	United Nations
UN HRC	United Nations Human Rights Committee
US	United States of America
VCLT	Vienna Convention on the Law of Treaties
WTO	World Trade Organization

1

Introduction

Has the European Court of Human Rights (ECtHR or Court) lost its legitimacy? The answer to this question is perhaps 'no'. If this was the case, the Contracting Parties would stop executing judgments of the Court, the applicants would stop bringing their complaints to the Court and, finally, the Contracting Parties would denounce the European Convention on Human Rights (ECHR or Convention). Another option might be that the ECtHR would continue to exist without having any real impact on human rights standards in Europe, and its judgments would lose much of their value. This has not yet happened.

International tribunals, including the ECtHR, face a substantial structural deficiency; they operate within systems that lack the coercive capacity to enforce their judgments. International courts thus depend, to a greater degree than domestic courts, on the legitimacy of their judgments as a basis upon which to encourage, and in effect coerce, compliance. The *prima facie* legitimacy of the ECtHR and its judgments were confirmed by the consent of the Contracting Parties. However, the Court cannot endlessly justify each and every judgment, especially since the original intent of the drafters has never played a primary role in the decision-making of the ECtHR. This point can be substantiated by the recent fierce attacks on the ECtHR that occurred in a few States and which were backed up by the arguments of illegitimate judicial interventions. For this reason, it must be seen whether legitimacy can be generated other than from the 'original consent' model. The key argument of this book is that European consensus can enhance the legitimacy of the ECtHR and its judgments. In order to achieve this, European consensus should be based on real evidence and it should be consistently applied in the case law.

European consensus is a tool of interpretation of the Convention that the ECtHR uses in its decision-making. The reason for the application of European consensus is that the meaning of some Convention terms can be linked to their common usage by the Contracting Parties. European consensus can be conceptualised as a tool of interpretation of the Convention which prioritises a particular solution to a complex human rights issue if this solution is supported by the majority of the 47 Contracting Parties. This support is identified through comparative analysis of the laws and practices of the Contracting Parties and international law. European consensus is a rebuttable presumption, which means that the Contracting Parties are presumed to be in violation of the Convention if their solution diverges from the solution adopted by the majority, unless they can provide sufficient and weighty reasons for such divergence.

This book is divided into two parts. The first part aims to establish how European consensus operates in the Court's reasoning. The overarching theme of this part is the method of application of European consensus. Chapters 2–4 explain the development of European consensus and examine how the Court has improved its methodology of identification and application of consensus. The central argument of this book is that only European consensus which is consistently applied and based on rigorous and verifiable data can enhance the legitimacy of the ECtHR. Chapters 2–4 mainly focus on the first part of the argument dealing with the application of European consensus.

It is suggested here that European consensus is actually not an entirely accurate term. The word 'consensus' presumes unanimity, while unanimity is nearly impossible to establish in real life and often it is useless for the Court's reasoning. Arguably, even if just one Contracting Party has a legal regulation which differs from the laws of all other Contracting Parties, then literal consensus cannot be established. One has to bear in mind that the consensus argument is often deployed by the ECtHR when the national legal norm or practice under scrutiny diverts from commonly accepted legal practices of the Contracting Parties. What the Court usually means by consensus is a 'trend'.

Identification of European consensus can be divided into three stages: preliminary stage, stage of assessment and stage of deployment. At the first stage, the Court prepares comparative law materials that describe the laws and practices of the Contracting Parties. It is a comparative exercise which happens behind the scenes, and the Court usually only includes a very short summary of often quite lengthy reports prepared by the Registry of the ECtHR. The Court's approach to comparative law has become much more professional in the last 10–15 years. The Court has invested resources in the creation and development of the Research and Library Division within the Court's Registry, which prepares independent comparative law reports upon the request of the judge-rapporteur[1] in cases of high importance. The fact that the ECtHR has access to verifiable and objective information creates a foundation for the proper application of real, not just perceived, European consensus.

At the second stage, the Court analyses the outcome of a comparative study and decides whether consensus can be established. The Court does not need nigh unanimity to establish consensus. In a number of cases, a trend in a particular direction has been enough to trigger the European consensus argument. This stage is not automatic, and the judges have to decide on a number of dilemmas, including whether the number of States is enough to constitute consensus and the level of abstraction that European consensus should be established on. European consensus is possible on the level of principles or rules. If consensus is established at the level of principles, it reflects a general agreement of the Contracting Parties in relation to a certain fundamental issue that might need further interpretation. For example, the Contracting Parties might agree that national minorities must be protected, but this principle can lead to various, even sometimes mutually exclusive rules that ensure such protection. In contrast, rules offer much more precise regulations that prescribe certain behaviour. The level at which consensus or the lack thereof is established might have an impact on the following stage because consensus on the level of rules is much more straightforward and can claim a higher degree of persuasiveness in comparison with consensus on the level of principles.

At the stage of deployment, the Court considers whether consensus or lack thereof should influence the outcome of the case. It is argued here that European consensus establishes a rebuttable presumption in favour of the regulation adopted by the majority of the Contracting Parties. This means that European consensus is not applied automatically, and the ECtHR judges retain a great deal of discretion in applying it. Having said that, the Court should not apply consensus arbitrarily, and if the Court decides not to follow consensus, it has to clearly and convincingly explain its reasons. The particularities of the historical and political development of a respondent State or moral sensitivity on the matter at issue are among these possible reasons.

---

[1] Pursuant to Rule 49-2 of Rules of Court where an application is made under Article 34 of the Convention and its examination by a chamber or a committee seems justified, the president of the section to which the case has been assigned shall designate a judge as judge-rapporteur, who shall examine the application.

Consensus is not homogeneous as the Court uses various sources in order to establish consensus: national law and practice, international treaties, opinion of the majority of people within the Contracting Party and expert opinion. While there are situations in which all or some of these types of consensus point in the same direction, a more complex scenario is when different types of consensus contradict each other and the Court has to choose one. This book argues that European consensus can enhance the legitimacy of the ECtHR by improving the predictability and foreseeability of the Court's judgment. In order to achieve this, the Court should establish clear rules of selection on the type of consensus to be followed. It is suggested that European consensus based on comparison of rules and practices of the Contracting Parties usually contains more precise regulations than consensus based on international treaties. The latter ordinarily requires implementation and therefore it cannot claim the same level of persuasiveness as consensus based on laws and practices of the Contracting Parties. Having said that, the Court might have reasons to follow the consensus based on international treaties, but these reasons again have to be clearly articulated. European consensus can also support a standard that is contrary to the beliefs that are held by the majority of the population in a particular State. In this case, the Court should be very careful about 'trumping' European consensus, as such 'trumping' can negatively impact the legitimacy and the credibility of the ECtHR.

The method of identification and application of consensus has been criticised by a number of commentators. This criticism is conceptualised as procedural criticism, and it is argued that the Court has taken such critical comments on board. The ECtHR has become more consistent in its application of European consensus in recent years. It now influences the outcomes of cases and it is based on rigorous comparative legal analysis.

The second part of the book deals with the value of European consensus. It mainly discusses why European consensus can be conceptualised as a tool that enhances legitimacy and whether it is perceived as such by the key decision-makers at the ECtHR. Chapters 5–7 aim to examine this argument.

This part opens the analysis of the substantive criticism of European consensus, which claims that it is normatively wrong to rely on counting States in human rights adjudication. The key theme of this criticism is the 'anti-majoritarian' argument, which questions the appropriateness of majoritarian decision-making in human rights adjudication. Human rights norms are anti-majoritarian because they are supposed to protect individuals who are often quite unpopular in society, such as minorities, prisoners or those on trial. Their interests are unlikely to be safeguarded through democratic majoritarian decision-making. Human rights are there to rectify this drawback of democracy. For that reason, one can argue that human rights are anti-majoritarian. At the same time, the European consensus argument relies upon what the majority of the Contracting Parties has decided; hence, it can be conceptualised as majoritarian decision-making. Those commentators who have developed the anti-majoritarian argument claim that this is a paradoxical situation, namely that a profoundly anti-majoritarian concept (human rights) relies on a majoritarian tool (European consensus) for its application. Chapter 5 argues that this description is not entirely accurate and that substantive criticism of European consensus is far-fetched.

This book offers a number of reasons in favour of rejecting the anti-majoritarian argument. The key counter-argument here is the manner in which the ECtHR has applied European consensus. It is not an absolute or automatic argument – even if European consensus is established, the Court continues to analyse the situation. If there are serious reasons to disregard or trump European consensus, it should be disregarded, but these reasons should be clearly articulated. If European consensus in fact endangers minority rights then it can be, and is likely to be, put aside by the Court. In contrast, this book shows that on a number of occasions consensual decision-making has been beneficial and furthers the protection of minority rights.

The anti-majoritarian argument does not take into account the fact that human rights are anti-majoritarian in the sense that they prevent arbitrary decision-making of the majority of people within a particular State or region. The Court does not normally take the opinion of the majority of the European population into account because it is very hard to identify, and the legitimacy of deployment of such opinion is doubtful. The Court uses norms and practices that have been approved by the authorities of the Contracting Parties. This is important for two reasons. First, it is presumed that national legal systems have domestic safeguards against human rights violations. It is perfectly possible that such a system has failed to operate in a particular case in a particular State but it is hard to imagine that it has failed across Europe. Second, European consensus operates in the European context, and there is a much higher average level of human rights protection in Europe than in some other regions or worldwide. Therefore, the threat to human rights protection as identified by the anti-majoritarian argument is far-fetched.

The proponents of the anti-majoritarian argument suggest replacing European consensus with reliance on the moral prevalence of human rights in legitimising the ECtHR judgments. Human rights norms are often abstract and do not offer a clear solution in hard cases. Moreover, people can disagree which solution is the most appropriate. This is the case especially if the Court wants to use evolutive interpretation to 'update' human rights protection to the current-day standards. European consensus offers the most objective and verifiable way of identifying the 'tipping point' necessary for evolution. Moreover, both the margin of appreciation and evolutive interpretation have been criticised for lacking clear and objective factors that would delineate their scope. This book argues that among the factors available to the ECtHR, European consensus is the most clear and objective if it is applied consistently.

After discussing the main strands of substantive criticism, the book turns to a discussion on the legitimacy of the ECtHR and shows why European consensus helps to minimise certain legitimacy challenges that the ECtHR is facing. European consensus is an implicit consent of the Contracting Parties to accept a particular solution as a common standard. Central to this book is the argument that European consensus integrates decisions made by national authorities within the Court's reasoning, thereby supporting a synergistic relationship between the ECtHR case law and the laws and practices of the Contracting Parties. Consensus is a means of dialogue between the ECtHR and the Contracting Parties, which can further their cooperation in the area of human rights protection.

It is also argued here that the Court's legitimacy can be improved if it is seen by the stakeholders as an institution that merely implements legal norms and not as an institution that pushes its own political agenda forward, concealing it behind a legalistic smokescreen. Human rights provisions are broad and they can often justify conflicting solutions for hard cases. The Court needs a more precise interpretatory mechanism that can be connected to the sources of international law. It is argued that European consensus can be linked to customary norms or to general principles of law, which are both sources of international law.

European consensus helps to enhance legitimacy through ensuring the Court's subsidiary function and preventing unacceptable judicial activism. The Contracting Parties continue to question the legitimacy of the Court's interferences into the areas which were traditionally covered by State sovereignty. The Contracting Parties even decided to include a reminder that the Court's role is subsidiary into the text of the Convention.[2] It seems that the Contracting Parties take subsidiarity seriously; this means that the States wish to participate in deciding complex and sensitive human rights issues. European consensus is an avenue for such participation. Through consensus, the Contracting Parties can influence the interpretation of the Convention, and perhaps this creates a sense of common ownership of the Convention case law.

This books ends with a discussion on the perceptions that judges have about the European consensus argument. Chapter 7 is mostly based on the interviews that were conducted with the sitting and former judges of the ECtHR. Thirty-three judges and many more lawyers of the Registry were interviewed for this project, and the most representative quotes from these interviews are incorporated into this chapter. The aim here is to prove that the judges consider European consensus as a legitimate tool of interpretation. This chapter presents the views of the judges about the reasons why the Court deploys European consensus. While the legitimacy of a particular aspect of a judgment is hard to prove, the book aims to determine whether the judges see European consensus as such. If so, it is safe to suggest that the Court will continue to use European consensus in its reasoning. The majority of the judges interviewed considered European consensus as a legitimate tool of interpretation but they also saw its limitations. European consensus is a persuasive argument and this is evident on at least two levels: it is persuasive for the judges sitting in the case and it can be persuasive for the authorities of the Contracting Parties which are supposed to execute the judgments. Finally, the judges expressed their views in relation to the identification of European consensus. The majority of the judges were very satisfied with the level of comparative law reports that they received from the Research Division and they confirmed that these reports were enough to establish consensus. The judges did not blindly follow the solution provided by European consensus and they considered this aspect of application of European consensus as a sufficient response to the anti-majoritarian argument.

---

[2] When Protocol 15 to the ECHR comes into force, the references to subsidiarity and the margin of appreciation will be included in the preamble to the Convention: 'Affirming that the High Contracting Parties, in accordance with the principle of subsidiarity, have the primary responsibility to secure the rights and freedoms defined in this Convention and the Protocols thereto, and that in doing so they enjoy a margin of appreciation, subject to the supervisory jurisdiction of the European Court of Human Rights established by this Convention.' Article 1 of Protocol 15.

The book is mainly built on the analysis of the case law of the ECtHR and academic commentaries. It argues that the benefits of legitimacy that flow from European consensus are undermined if the concept is unclear and its application by the ECtHR is incoherent. If this is so, it would be perceived as an arbitrary and illegitimate concept which does not amount to a legal standard. This book will seek to clarify the ECtHR's approach to European consensus by analysing its use in the case law and outlining its possible implications on the legitimacy of the ECtHR judgments. In order to do this, all cases of the Grand Chamber of the ECtHR, starting from the creation of the permanent court in 1998, will be analysed. Some key Chamber judgments and judgments of the ECtHR delivered before 1998 will be reviewed. The book analyses the judgments that were issued by the ECtHR up to 1 January 2014.

2

The concept of European consensus

2.1 Introduction

This chapter opens the discussion on the concept of European consensus in the case law of the European Court of Human Rights (ECtHR or Court). It sets the scene for deeper analysis of the rationale for European consensus and how it can improve the legitimacy of the Court's decisions. It also aims to identify patterns in the application of consensus by the ECtHR, to rationalise these patterns and to propose certain improvements to the Court's practice.

This chapter seeks to conceptualise European consensus as a presumption that favours the solution to a human rights issue which is adopted by the majority of the Contracting Parties. This presumption can be rebutted if the Contracting Party in question offers a compelling justification. Such a conceptualisation implies that European consensus has a strong persuasive effect and its rebuttal should be supported by convincing and lucid reasons.

Principles such as transparency, clarity and consistency are key facets of the process legitimacy of the Court's decisions.[1] European consensus is assessed through these principles, and the proposals offered in this chapter are predicated upon them. It will be argued that, while there are discernible patterns to the Court's application of consensus, its methodology would be strengthened by clarification.

Section 2.2 of this chapter assesses the terminology that the Court uses to refer to European consensus. The Court calls consensus by 'many names', and, because of this, it will be argued that it should be more consistent in using this terminology. The Court should also consistently employ a single well-defined term to avoid confusion. Moreover, the concept of consensus is criticised for not reflecting the word's literal meaning. Section 2.3 of this chapter demonstrates that European

---

[1] This point is discussed in more detail in Chapter 6.

consensus is not an *ad hoc* argument but a well-established doctrine of interpretation of the European Convention on Human Rights (ECHR or Convention). Having said that, it cannot be applied in every case due to its 'elitist' nature: it is not required in cases of repetitive applications[2] or in unique cases.[3]

Section 2.4 of this chapter explains how the Court applies European consensus, and it is argued that the application of consensus can be conceived in three stages: (1) preliminary stage, (2) stage of assessment and (3) stage of deployment. This conceptualisation helps to identify certain specific challenges in each of these stages.

In the preliminary stage, the Court collects comparative law materials. This is followed by an assessment of these materials where the Court confirms whether or not there is consensus. Finally, at the stage of deployment, the Court considers how decisive consensus might be for the outcome of the case. This section principally addresses the stages of assessment and deployment, while the preliminary stage is analysed in Chapter 4. The preliminary stage is separated from the stages of assessment and deployment because the latter ones are in the spotlight and can be examined by analysing the reasoning of the Court, while the preliminary stage is hidden and requires particular attention.

2.2 Definition of European consensus

2.2.1 Terminology

The consistent and coherent application of any legal concept is difficult if its scope remains unclear.[4] Therefore, the fact that the Court has not

---

[2] The case *Burdov (no 2) v. Russia* has identified a structural problem of non-execution of final national judgments. The Court pointed out that '[t]he State has thus been very frequently found to considerably delay the execution of judicial decisions ordering payment of social benefits such as pensions or child allowances, of compensation for damage sustained during military service or of compensation for wrongful prosecution. The Court cannot ignore the fact that approximately seven hundred cases concerning similar facts are currently pending before it against Russia.' *Burdov (no 2) v. Russia*, Application No 33509/04, Judgment of 15 January 2009, para. 133.

[3] See, *Broniowski v. Poland*, Application No 31443/96, Judgment of 22 June 2004.

[4] Clarity of legal concepts is an important aspect of the rule-of-law principle. Fallon argues that '[t]he Rule of Law is an ideal that can be used to evaluate laws, judicial decisions, or legal systems'. R.J. Fallon, '"The Rule of Law" as a Concept in Constitutional Discourse', *Columbia Law Review*, 97 (1997) 1, 8–9. The rule-of-law principle should be applicable to the ECtHR's methods of adjudication. See, J.A. Brauch, 'The Margin of Appreciation and the Jurisprudence of the European Court of Human Rights: Threat to the Rule of Law', *Columbia Journal of European Law*, 11 (2004), 113, 124–5. For more detailed discussion of

defined the term 'European consensus' in its judgments is an issue. Wildhaber, Hjartarson and Donnelly argue that it was the Court's intention to keep the concept 'fuzzy enough to avoid the consequences of adopting one particular theory out of the many held by judges and academics'.[5] Whilst it may be true that the Court has intentionally avoided providing clear parameters for European consensus, such reluctance should not be endorsed. Lack of a clear, consistent and, to a reasonable extent, predictable definition of consensus reduces its capacity to enhance the process legitimacy of the Court and its judgments. A lack of clarity in defining European consensus has also led some commentators to express the view that the Court's 'experience of over 30 years in hundreds of cases demonstrates that it is simply unable to articulate and apply a clear, predictable, and workable consensus standard'.[6]

The Court has deployed various terms to indicate the presence or absence of a common European approach. These include 'international consensus amongst the Contracting States of the Council of Europe',[7] 'any European consensus',[8] 'common standard amongst the Member States of the Council of Europe',[9] 'common European standard'[10] and 'general trend'.[11] For the purposes of this book, these terms are all included within the overarching phrase 'European consensus'. Until now, the Court has referred to European consensus in the majority of cases, and this book follows the Court's approach even though it is open to criticism.

The word 'consensus' is of Latin origin, and a contemporary English dictionary defines it as an 'agreement in opinion; the collective

---

the rule-of-law principle, see, for example, B.Z. Tamanaha, *On the Rule of Law* (Cambridge University Press, 2004); A.V. Dicey, *Introduction to the Study of the Law of the Constitution* (Liberty Fund Inc., 1982), p. 110; F.A. Hayek, *The Road to Serfdom* (Routledge Press, 1944).

[5] L. Wildhaber, A. Hjartarson and S. Donnelly, 'No Consensus on Consensus? The Practice of the European Court of Human Rights', *Human Rights Law Journal*, 33 (2013), 248, 249.

[6] J.A. Brauch, 'The Dangerous Search for an Elusive Consensus: What the Supreme Court Should Learn from the European Court of Human Rights', *Howard Law Journal*, 52 (2008–2009), 277, 278.

[7] *Lee* v. *the United Kingdom*, Application No 25289/94, Judgment of 18 January 2001, para. 95.

[8] *Evans* v. *the United Kingdom*, Application No 6339/05, Judgment of 10 April 2007, para. 45.

[9] *T.* v. *the United Kingdom*, Application No 24724/94, Judgment of 16 December, para. 72.

[10] *X., Y. and Z.* v. *the United Kingdom*, Application No 21830/93, Judgment of 22 April 1997, para. 44.

[11] *Ünal Tekeli* v. *Turkey*, Application No 29865/96, Judgment of 16 November 2004, para. 61.

unanimous opinion of a number of persons'.[12] The inclusion of unanimity in this definition suggests that consensus can be found only if everyone agrees on a certain point. Therefore, in the context of the ECtHR, European consensus can be identified only if all the Member States regulate an issue in an identical or significantly similar way. Arguably, even if only one Contracting Party[13] has a different solution, consensus is not present, if 'consensus' is given its literal meaning.

In the majority of cases, however, 'European consensus' has been employed to indicate a trend. The members of the organising committee[14] of the Conference on European Consensus in the ECtHR Jurisprudence came to a similar conclusion:

> It is clear that consensus in the Convention sense does not mean the unanimity that is needed for treaty amendment. It is more an expression of the common ground required for the collective approach underlying the Convention system and the interaction between the European and domestic systems.[15]

The ECtHR does not necessarily wait for unanimity; it can be satisfied with the existence of a trend in the laws of the Contracting Parties.[16] The word 'trend' is defined as 'a general direction in which something is developing or changing'.[17] Here, the Court is not looking for identical legal rules but rather tracing a convergence among States. For example, in *X., Y. and Z. v. the United Kingdom*, the Court identified 'a clear trend within the Contracting States towards the legal recognition of gender reassignment'.[18]

---

[12] C. Soanes and A. Stevenson (eds.), *The Oxford Dictionary of English* (Oxford University Press, 2005).

[13] It might be the respondent State in a particular case.

[14] Anatoly Kovler, Vladimiro Zagrebelsky, Lech Garlicki, Dean Spielmann, Renate Jaeger and Roderick Liddell.

[15] A. Kovler et al., 'The Role of Consensus in the System of the European Court of Human Rights' in *Dialogues between Judges* (Council of Europe, 2008), p. 27.

[16] Thirty-three judges were interviewed for this book. Currently sitting judges are not named – their identity is not revealed. Judge 18 points out that 'we are not a law-making body. We cannot replace the national parliaments. What national parliaments do is very relevant. We have to interpret the Convention in light of present day circumstances and therefore we look on those present days circumstances having regard to consensus. But we have in our case law judgments where there admittedly was no consensus. Mere fact that there is no consensus or not yet a consensus does not mean that we should not take the lead. As to the new solutions we need a trend.' K. Dzehtsiarou, *Interview with Judge 18* (European Court of Human Rights, Strasbourg).

[17] Soanes and Stevenson, *The Oxford Dictionary of English*.

[18] *X., Y. and Z. v. the United Kingdom*, para. 40.

Similarly, in *Christine Goodwin v. the United Kingdom*, the Court examined tendencies in the legal recognition of transsexual surgery under the title '[t]he state of any European and international consensus'.[19] However, this does not mean that consensus in the sense of unanimity has not been used by the Court. It can happen if the Court deals with more abstract principle values – in other words, consensus on the level of principles, such as protection of children's rights and protection of victims of sexual violence.[20] This is discussed in the following section. However, such consensus has to be further interpreted, and the same principle can justify a few different outcomes in a case.

The fact that it is very difficult to reach literal consensus in real life was also emphasised by the dissenting judges in *X. and others v. Austria*. In that case, the Court was called upon to consider whether Austrian legislation prohibiting second-parent adoption by same-sex couples violated the Convention. Dissenting judges Casadevall, Ziemele, Kovler, Jočienė, Šikuta, De Gaetano and Sicilianos questioned the Court's deployment of consensus:

> [S]hould we always adhere to the somewhat restrictive notion of 'consensus', which is rarely encountered in real life? Would it not be more appropriate and simpler to speak in terms of a 'trend'?[21]

Some commentators have taken up these concerns and have argued that the Court should use the term 'trend' instead of 'consensus'.[22] While the term 'trend' better reflects the reality, this book will continue to use the term 'consensus' as it has been employed more often by the Court in its case law. However, this does not constitute an endorsement of this term.

European consensus is primarily identified at two levels. First, it can be identified at the level of rules, by which I mean the specific implementing measures which are undertaken to give effect to a legal principle in a particular system. Second, consensus can operate at the level of principles, by which I mean those general concepts which underpin legal standards.

---

[19] *Christine Goodwin v. the United Kingdom*, Application No 28957/95, Judgment of 11 July 2002, para. 84–5.
[20] See, Section 2.2.3.
[21] *X. and others v. Austria*, Application No 19010/07, Judgment of 19 February 2013, Dissenting opinion of judges Casadevall, Ziemele, Kovler, Jočienė, Šikuta, De Gaetano and Sicilianos, para. 15.
[22] P. Mahoney and R. Kondak, 'Common Ground: A Starting Point or Destination for Comparative-Law Analysis by the European Court of Human Rights?' (Unpublished, on file with the author).

2.2.2 Level of consensus

This section analyses the two levels of consensus: rules and principles. Some commentators conceptualise this phenomenon as a level of abstraction in comparative law. Ambrus argues that

> in some cases the Court examines the countries' general direction concerning the disputed issue, while in other cases it requires that the member states' approach be comparable in terms of concrete provisions or measures.[23]

Various levels of abstraction that consensus can be identified on were also discussed by the judges of the ECtHR. In *Zaunegger v. Germany*, the Court was asked to check whether the impossibility of securing judicial review of custody of a child born out of wedlock discriminated against the father. In this case, the Court found

> in this context that although there exists no European consensus as to whether fathers of children born out of wedlock have a right to request joint custody even without the consent of the mother, the common point of departure in the majority of Member States appears to be that decisions regarding the attribution of custody are to be based on the child's best interest and that in the event of a conflict between the parents such attribution should be subject to scrutiny by the national courts.[24]

It seems that there is consensus in this case at the level of principles – namely agreement that the State should act in the best interest of the child. However, there are rules which are much more precise that regulate the rights of fathers in relation to children born outside wedlock. The Court placed an emphasis on the abstract principle and disregarded the diverse legal regulations. It concluded that there was a violation of Article 14 taken in conjunction with Article 8 of the Convention.

In his dissenting opinion, Judge Schmitt examined the abstraction of consensus and observed that there was no 'proper' consensus on the issue. He concluded that

> [w]here there is no uniform approach it has to be accepted in my opinion that there are a number of possible ways of solving the conflict between the different interests at stake. Moreover, the common starting-point of the legislation in the member States is, as in Germany, the child's best

---

[23] M. Ambrus, 'Comparative Law Method in the Jurisprudence of the European Court of Human Rights', *Erasmus Law Review*, 2 (2009) 353, 365. See also, E. Brems, *Human Rights: Universality and Diversity* (Springer, 2001), pp. 417–8.

[24] *Zaunegger v. Germany*, Application No 22028/04, Judgment of 3 December 2009, para. 60.

interests. With regard to this common goal and the non-existent consensus among the member States, I am not convinced that providing the father with the possibility of obtaining joint custody by court order against the will of the mother should be the only legal solution in accordance with the Convention.[25]

In this approach, the choice of the level of abstraction may impact upon the outcome of the case, as shown in *Zaunegger* v. *Germany*. It seems that it is an obligation of the Court to explain why it deploys consensus at a certain level.

2.2.2.1   Consensus at the level of rules

In the case of rules, the Court often identifies a trend rather than putting the issue 'on hold' until unanimity is established. Having said that, the Court can establish nigh unanimity at the level of rules. In *Ünal Tekeli* v. *Turkey*, for example, the Court stated that Turkish legislation prohibiting married women from retaining their maiden names was the last such law in Europe.[26] In *Bayatyan* v. *Armenia*, the Court stated that at the time of interference only four States did not provide for alternative military service on the basis of conscientious objections.[27] These cases, however, are rare examples in which European consensus means nigh unanimity, and concerns rules, not principles.

In a different context, the Court was satisfied when a much less overwhelming majority existed. In *M.C.* v. *Bulgaria*, the Court considered whether a lack of resistance on the part of a victim could negate the charge of rape. It held that

> historically, proof of physical force and physical resistance was required under domestic law and practice in rape cases in a number of countries. The last decades, however, have seen a clear and steady trend in Europe and some other parts of the world towards abandoning formalistic definitions and narrow interpretations of the law in this area.[28]

The level of consensus should predetermine the weight of consensus in the Court's reasoning. If there is a consensus at the level of rules, the respondent State should provide very convincing justification for diverging from that consensus.[29] Moreover, if the Court decides to disregard such consensus, it should explicitly and convincingly explain what

---

[25] Ibid., Dissenting opinion of Judge Schmitt, para. 5.
[26] *Ünal Tekeli* v. *Turkey*, para. 61.
[27] *Bayatyan* v. *Armenia*, Application No 23459/03, Judgment of 7 July 2011, para. 103.
[28] *M.C.* v. *Bulgaria*, Application No 39272/98, Judgment of 4 December 2003, para. 156.
[29] See, *A., B. and C.* v. *Ireland*, Application No 25579/05, Judgment of 16 December 2010.

reasons trumped consensus. If consensus on the level of rules is established, it clearly signals that the Contracting Parties consent to a particular approach to the matter at issue. That said, the establishment of European consensus at the level of rules is comparatively rare due to the fact that a legal matter can be dealt with in various different ways. Therefore, if a precise European consensus at the level of rules is established, it will be considered by the Court as highly persuasive, if not decisive.[30] This is less so in case of consensus at the level of principles. In the latter case, the Contracting Parties agree to a set of vaguely defined values and they can still justifiably claim a broad margin of appreciation in relation to precise regulation of the matter at issue.

2.2.2.2 Consensus at the level of principles

At the level of principles, the Court uses 'consensus', understood as unanimity, to clarify the meaning of vague terms enshrined in the Convention. In *Selmouni v. France*, the Court used consensus to clarify the meaning of Article 3 of the Convention by comparing it with the United Nations Convention against Torture and Other Cruel, Inhuman or Degrading Treatment or Punishment.[31]

The identification of a consensus in principle is significantly easier than identifying consensus in the application of a principle, that is at the level of rules. In some cases, the Court requires convergence of rules in addition to the consensus at the level of principles to influence the outcome of a particular case. In *Chapman v. the United Kingdom*, the ECtHR stated that

> the Court is not persuaded that the consensus is sufficiently concrete for it to derive any guidance as to the conduct or standards which Contracting States consider desirable in any particular situation. The framework convention, for example, sets out general principles and goals but the signatory States were unable to agree on means of implementation.[32]

The Court subsequently reconsidered this matter in *D. H. and others v. the Czech Republic*,[33] where it was satisfied with the level of consensus in relation to protection of minorities in order to find a violation. The Court should clarify its approach as to the level of concreteness that

---

[30] K. Dzehtsiarou, *Interview with Judge 12* (European Court of Human Rights, Strasbourg).
[31] *Selmouni* v. *France*, Application No 25803/94, Judgment of 28 July 1999, para. 97–100.
[32] *Chapman* v. *the United Kingdom*, Application No 27238/95, Judgment of 18 January 2001, para. 94.
[33] *D.H. and others* v. *the Czech Republic*, Application No 57325/00, Judgment of 13 November 2007.

consensus should achieve in order to form part of a compelling argument.[34] Unlike consensus at the level of rules, consensus at the level of principles requires further interpretation and implementation by rules and cannot claim the same degree of persuasive value as the consensus at the level of rules.

2.3 Spread of European consensus

2.3.1 Importance of consensus

European consensus, in terms of both rules and principles, has been deployed throughout the jurisprudence of the ECtHR. This section aims to show that European consensus is not an accidental or *ad hoc* argument. European consensus has become one of the tools of interpretation of the ECHR alongside evolutive interpretation, margin of appreciation, autonomous meaning of the Convention and proportionality. Consensus is used to interpret a wide range of rights enshrined in the Convention and Protocols. The unconditional nature of the rights protected (e.g. Article 3) does not leave much scope for the Court to assess European consensus in relation to them. However, the Court has still managed to deploy it in the interstices. Here follows a short summary of the use of European consensus or lack thereof as regards the key provisions of the Convention.

Right to life (Article 2) The Court has applied European consensus in cases where it has attempted to define the moment when life begins,[35] or whether the right to die and euthanasia are guaranteed by Article 2.[36] The Court has also deployed European consensus to determine the scope of positive obligations of the Contracting Parties to protect life.[37]

---

[34] Brauch points out that '[t]here are several vital but unanswered questions: (1) what is needed to satisfy the consensus requirement – a trend or a consensus? (2) where must that trend or consensus be found, in Europe or in the world as a whole?; and (3) how will anyone, individuals or member States, know when a trend or consensus exists?' Brauch, 'The Margin of Appreciation', 145. See also, A. McHarg, 'Reconciling Human Rights and the Public Interest: Conceptual Problems and Doctrinal Uncertainty in the Jurisprudence of the European Court of Human Rights', *Modern Law Review*, 62 (1999), 671, 691.

[35] See, for example, *Vo* v. *France*, Application No 53924/00, Judgment of 8 July 2004, para. 82; *Evans* v. *the United Kingdom*, para. 54.

[36] *Pretty* v. *the United Kingdom*, Application No 2346/02, Judgment of 29 April 2002, para. 48.

[37] *Opuz* v. *Turkey*, Application No 33401/02, Judgment of 9 June 2009, para. 138.

Prohibition of torture (Article 3) The Court has made references to consensus when it defined torture[38] and while examining the scope of positive obligations imposed by Article 3 on the Contracting Parties.[39]

Prohibition of slavery and forced labour (Article 4) The Court has used European consensus to establish positive obligations of the Contracting Parties to investigate and prosecute instances of servitude and forced labour.[40]

Right to liberty and security (Article 5) The Court has examined European consensus in relation to the tariff system for prisoners serving life imprisonment.[41] The Court has also deployed European consensus in the cases where the ECtHR considered compatibility of irreducible life sentences with the Convention.[42]

Right to fair trial (Article 6) The Court has employed European consensus in cases concerning both the civil and criminal components of Article 6. European consensus was one of the reasons that the Court developed Article 6 guarantees in pre-trial measures in civil procedure.[43] In relation to criminal proceedings, European consensus has been found to be relevant in the assessment of whether certain types of evidence were admissible.[44]

Right to privacy (Article 8) Articles 8–11 allow the Contracting Parties to limit the exercise of rights granted under the Convention. The Court has often used consensus to examine if this interference is disproportionate. European consensus has been considered in relation to various aspects of Article 8. The Court has deployed consensus in cases

---

[38] *Selmouni v. France*, para. 96–100; *V. v. the United Kingdom*, Application No 24888/94, Judgment of 16 December 1999, para. 73.
[39] *M.C. v. Bulgaria*, para. 154–5; *M.S.S. v. Belgium and Greece*, Application No 30696/09, Judgment of 21 January 2011, para. 251.
[40] *Siliadin v. France*, Application No 73316/01, Judgment of 26 July 2005, para. 111–2.
[41] *Stafford v. the United Kingdom*, Application No 46295/99, Judgment of 28 May 2002, para. 68–9.
[42] *Vinter and others v. the United Kingdom*, Application No 66069/09, 130/10 and 3896/10, Judgment of 9 July 2013, para. 117.
[43] *Micallef v. Malta*, Application No 17056/06, Judgment of 15 October 2009, para. 78.
[44] *Gäfgen v. Germany*, Application No 22978/05, Judgment of 1 June 2010, para. 174.

concerning, *inter alia*, adoption,[45] abortion,[46] LGBT rights,[47] protection of personal data[48] and gender equality.[49]

Freedom of religion (Article 9) The Court considered whether European consensus existed in the case concerning the legal prohibition on wearing religious headscarves in universities.[50] Consensus was discussed in *Lautsi v. Italy*, where the Court was called upon to assess the compatibility of Italian laws regarding the display of crucifixes in public schools with Article 9 of the Convention.[51]

Freedom of expression (Article 10) The Court has deployed European consensus in cases involving the protection of morality.[52] European consensus was considered when the Court balanced freedom of speech with the protection of State secrets[53] and when it dealt with the prohibition of a TV advertisement.[54]

Freedom of association (Article 11) The Court deployed consensus at the definitional stage of this article. For example, the Court considered whether civil servants were entitled under Article 11 to form trade unions.[55] It also used consensus at the stage of assessment of the State interference, for example whether the waiting period for the official registration of a religious organisation was excessive.[56]

---

[45] See, for instance, *E.B. v. France*, Application No 43546/02, Judgment of 22 January 2008; *Fretté v. France*, Application No 36515/97, Judgment of 26 February 2002; *Kearns v. France*, Application No 35991/04, Judgment of 10 January 2008.
[46] *A., B. and C. v. Ireland*, para. 231–40.
[47] *Christine Goodwin v. the United Kingdom*, para. 85–6; *Dudgeon v. the United Kingdom*, Application No 7525/76, Judgment of 23 September 1981, para. 45.
[48] *S. and Marper v. the United Kingdom*, Application No 30562/04 and 30566/04, Judgment of 4 December 2008, para. 112.
[49] *Ünal Tekeli v. Turkey*, para. 61.
[50] *Leyla Şahin v. Turkey*, Application No 44774/98, Judgment of 10 November 2005, para. 109.
[51] *Lautsi and others v. Italy*, Application No 30814/06, Judgment of 18 March 2011, para. 70.
[52] *Handyside v. the United Kingdom*, Application No 5493/72, Judgment of 7 December 1976, para. 48.
[53] *Stoll v. Switzerland*, Application No 69698/01, Judgment of 10 December 2007, para. 155.
[54] *Murphy v. Ireland*, Application No 44179/98, Judgment of 10 July 2003, para. 81; *Animal Defenders International v. the United Kingdom*, Application No 48876/08, Judgment of 22 April 2013, para. 123.
[55] *Demir and Baykara v. Turkey*, Application No 34503/97, Judgment of 12 November 2008, para. 85, 106.
[56] *Kimlya and others v. Russia*, Application No 76836/01 and 32782/03, Judgment of 1 October 2010, para. 98.

Right to marry (Article 12) Consensus has been considered in cases dealing with same-sex marriages[57] and the right to marry for transsexuals.[58]

Property rights (Article 1, Protocol 1) The Court has deployed consensus in its consideration of the scope of protection afforded by Article 1, Protocol 1, for example in cases concerning adverse possession[59] and inheritance.[60]

Right to education (Article 2, Protocol 1) The Court has analysed consensus in relation to non-discrimination of minorities in their access to education.[61]

Voting rights (Article 3, Protocol 1) The Court has utilised consensus in its assessment of the composition and functioning of administrative electoral bodies.[62] The Court has also incorporated the concept of European consensus in its consideration of prisoners' right to vote.[63]

While this outline of the Court's case law is far from exhaustive, it shows that European consensus has not been solely attributed, as it is sometimes suggested, to the personal rights enshrined in Articles 8–11 of the ECHR.[64] Rather, the consensus tool has been used when construing a broad range of rights; almost all Convention rights were mentioned in the list above. European consensus has no exclusive connection to any particular right. Moreover, consensus has been used by the Court in different contexts and linked to different methods of interpretation.[65]

---

[57] *Schalk and Kopf* v. *Austria*, Application No 30141/04, Judgment of 24 June 2010, para. 58; *H.* v. *Finland*, Application No 37359/09, Judgment of 13 November 2012, para. 49.

[58] *Christine Goodwin* v. *the United Kingdom*, para. 84–5.

[59] *J.A. Pye (Oxford) Ltd and J.A. Pye (Oxford) Land Ltd* v. *the United Kingdom*, Application No 44302/02, Judgment of 30 August 2007, para. 78.

[60] *Mazurek* v. *France*, Application No 34406/97, Judgment of 1 February 2000, para. 31.

[61] *D.H. and others* v. *the Czech Republic*, para. 181.

[62] *Georgian Labour Party* v. *Georgia*, Application No 9103/04, Judgment of 8 July 2008, para. 53.

[63] *Hirst* v. *the United Kingdom (No. 2)*, Application No 74025/01, Judgment of 6 October 2005, para. 81.

[64] A.A. Ostrovsky, 'What's So Funny about Peace, Love, and Understanding? How the Margin of Appreciation Doctrine Preserves Core Human Rights within Cultural Diversity and Legitimises International Human Rights Tribunals', *Hanse Law Review*, 1 (2005), 47, 50; B. Wilkins, 'International Human Rights and National Discretion', *Journal of Ethics*, 6 (2002), 373, 377.

[65] The Court has deployed European consensus to determine, for instance, evolutive interpretation and the margin of appreciation.

2.3.2 Reasons for limited deployment of consensus

Despite the broad application of the European consensus argument across the rights enshrined in the Convention, it has been deployed in less than 5 per cent of all judgments delivered by the ECtHR.[66] It is suggested that there are four possible reasons for this. First, the Court deploys European consensus only in cases of major importance[67] that concern difficult questions of interpretation of the Convention. Whilst consensus is more often utilised by the Grand Chamber[68] than the Chambers, it is not exclusive to it.[69] The Court does not apply consensus in cases of repetitive violations where the outcome is predetermined by established case law of the ECtHR and requires only a minimum of additional reasoning. Moreover, consensus is not useful in relation to inadmissible cases. The decisions in these cases are often made on the basis of whether the application complies with the formal rules in Articles 34 and 35 of the ECHR. Given that these repetitive and inadmissible applications constitute the vast majority of the Court's docket,[70] it is understandable that consensus is deployed relatively rarely by the Court.

---

[66] The Court did not deploy uniform terminology in relation to European consensus. Therefore, it is hardly possible to examine all Chamber and Grand Chamber cases where European consensus was mentioned. The author has conducted an estimation of the number of cases that mentioned keywords 'European consensus', 'common standards' and 'comparative law'. It appears that these keywords are mentioned in the context relevant to this research in less than 5 per cent of all judgments and decisions of the ECtHR published in English.

[67] Judge Myjer points out that 'most of the cases we are dealing with in the chamber are the clone cases. Thinking of the cases where we need consensus, these are cases about serious interpretation of the Convention which are the Grand Chamber cases and are the cases where we normally ask for comparative law study.' K. Dzehtsiarou, *Interview with Judge Egbert Myjer* (European Court of Human Rights, Strasbourg, 2009). At the High Level Conferences on the Future of the European Court of Human Rights in Interlaken, Izmir and Brighton, the Contracting Parties emphasised that the Court's backlog crisis is mainly due to an increasing amount of repetitive cases. See, Interlaken Declaration, adopted on 19 February 2010, para. 7; Izmir Declaration, adopted on 27 April 2011, section E; Brighton Declaration, adopted on 20 April 2012.

[68] A case can be relinquished to the Grand Chamber by the Chamber (Article 30 of the ECHR) or a case can be referred to the Grand Chamber (Article 43 of the ECHR).

[69] In 2013, the Grand Chamber delivered 12 judgments; 8 contained references to European consensus (HUDOC database). See, Chapter 4.

[70] In 2013, the Court declared inadmissible 89,737 applications. According to the Court's analysis of statistics, the Court has delivered judgment 'in respect of 3,659 applications (compared with 1,678 in 2012 – an increase of 118%). A significant proportion of these applications were joined, with the result that the number of judgments actually delivered was 916, a decrease of 16%. 219 judgments were adopted by a three-judge Committee formation under the procedure, introduced by Protocol 14. These judgments accounted

Second, some cases present unique legal and/or factual situations in a respondent State that cannot be compared with any other country due to historical or other particular reasons. In this respect, Judge Garlicki mentioned *Broniowski v. Poland*.[71] This case dealt with a unique historical situation, and it was hardly possible to deploy consensus to the facts of this case. The Court considered whether the failure of the Polish authorities to compensate Polish citizens for their property that was nationalised in Western Ukraine in 1939 complied with the ECHR.[72]

Third, methodologically sound comparative analysis is costly in time and manpower.[73] The Court, especially in the past, has used non-governmental organisation (NGO) reports or parties' submissions which contain comparative analyses rather than its own independent research. Only after the Research Division was created did the Court begin to conduct such research.[74] However, the resources available to the Research Division are limited.[75] The parties to the case or third parties continue to submit their reports. These can contain comparative data but they must be verified.[76] Such verification can also be burdensome, and this limits the capacity of the Court to deploy European consensus. This means that the ECtHR needs to strategically select those cases where comparative legal analysis can be meaningfully applied.

---

for 75% of the applications. 81% of those applications concerned the Ukrainian non-enforcement cases.' *Analysis of Statistics 2013* (European Court of Human Rights, 2014).

[71] *Broniowski v. Poland*.

[72] K. Dzehtsiarou, *Interview with Judge Lech Garlicki* (European Court of Human Rights, Strasbourg, 2009).

[73] Dzehtsiarou, *Interview with Judge 12*.

[74] The date of creation of the Research Division of the Court is not mentioned in open sources of the ECtHR. The current head of the Research Division, Montserrat Enrich-Mas, informed the author that 'it is not easy to trace the exact date of the formation of the Division, since the research function was in the Court yet in the old Commission days. However, until about year 2000 this function was vested in an employee, rather than a division, since there was much less work to do. From about year 2000 the need to form a separate division emerged.'

[75] See, Chapter 4 for more in-depth discussion of comparative law at the ECtHR.

[76] Judge 12 points out that the Court sometimes had to verify data provided by the parties of the case and third parties. He stated that 'in the past you could rely on the parties to provide a lot of comparative information about the legal situation in other countries. That was not unproblematic. One of the problems was how you verify the accuracy of the information. And often the information that we got we could not really use for that reason. We did not have the time and resources to check it ourselves. Often the information we got was extremely detailed based on research carried out by governments using their networks of embassies to provide information on comparative or international law. Therefore you could stand over that and rely on it as being pretty accurate especially if it was not challenged by the other side.' Dzehtsiarou, *Interview with Judge 12*.

Fourth, the human element should not be ignored: some judges are more inclined towards comparative research than others. The judge-rapporteur[77] is empowered to request the comparative survey from the Research Division. If the judge-rapporteur is not inclined towards comparative research, it is less likely that European consensus will appear in the final judgment. For example, one of the judges interviewed by the author has stated that he does not consider European consensus to be a compelling argument and that he has never requested comparative law research.[78]

The reasons listed, however, do not undermine the role of consensus in the cases dealing with novel and constitutional issues.[79] In these cases, the Court develops and clarifies the standards of human rights protection of Europe.

2.4 Application of European consensus

This section outlines how European consensus functions in the ECtHR's reasoning. Morawa correctly observed that the most common way that European consensus is applied is as a means of mediation between dynamic interpretation and the margin of appreciation. According to him, European consensus is

> a comparative survey of both the laws and practices of member states illustrating that there is a widely accepted standard with respect to the treatment of a certain issue or procedure may be the basis for ... a dynamic interpretation, while no or little common ground between the

---

[77] According to Rule 49 of Rules of Court, '[w]here an application is made under Article 34 of the Convention and its examination by a Chamber or a Committee exercising the functions attributed to it under Rule 53 § 2 seems justified, the President of the Section to which the case has been assigned shall designate a judge as Judge Rapporteur, who shall examine the application. In their examination of applications, Judge Rapporteurs (a) may request the parties to submit, within a specified time, any factual information, documents or other material which they consider to be relevant; (b) shall, subject to the President of the Section directing that the case be considered by a Chamber or a Committee, decide whether the application is to be considered by a single-judge formation, by a Committee or by a Chamber; (c) shall submit such reports, drafts and other documents as may assist the Chamber or the Committee or the respective President in carrying out their functions.'

[78] K. Dzehtsiarou, *Interview with Judge 22* (European Court of Human Rights, Strasbourg).

[79] For a discussion of the constitutionalist and adjudicatory functions of the ECtHR see, K. Dzehtsiarou and A. Greene, 'Restructuring the European Court of Human Rights: Preserving the Right of Individual Petition and Promoting Constitutionalism', *Public Law* (2013), 710, 713–6.

states parties allows a respondent state to exercise its discretion within a rather wide margin of appreciation.[80]

European consensus can be conceptualised as a tool that can bring forward a particular human rights issue from the margin of appreciation and trigger evolutive interpretation.[81] Nevertheless, the consensus decision-making mechanism is not limited solely to this particular role. European consensus can be a useful factor for testing the proportionality of interference.[82] In a case where no consensus is identified, the Court can resort to autonomous interpretation.[83]

2.4.1 European consensus in action

As stated above, the process of application of European consensus by the ECtHR can be divided into three stages: (1) preliminary stage, (2) stage of assessment and (3) stage of deployment. These three stages will now be considered in turn.

At the first stage, the ECtHR collects comparative law materials. The Court compares the laws and practices of the Contracting Parties, relevant general international law and relevant laws and practices of States that are not members of the Council of Europe. Chapter 4 discusses this stage of the process of consensus identification in greater detail.

At the second stage, the Court decides whether the comparative law report can substantiate one of the following conclusions: (1) there is a lack of European consensus; (2) European consensus is established, and the law or practice at hand is a part of it; (3) neither European consensus nor lack thereof can be decisively established; or (4) European consensus is established, and the law or practice at hand contradicts European consensus.

The Court establishes a lack of consensus if there is a substantive discrepancy in the legal regulation of a particular issue in Europe. For example, in *Vo* v. *France*, the Court stated that there was no consensus on

---

[80] A. Morawa, 'The "Common European Approach", "International Trends", and the Evolution of Human Rights Law. A Comment on *Goodwin and I. v. the United Kingdom*', *German Law Journal*, 3 (8) (2002).
[81] K. Dzehtsiarou, 'European Consensus and the Evolutive Interpretation of the European Convention on Human Rights', *German Law Journal*, 12 (2011), 1730.
[82] *Kimlya and others v. Russia*, para. 98.
[83] J. Gerards, 'Judicial Deliberations in the ECtHR' in N. Huls, M. Adams and J. Bomhoff (eds.), *The Legitimacy of Highest Courts' Rulings. Judicial Deliberations and Beyond* (Cambridge University Press, 2009), available at http://papers.ssrn.com/sol3/papers.cfm?abstract_id=1114906, accessed on 6 August 2014.

2.4 APPLICATION OF EUROPEAN CONSENSUS 25

the moment when life begins;[84] in *Schalk and Kopf* v. *Austria* (and more recently in *Vallianatos and others* v. *Greece*), the Court affirmed that there was no consensus in relation to same-sex marriages;[85] and in *Animal Defenders International* v. *the United Kingdom*, the Court did not find there to be a consensus on how to regulate paid political advertising in broadcasting.[86]

Second, the Court can establish European consensus and confirm that the law under scrutiny is in line with it. In *Stoll* v. *Switzerland*,[87] the applicant argued that the State had breached its Convention obligation under Article 10 (freedom of expression) by imposing a criminal sanction for disclosure of confidential information. The Court stated that 'a consensus appears to exist among the Member States of the Council of Europe on the need for appropriate criminal sanctions to prevent the disclosure of certain confidential items of information'.[88] After holding that the Swiss law was similar to the laws in the majority of European States, the ECtHR found that the fine for the disclosure of information was proportionate and there was no violation of Article 10. Thus, if the Court finds that the law is in line with a European consensus, it does not immediately mean that there is no violation, although it is a likely outcome.

The position of municipal law as a part of European consensus does not always guarantee that the ECtHR will find there to be no violation of the Convention in all cases. In *B. and L.* v. *the United Kingdom*,[89] the complaint concerned the inability of a former father-in-law to marry his former daughter-in-law according to UK law. The Court concluded that a prohibition similar to the UK one could be found in the laws of a large number of the Contracting Parties.[90] Nevertheless, the Court further stated that

> [t]he Court must however examine the facts of the case in the context pertaining in the United Kingdom. It observes that this bar on marriage is aimed at protecting the integrity of the family (preventing sexual rivalry between parents and children) and preventing harm to children who may be affected by the changing relationships of the adults around them. These

---

[84] *Vo* v. *France*, para. 82.   [85] *Schalk and Kopf* v. *Austria*, para. 58.
[86] *Animal Defenders International* v. *the United Kingdom*, para. 123; *Vallianatos and others* v. *Greece*, Application No. 29381/09 and 32684/09, Judgment of 7 November 2013, para. 91.
[87] *Stoll* v. *Switzerland*.   [88] Ibid., para. 155.
[89] *B. and L.* v. *the United Kingdom*, Application No 36536/02, Judgment of 13 September 2005.
[90] Ibid., para. 36.

are, without doubt, legitimate aims. [However, u]nder United Kingdom law the bar on a marriage of this degree of affinity is not subject to an absolute prohibition. Marriages can take place, pursuant to a personal Act of Parliament. From the information before the Court, it transpires that individuals in a similar situation to these applicants have been permitted to marry ... where there were also children in the household, it was declared that the impediment placed on the marriage served no useful purpose of public policy. The inconsistency between the stated aims of the incapacity and the waiver applied in some cases undermines the rationality and logic of the measure.[91]

In this case, the Court refocused its analysis from considering the ban on marrying a daughter-in-law and other relatives, for which a European consensus in favour of a ban did indeed exist, to the particular procedure for getting an exception from this rule, as prescribed under British law. The ban itself was not considered to be in breach of the Convention but the realisation of the exception procedure was.

If a law under scrutiny is in line with European consensus, it is highly likely that the Court will agree that this law is in compliance with the ECHR.[92] There are not many cases where the law under scrutiny formed a part of European consensus. It is likely that these cases are considered by the Court as manifestly ill-founded and they are eliminated at the stage of admissibility. Many such decisions are not published and they are not available for further scrutiny.

Third, the Court can conclusively establish neither the presence nor absence of European consensus. This unusual situation can take place where only a very limited number of States have regulated a particular issue and the outcome of comparative analysis cannot establish presumption either way. In *X. v. Austria*, the Court considered whether the impossibility of second-parent adoption in a same-sex relationship was discriminatory in comparison with a situation of unmarried different-sex couples. In this case, the Court stated that

> solely in order to respond to the Government's assertion that no European consensus exists, it has to be borne in mind that the issue before the Court is not the general question of same-sex couples' access to second-parent adoption, but the difference in treatment between unmarried different-sex couples and same-sex couples in respect of this type of adoption. Consequently, only those ten Council of Europe member States which allow second-parent adoption in unmarried couples may be regarded as a basis for comparison. Within that group, six States treat heterosexual

---

[91] Ibid.   [92] Dzehtsiarou, *Interview with Judge 12*.

couples and same-sex couples in the same manner, while four adopt the same position as Austria. The Court considers that the narrowness of this sample is such that no conclusions can be drawn as to the existence of a possible consensus among Council of Europe member States.[93]

The Court concluded that consensus or lack thereof was not helpful in consideration of the matter at hand. Therefore, the Court continued a discussion of the issue using other methods of interpretation and found a violation of Article 14 taken in conjunction with Article 8 of the Convention.

The fourth situation emerges when the State legislation under consideration by the Court contradicts European consensus. The Court does not wait for total unanimity to confirm that there is consensus in a particular case. In *Stanev* v. *Bulgaria*,[94] the Court established that 18 Contracting Parties out of 20 that were studied allowed direct access to national courts to partially incapacitated persons. These data led the ECtHR to confirm that there was a trend in Europe.[95] One can argue that the sample is quite small in this case and perhaps that is the reason why the Court did not claim there to be consensus. In some cases, the Court did not specify the exact number of States that had adopted the measure in question.[96] The best practice of the Court is when European consensus is based on comprehensive and transparent analysis of the Contracting Parties' legislation. For instance, in *Fabris* v. *France*, the respondent State was one of the very few exceptions to the rule that inheritance rights of a child should not depend on the marital status of his or her parents.[97]

Once established, neither the presence nor absence of consensus is applied automatically to the case at hand. At the stage of deployment of consensus, the Court usually considers the consequences of such consensus on the matter at issue. It is argued that the presence or absence of consensus creates a rebuttable presumption: lack of consensus

---

[93] *X. and others* v. *Austria*, para. 149.
[94] *Stanev* v. *Bulgaria*, Application No 36760/06, Judgment of 17 January 2012.
[95] Ibid., para. 243.
[96] In *Demir and Baykara* v. *Turkey*, the Court stated: '[a]s to the practice of European States, it can be observed that, in the vast majority of them, the right for public servants to bargain collectively with the authorities has been recognised, subject to various exceptions so as to exclude certain areas (disciplinary procedures, pensions, medical insurance, wages of senior civil servants) or certain categories of civil servants who hold exclusive powers of the State (members of the armed forces and of the police, judges, diplomats, career civil servants at federal level)'. *Demir and Baykara* v. *Turkey*, para. 52.
[97] *Fabris* v. *France*, Application No 16574/08, Judgment of 7 February 2013, para 34.

presumes in favour of the margin of appreciation.[98] For example, in *Evans v. the United Kingdom*, the Court stated '[w]here ... there is no consensus within the Member States of the Council of Europe, either as to the relative importance of the interest at stake or as to the best means of protecting it, particularly where the case raises sensitive moral or ethical issues, the margin will be wider'.[99] A wide margin of appreciation means that the Court will not find the law or practice of the Member State to be in breach of the Convention and that 'the Court would generally respect the legislature's policy choice unless it is manifestly without reasonable foundation'.[100]

The ECtHR has not provided a definition of what it considers to be an intervention that is 'manifestly without reasonable foundation'. In *TV Vest As and Rogaland Pensjonistparti v. Norway*,[101] the Court dealt with a prohibition on television broadcasting of political advertising in the domestic law of Norway. The Court confirmed that there was no consensus in the area and that a wide margin of appreciation was afforded to the Member States.[102] Nevertheless, the Court found a breach of Article 10 of the Convention, noting that the legislation in question was intended to remove disadvantages between political parties that had disparate financial resources; otherwise, parties with small budgets would be under-represented on television. However, the law in question failed to achieve this aim. In contrast to the major political parties, which were given a large amount of attention in the edited television coverage, small parties were barely mentioned. For that reason, paid advertising on television became the only way for these parties to communicate their message to the public through that type of media.[103] Therefore, the Court found a violation of the Convention, as this was an example of a law without reasonable foundation.

In *Hirst v. the United Kingdom (No. 2)*,[104] the ECtHR examined a legal provision according to which convicted prisoners would be automatically deprived of the right to vote. Following a comparative analysis, the Court found there to be no European consensus but held that the lack of

---

[98] *Vo v. France*, para. 82. [99] *Evans v. the United Kingdom*, para. 77.
[100] *Dickson v. the United Kingdom*, Application No 44362/04, Judgment of 4 December 2007, para. 78.
[101] *TV Vest AS and Rogaland Pensjonistparti v. Norway*, Application No 21132/05, Judgment of 11 December 2008.
[102] Ibid., paras. 65–6. [103] Ibid., paras. 70–5.
[104] *Hirst v. the United Kingdom (No 2)*.

2.4 APPLICATION OF EUROPEAN CONSENSUS

consensus was not decisive. The Court affirmed that, while the margin of appreciation was wide, it was not all-embracing:

> The [relevant] provision imposes a blanket restriction on all convicted prisoners in prison. It applies automatically to such prisoners, irrespective of the length of their sentence and irrespective of the nature or gravity of their offence and their individual circumstances. Such a general, automatic and indiscriminate restriction on a vitally important Convention right must be seen as falling outside any acceptable margin of appreciation, however wide that margin might be, and as being incompatible with Article 3 of Protocol No. 1.[105]

Therefore, lack of consensus does not automatically leave the issue within the area of State discretion. It allows the Court to establish a presumption in favour of the solution adopted by the respondent State, which may be rebutted. The ECtHR can examine the law to determine whether it is manifestly unreasonable and appropriate to allow a wide margin of appreciation.

The presence of European consensus also establishes a presumption in favour of the solution adopted in the majority of the Contracting Parties and usually against the solution adopted by a diverging respondent State. This presumption is also rebuttable[106] if a strong justification for divergence is submitted. The following section deals with the reasons that can justify rebuttal of such a presumption.

Mahoney and Kondak describe an approach to European consensus similar to the one proposed here. They argue that all cases in which the Court deploys European consensus can be divided into four groups: two rules and two exceptions. The first group enshrines those judgments where European consensus supports finding a violation. Exceptions to this rule, namely that there is consensus but no violation was found, are placed in the second group. The third group contains the judgments that follow the rule which provides that a lack of European consensus leads to a broad margin of appreciation and to finding no violation.[107] Finally, the fourth group contains exceptions to the latter rule: the Court declares a violation despite the lack of consensus.[108] This approach is similar to understanding European consensus as a presumption. However, the latter suggests that the Court has to justify the rebuttal of

---

[105] Ibid., para. 82.
[106] Brems, *Human Rights*, p. 420. See also, *Sitaropoulos and Giakoumopoulos v. Greece*, Application No. 42202/07, Judgment of 15 March 2012, para. 74.
[107] Mahoney and Kondak, 'Common Ground'.
[108] *Christine Goodwin v. the United Kingdom*.

such a presumption. If a failure to apply European consensus is seen as an exception, then such justification is not immediately presumed. For the sake of predictability and clarity, the Court has to use clear and convincing arguments to support its decision to depart from what consensus or lack thereof provides.

2.4.2 Limits of application of the European consensus argument

This section analyses those reasons that can be seen by the Court as sufficiently weighty to countervail measures adopted by the majority of the Contracting Parties. Where a European consensus is identified, the Member State's law may fall outside European consensus without reasonable justification. In this situation, the consequences are often clear: the Court normally finds a violation of the Convention right.[109] Alternatively, the Member State may have a particularly strong justification for the law in question even if this law is different to the European consensus. The limits outlined below are not exhaustive and their content can vary depending on the facts of the case. The strength of these limits,[110] surrounding factors[111] and concreteness of European consensus[112] can determine the decision of the Court.

2.4.2.1 Text of the Convention and Protocols

In the unlikely event of a contradiction between the text of the Convention (including its Protocols) and European consensus, the Court will apply the former. Those issues that are clear in

---

[109] See, for example, *Ünal Tekeli v. Turkey*; *Tănase v. Moldova*, Application No 7/08, Judgment of 27 April 2010; *D.H. and others v. the Czech Republic*; *Micallef v. Malta*.

[110] It depends how clearly these limits are established and how relevant they are to the matter at issue. In *A., B. and C.*, the Court agreed that legal regulation of abortion is particularly morally sensitive. *A., B. and C. v. Ireland*, para. 233–4.

[111] In *Republican Party of Russia v. Russia*, the Court confirmed that the historical and political particularities of some Contracting Parties can justify their divergence from the solution supported by European consensus. However, this justification is temporal. If the divergence exists for a long period of time, it has to be supported with increasingly strong justification. *Republican Party of Russia v. Russia*, Application No 12976/07, Judgment of 12 April 2011, para. 127–30.

[112] As outlined in the previous section, consensus at the level of rules is arguably more convincing than consensus at the level of principles. Moreover, the number of the Contracting Parties which adopted a particular solution would also arguably affect the persuasiveness of European consensus. Dzehtsiarou, *Interview with Judge 12*.

the Convention do not require consensus.[113] Moreover, the Court has refrained from the application of European consensus if the Contracting States had commenced drafting a new Protocol to deal with the matter. Mowbray correctly points out that 'where States have signalled their intention to extend Convention rights/freedoms by means of additional Protocols, the Court has adopted great caution in not transgressing into these areas through over-creative interpretations of the existing text'.[114] This reasoning was used by the ECtHR in *Soering v. the United Kingdom*. In this case, the Court considered whether extradition to a country where the death penalty existed would violate Article 3 of the ECHR. The Court held that

> [t]he Convention is to be read as a whole and Article 3 should therefore be construed in harmony with the provisions of Article 2. On this basis, Article 3 evidently cannot have been intended by the drafters of the Convention to include a general prohibition of the death penalty since that would nullify the clear wording of Article 2 § 1. Subsequent practice in national penal policy, in the form of a generalised abolition of capital punishment, could be taken as establishing the agreement of the Contracting States to abrogate the exception provided for under Article 2 § 1 and hence to remove a textual limit on the scope for evolutive interpretation of Article 3. However, Protocol No. 6, as a subsequent written agreement, shows that the intention of the Contracting Parties as recently as 1983 was to adopt the normal method of amendment of the text in order to introduce a new obligation to abolish capital punishment in time of peace and, what is more, to do so by an optional instrument allowing each State to choose the moment when to undertake such an engagement. In these conditions, notwithstanding the special character of the Convention, Article 3 cannot be interpreted as generally prohibiting the death penalty.[115]

This limitation to European consensus was again considered in *Öcalan v. Turkey*, where the ECtHR came to a similar conclusion.[116] These cases

---

[113] K. Dzehtsiarou, *Interview with Judge Christos Rozakis* (European Court of Human Rights, Strasbourg, 2010).

[114] A. Mowbray, 'The Creativity of the European Court of Human Rights', *Human Rights Law Review*, 5 (2005), 57, 69.

[115] *Soering v. the United Kingdom*, Application No 14038/88, Judgment of 7 July 1989, para. 103.

[116] The Court stated that 'the fact that there is still a large number of States who have yet to sign or ratify Protocol No 13 may prevent the Court from finding that it is the established practice of the Contracting States to regard the implementation of the death penalty as inhuman and degrading treatment contrary to Article 3 of the Convention, since no derogation may be made from that provision, even in times of war. However, the Grand Chamber agrees with the Chamber that it is not necessary for the Court to reach any firm

establish that the explicit text of the Convention and the Protocols overrides the necessity for establishing European consensus. The Court again considered the issue of the death penalty in the more recent case of *Al-Saadoon and Mufdhi v. the United Kingdom*. The ECtHR took into account the fact that a growing number of the Contracting Parties had signed and ratified Protocol 13, which prohibited the death penalty under any circumstances. This fact influenced the Court's position in relation to the compliance of the death penalty with Articles 2 and 3. The Court stated that

> the Grand Chamber in *Öcalan* did not exclude that Article 2 had already been amended so as to remove the exception permitting the death penalty. Moreover, as noted above, the position has evolved since then. All but two of the Member States have now signed Protocol No. 13 and all but three of the States which have signed have ratified it. These figures, together with consistent State practice in observing the moratorium on capital punishment, are strongly indicative that Article 2 has been amended so as to prohibit the death penalty in all circumstances. Against this background, the Court does not consider that the wording of the second sentence of Article 2 § 1 continues to act as a bar to its interpreting the words 'inhuman or degrading treatment or punishment' in Article 3 as including the death penalty.[117]

Even though the Court ultimately applied a dynamic interpretation in relation to the death penalty, it happened due to an increasing number of ratifications of Protocol 13 and not due to changes in the national laws of the Contracting Parties. This means that the *de facto* amended text of the Convention was in line with the new approach to the death penalty in Europe. The ECtHR has been reluctant to amend the text of the Convention through judicial doctrine even if such amendment would be supported by the great majority of the Contracting Parties.[118]

2.4.2.2 Historical and political justification

The Court has identified another theoretical limitation to European consensus – historical and political justification. In the cases analysed

---

conclusion on these points since, for the following reasons, it would be contrary to the Convention, even if Article 2 were to be construed as still permitting the death penalty, to implement a death sentence following an unfair trial.' *Öcalan* v. *Turkey*, Application No 46221/99, Judgment of 12 May 2005, para. 165.

[117] *Al-Saadoon and Mufdhi* v. *the United Kingdom*, Application No 61498/08, Judgment of 2 March 2010, para. 120.

[118] See also, *Johnston and others* v. *Ireland*, Application No 9697/82, Judgment of 18 December 1986.

2.4 APPLICATION OF EUROPEAN CONSENSUS 33

below, this justification was not considered strong enough to overcome European consensus. In *Tănase* v. *Moldova*, the Court scrutinised Moldovan electoral legislation according to which persons with dual citizenship could not be elected to the national parliament. The ECtHR stated that

> a review of practice across Council of Europe Member States reveals a consensus that where multiple nationalities are permitted, the holding of more than one nationality should not be a ground for ineligibility to sit as a member of Parliament, even where the population is ethnically diverse and the number of MPs with multiple nationalities may be high. However, notwithstanding this consensus, a different approach may be justified where special historical or political considerations exist which render a more restrictive practice necessary.[119]

The Court considered the historical and political circumstances of Moldova and came to the conclusion that they did not justify the departure from European consensus in this case. Similarly, in *Republican Party of Russia* v. *Russia*,[120] the Court considered whether the Russian ban on regional parties complied with the ECHR. The Court stated that

> very few Council of Europe member States prohibit regional parties or require that a political party should have a certain number of regional or local branches. Georgia is the only country that explicitly prohibits regional political parties. Two countries, Ukraine and Armenia, require that a political party have a certain number of regional branches, while two more countries, Moldova and Romania, require political parties to have members domiciled in a certain number of regions. The Court considers that a review of practice across Council of Europe member States reveals a consensus that regional parties should be allowed to be established. However, notwithstanding this consensus, a different approach may be justified where special historical or political considerations exist which render a more restrictive practice necessary.[121]

The Court again did not agree that the historical and cultural justification in this case could limit the European consensus identified, since the ban at hand was imposed for an unlimited period of time and indiscriminately to every regional political party.[122] However, the Court confirmed that a historical and political justification could in theory justify divergence from the solution adopted by the majority of the

---

[119] *Tănase* v. *Moldova*, para. 172. [120] *Republican Party of Russia* v. *Russia*.
[121] Ibid., para. 126. [122] Ibid., paras. 127–30.

Contracting Parties.[123] Despite the Court's repeated insistence that historical and political factors could justify a divergence from European consensus, it seems that this threshold has not yet been reached.

2.4.2.3 Moral sensitivity of the matter at issue

A rule that has been established by the case law of the ECtHR is that a respondent State enjoys a wide margin of appreciation in morally sensitive cases unless European consensus is established. For example, the Court identified consensus in *Dudgeon v. the United Kingdom* when considering whether the criminalisation of homosexual relations was in compliance with the ECHR. The Court stated that

> [a]s the Government correctly submitted, it follows that the moral climate in Northern Ireland in sexual matters, in particular as evidenced by the opposition to the proposed legislative change, is one of the matters which the national authorities may legitimately take into account in exercising their discretion ... Nevertheless, this cannot of itself be decisive as to the necessity for the interference with the applicant's private life resulting from the measures being challenged ... As compared with the era when that legislation was enacted, there is now a better understanding, and in consequence an increased tolerance, of homosexual behaviour to the extent that in the great majority of the member States of the Council of Europe it is no longer considered to be necessary or appropriate to treat homosexual practices of the kind now in question as in themselves a matter to which the sanctions of the criminal law should be applied; the Court cannot overlook the marked changes which have occurred in this regard in the domestic law of the member States.[124]

The moral sentiments of the citizens of Northern Ireland were disregarded because a European consensus supported an alternative outcome. The rule that the respondent State enjoys a wide margin of appreciation unless European consensus is established was reconsidered in *A., B. and C. v. Ireland*. In this case, the ECtHR assessed whether the Irish ban on abortion violated several provisions of the ECHR. In 2005, three Irish women travelled to England for abortions on health and/or well-being grounds. They complained that 'restrictive and unclear Irish laws'[125] violated the ECHR.

---

[123] In *Tănase v. Moldova*, the Court stated that it 'does not exclude that in the immediate aftermath of the Declaration of Independence by Moldova in 1991, a ban on multiple nationals sitting as members of Parliament could be justified'. *Tănase* v. *Moldova*, para. 173.
[124] *Dudgeon* v. *the United Kingdom*, para. 56–60.
[125] S.K. Calt, '*A., B. and C.* v. *Ireland*: "Europe's *Roe* v. *Wade*"?', *Lewis and Clark Law Review*, 14 (2010), 1189, 1189.

2.4 APPLICATION OF EUROPEAN CONSENSUS

The Court considered European consensus in its assessment of the width of the margin of appreciation to be applied in the case. Morality and European consensus were considered as conflicting variables determining the scope of the margin of appreciation. The Court stated that

> [t]here can be no doubt as to the acute sensitivity of the moral and ethical issues raised by the question of abortion or as to the importance of the public interest at stake. A broad margin of appreciation is, therefore, in principle to be accorded to the Irish State in determining the question whether a fair balance was struck between the protection of that public interest ... and the conflicting rights ... under Article 8 of the Convention. However, the question remains whether this wide margin of appreciation is narrowed by the existence of a relevant consensus.[126]

The Court confirmed that there was a consensus amongst a substantial majority of the Contracting States of the Council of Europe towards allowing abortion on broader grounds than accorded under Irish law.[127] However, the Court further stated that this consensus did not decisively narrow the State's margin of appreciation.[128] The ECtHR held that the wide margin of appreciation accorded to a State's protection of the unborn necessarily translated into a margin of appreciation for that State as to how it balanced the conflicting rights of the mother. Finally, the Court concluded that consensus in this case did not mean that the Irish State did not strike a fair balance between conflicting rights. The Court stated that

> even if it appears from the national laws referred to that most Contracting Parties may in their legislation have resolved those conflicting rights and interests in favour of greater legal access to abortion, this consensus cannot be a decisive factor in the Court's examination of whether the impugned prohibition on abortion in Ireland for health and well-being reasons struck a fair balance between the conflicting rights and interests, notwithstanding an evolutive interpretation of the Convention.[129]

The Court shifted the subject of consensus from deciding whether Irish abortion law was excessively restrictive to the legal issue of the moment of the beginning of life. This point was underlined by the dissenting judges.[130] The Court stated that the prohibition of abortion for health

---

[126] A., B. and C. v. Ireland, para. 233-4.   [127] Ibid., para. 235.   [128] Ibid., para. 236.
[129] Ibid., para. 237.
[130] In joint partly dissenting opinion, Judges Rozakis, Tulkens, Fura, Hirvelä, Malinverni and Poalelungi argued that the Court was not called upon in the case to answer the difficult question of 'when life begins'. This was not the issue before the Court, and undoubtedly the Court is not well equipped to deal effectively with it. The issue before

and well-being reasons in Ireland, based as it was on the profound moral views of the Irish people as to the nature of life and as to the consequent protection to be accorded to the right to life of the unborn, did not exceed the margin of appreciation accorded in that respect to the Irish State. The dissenting judges pointed out that the Court disregarded European consensus on the ground of profound moral views.[131]

It is suggested that the Court needs to clarify its policy as to whether it can disregard European consensus in cases that involve morally sensitive issues. The Court has reiterated many times that the area of margin of appreciation is wide in such cases, save in the situation where European consensus can be identified.[132] *A., B. and C. v. Ireland* arguably changed this approach. The dissenting judges rightly pointed out that *A., B. and C.* was a dangerous departure from the previous case law of the ECtHR. However, the fact that the Court itself did not clearly state that the moral sensitivity of the case could overrule European consensus makes it possible to argue that the Court will reconsider the initial rule. This case also shows that European consensus can be trumped if a particular moral stand is supported by the majority of people in a particular country. The dangers of such a situation are further discussed in Chapter 3.

2.5 Conclusion

This section has discussed how European consensus operates within the practice of the ECtHR. It is argued here that European consensus is a

---

the Court was whether, regardless of when life begins – before birth or not – the right to life of the foetus can be balanced against the right to life of the mother, or her right to personal autonomy and development, and possibly found to weigh less than the latter rights or interests. And the answer seems to be clear: there is an undeniably strong consensus among European States ... to the effect that, regardless of the answer to be given to the scientific, religious or philosophical question of the beginning of life, the right to life of the mother, and, in most countries' legislation, her well-being and health, are considered more valuable than the right to life of the foetus. Ibid., Joint Partly Dissenting Opinion of Judges Rozakis, Tulkens, Fura, Hirvelä, Malinverni and Poalelungi, para. 2.

[131] The dissenting judges argued that it is the first time that the Court has disregarded the existence of a European consensus on the basis of 'profound moral views'. Even assuming that these profound moral views are still well embedded in the conscience of the majority of Irish people, to consider that this can override the European consensus, which tends in a completely different direction, is a real and dangerous new departure in the Court's case law. Ibid., para. 6.

[132] In *Vo v. France*, the Court stated, '[i]t is not only legally difficult to seek harmonisation of national laws at Community level, but because of lack of consensus, it would be inappropriate to impose one exclusive moral code'. *Vo v. France*, para. 82.

2.5 CONCLUSION

rebuttable presumption in favour of the solution adopted by a significant majority of the Contracting Parties, which is identified on the basis of comparative analysis of laws and practices of these Parties. New consensus can support the Court's dynamic interpretation. A lack of consensus establishes a presumption in favour of diversity and justifies a broader margin of appreciation.

3

Types of consensus

3.1 Introduction

The European Court of Human Rights (ECtHR or Court) utilises various sources to establish consensus and attaches different weight to different types of consensus. In the interests of clarity and foreseeability of ECtHR judgments, the types of consensus should be clearly distinguished.

It is argued that consensus can be divided into four types, depending on the source the Court uses to identify this consensus: national law, international law, attitude of people within the Contracting Party or expert opinion. Examining the type of consensus which is deployed is not just a theoretical puzzle. The practical application of this exercise comes to the fore when the Court reveals contradictions between two or more types of consensus. When this happens, the Court has to choose one of the types of consensus, and this has to be accomplished on a principled basis. This chapter aims to shed light on the typology of the consensus argument and the interaction between the types of consensus in the case law of the ECtHR.

Section 3.2 explains the rationale behind the typology and analyses how the Court integrates different types of consensus in its reasoning. Section 3.3 considers the possible interactions between the different types of consensus. Preference for one type of consensus over another can create legitimacy concerns if the Court does not clearly state the reasons for its preferred choice. If the Court decides to 'trump' European consensus with internal consensus, it places the legitimacy of the Court at risk. Therefore, such 'trumping' should be avoided when possible. It should be noted that interaction between expert consensus and other types of consensus is not considered in this section due to the rather infrequent deployment of expert consensus, as well as its predominantly technical character.

3.2 Typology of consensus

Throughout its existence, the Court has used different types of consensus in its reasoning and has not clearly distinguished between them, thus leaving some uncertainty as to both the precise meaning of consensus and the relative weighting of the different kinds of consensus deployed. This ambiguity can undermine the process legitimacy of the judgments in which European consensus is used, and generally this 'flexible' approach of the Court to consensus has attracted criticism. Murray is one of these critics. He stated that

> [t]here is also the more flexible, if not lax, approach to the objective indicia used to discern consensus. From the inception of the consensus doctrine, the Court has taken a flexible approach, relying not only on specific legislation in the national systems of the Contracting Parties but also looking to other sources such as international conventions. Nor has the Court required that consensus be overwhelming or long-established: indeed, it is frequently the case that a decision refers to trends in a given direction rather than concrete consensus based on analysis of national systems.[1]

The aim of this chapter is to draw a clear line between the different types of consensus. The ECtHR deploys four types of consensus:

1. consensus based on comparative analysis of the laws and practices of the Contracting Parties;
2. consensus based on international treaties;
3. internal consensus in the respondent Contracting Party;
4. expert consensus.[2]

Only the first type can be truly called *European* consensus. Consensus based on comparative analysis is a summary of the laws and practices of the Contracting Parties and therefore represents the common standards adopted by the European States. Consensus based on international treaties is usually identified through analysis of the treaties ratified, or at least signed, by the Contracting Parties. In establishing this type of consensus, the Court can also rely on soft law mechanisms adopted by international

---

[1] J.L. Murray, 'Consensus: Concordance, or Hegemony of Majority' in *Dialogues between Judges* (Council of Europe, 2008), p. 52.

[2] K. Dzehtsiarou, 'Does Consensus Matter? Legitimacy of European Consensus in the Case Law of the European Court of Human Rights', *Public Law* (2011), 534, 548. See also E. Myjer, 'Pierter Van Dijk and His Favourite Strasbourg Judgment' in M. van Roosmalen et al. (eds.), *Fundamental Rights and Principles* (Intersentia, 2013), p. 69.

organisations.[3] This type of consensus is more international than European, although it can also be called European in some instances when the ECtHR mentions treaties and other documents drafted and adopted within the Council of Europe[4] or if these treaties are ratified by the majority of the Contracting Parties. Internal consensus and expert consensus are clearly not *European* types since they represent the attitudes of the public to a particular issue within a sole respondent State or expert opinion. However, all types of consensus should be identified here, since 'non-European' types of consensus can contradict European consensus.[5] In such cases, the Court should explain why it chooses one type over another. Each of these types will now be considered in turn.

3.2.1 Consensus based on comparative analysis of the laws and practices of the Contracting Parties

The first type of consensus is based on comparative analysis of the national laws of the Contracting Parties.[6] Chapters 2 and 4 mainly describe the application and methodology of this type of consensus.

Over the years, the Court's approach to identification of European consensus has changed considerably. In early cases, in order to establish European consensus, the Court could rely on the perception of judges about common values which existed in the Contracting Parties. The Court could accept that these values were in the process of development and encourage such development.[7] However, the flexibility of the Court's approach to identification of the European consensus has been widely

---

[3] See, for example, *Scordino v. Italy (No 1)*, Application No 36813/97, Judgment of 29 March 2006, para. 73–4.

[4] See, for example, *Ramanauskas v. Lithuania*, Application No 74420/01, Judgment of 5 February 2008, para. 35–7.

[5] See, for example, *A., B. and C. v. Ireland*, Application No 25579/05, Judgment of 16 December 2010; *Tyrer v. the United Kingdom*, Application No 5856/72, Judgment of 25 April 1978.

[6] See, for example, *Ünal Tekeli v. Turkey*, Application No 48616/99, Judgment of 16 November 2004; *A., B. and C. v. Ireland*; *Republican Party of Russia v. Russia*, Application No 12976/07, Judgment of 12 April 2011.

[7] Letsas argues that this approach was deployed in *Marckx v. Belgium*, where the Court 'invoke[d] some abstract common standard, evidenced by the existence of a couple of international conventions which had not been ratified by the majority, let alone all, of the contracting states'. G. Letsas, 'The ECHR as a Living Instrument: Its Meaning and Legitimacy' in A. Føllesdal, B. Peters and G. Ulfstein (eds.), *Constituting Europe: The European Court of Human Rights in a National, European and Global Context* (Cambridge University Press, 2013), p. 115.

3.2 TYPOLOGY OF CONSENSUS

criticised by academic commentators.[8] The ECtHR has gradually changed its methodology of consensus identification. The Court now bases its conclusions of presence or absence of European consensus not on vague and unsubstantiated perceived common values but on comparative statistical analysis of laws and practices of the Contracting Parties. This argument can be substantiated first by reference to the establishment of the Research Division. This is a part of the Registry of the Court, and one of its objectives is to prepare comparative legal research upon the Court's request. The *modus operandi* of this division will be discussed in more detail in Chapter 4. Second, a more 'statistical' approach can be further proved by the fact that the Court includes comprehensive comparative surveys in its judgments and relies on them in establishing consensus.

The Court not only has detailed comparative data at its disposal but also reproduces the summary of these data in its judgments. In 2013, for example, the ECtHR referred to consensus based on analysis of domestic laws and practices in no less than 13 judgments.[9] Of course, this number is very low, especially compared to the overall number of judgments that the ECtHR delivers every year.[10] Having said that, the ECtHR includes comparative law provisions only in the judgments concerned with legal questions which have not been dealt with by the Court before or where there is a chance that its case law can be changed. The following analysis of the case law of the ECtHR from 2013 demonstrates two main points: first, the Court bases a decision about consensus on comparative law which is capable of substantiating either presence or absence of

---

[8] Y. Arai-Takahashi, *The Margin of Appreciation Doctrine and the Principle of Proportionality in the Jurisprudence of the ECHR* (Intersentia, 2002), pp. 192–3. See also, P. Mahoney, 'The Comparative Method in Judgments of the European Court of Human Rights: Reference Back to National Law' in G. Canivet, M. Andenas and D. Fairgrieve (eds.), *Comparative Law before the Courts* (British Institute of International and Comparative Law, 2004), p. 149; H.C. Yourow, *The Margin of Appreciation Doctrine in the Dynamics of European Human Rights Jurisprudence* (Brill, 1995), p. 195; P. Martens, 'Perplexity of the National Judge Faced with the Vagaries of European Consensus' in *Dialogues between Judges* (Council of Europe, 2008), p. 79; L.R. Helfer, 'Consensus, Coherence and the European Convention on Human Rights', *Cornell International Law Journal*, 23 (1993), 133, 138–41; T. Zwart, 'More Human Rights Than Court: Why the Legitimacy of the European Court of Human Rights Is in Need of Repair and How It Can Be Done' in S. Flogaitis, T. Zwart and J. Fraser (eds.), *The European Court of Human Rights and Its Discontents* (Edward Elgar, 2013), p. 93.

[9] Only final judgments were considered. Those referred to the Grand Chamber are not taken into account.

[10] For instance, in 2013 the ECtHR delivered judgments in respect of 3,659 applications. *Analysis of Statistics 2013* (European Court of Human Rights, 2014).

consensus; second, European consensus or lack thereof influences the outcome of the case.

A significant disparity in legal regulation in Europe, in other words, a lack of European consensus, often leads to finding no violation of the European Convention on Human Rights (ECHR or Convention). In *Animal Defenders International* v. *the United Kingdom*, the majority of the Grand Chamber of the ECtHR emphasised that there was no common European approach to regulation of paid political advertisements, and this allowed the Court to conclude that a wide margin of appreciation should be reserved for the respondent Party.[11] In this case, the ECtHR analysed laws of 34 Contracting Parties.[12]

In *Sindicatul 'Păstorul cel Bun'* v. *Romania*, the ECtHR found no violation of Article 11. Members of the Romanian clergy tried to form a trade union but the State refused to register it. The Court here concluded that there were many ways of governing relations between churches and States in Europe. The Court provided a number of examples of such relations in its judgments.[13] A lack of consensus led the Court to confirm a wide margin of appreciation which justified finding no violation in this case.[14] Similarly, no violation due to a lack of consensus was found in *Allen* v. *the United Kingdom*,[15] *Shindler* v. *the United Kingdom*[16] and *Mehmet Şentürk and Bekir Şentürk* v. *Turkey*.[17]

In a number of cases, the Court supported its judgment by reference to the clear and overwhelming mathematical majority of States in favour of finding a violation. In the Grand Chamber judgment of *Vallianatos and others* v. *Greece*, the Court stated that there was European consensus on the issue of allowing same-sex couples to form civil partnerships:

> [O]f the nineteen States which authorise some form of registered partnership other than marriage, Lithuania and Greece are the only ones to reserve it exclusively to different-sex couples. In other words, with two exceptions, Council of Europe member States, when they opt to enact legislation introducing a new system of registered partnership as an

---

[11] *Animal Defenders International* v. *the United Kingdom*, Application No 48876/08, Judgment of 22 April 2013, para. 123.
[12] Ibid., para. 72.
[13] *Sindicatul 'Păstorul cel Bun'* v. *Romania*, Application No 2330/09, Judgment of 9 July 2013, para. 171.
[14] Ibid., para. 61.
[15] *Allen* v. *the United Kingdom*, Application No 25424/09, Judgment of 12 July 2013.
[16] *Shindler* v. *the United Kingdom*, Application No 19840/09, Judgment of 7 May 2013.
[17] *Mehmet Şentürk and Bekir Şentürk* v. *Turkey*, Application No 13423/09, Judgment of 9 April 2013.

3.2 TYPOLOGY OF CONSENSUS

alternative to marriage for unmarried couples, include same-sex couples in its scope.[18]

The ECtHR found a violation of Article 14 in conjunction with Article 8 in this case.

In *Vinter and others v. the United Kingdom*, the Court concluded that there were only six States in Europe which allowed life sentences without parole.[19] Therefore, the Court agreed that

> a large majority of Contracting States either do not impose life sentences at all or, if they do impose life sentences, provide some dedicated mechanism, integrated within the sentencing legislation, guaranteeing a review of those life sentences after a set period.[20]

The Court found a violation of Article 3 of the Convention in this case. In *Fabris* v. *France*, the ECtHR established a strong consensus (40 States out of 42)[21] that a child's status for inheritance purposes should be independent of the marital status of his or her parents. The Court stated that the French law which diverged from this general trend violated the Convention. In *Şükran Aydın and others* v. *Turkey*, none of the 22 Contracting Parties surveyed criminally banned the use of minority languages during the elections.[22] This led the Court to finding a violation of the Convention.[23] A similar method was deployed by the Court in the case of *Nataliya Mikhaylenko* v. *Ukraine*.[24]

In three judgments, the Court used slightly different reasoning but the Court's decisions were nevertheless substantiated by comparative data. In *Berisha* v. *Switzerland*, the Court established that there was European consensus on the level of the principle that all decisions concerning children should be in their best interest.[25] In this judgment, the Court did not offer comparative data but referred to a previously decided case where this principle was substantiated.[26] The Court concluded that the

---

[18] *Vallianatos and others* v. *Greece*, Application No 29381/09 and 32684/09, Judgment of 7 November 2013, para. 91.
[19] *Vinter and others* v. *the United Kingdom*, Application No 66069/09, 130/10 and 3896/10, Judgment of 9 July 2013, para. 68.
[20] Ibid., para. 117.
[21] *Fabris* v. *France*, Application No 16574/08, Judgment of 7 February 2013, para. 34.
[22] *Şükran Aydın and others* v. *Turkey*, Application No 49197/06, 23196/07, 50242/08, 60912/08 and 14871/09, Judgment of 22 January 2013, para. 36.
[23] Ibid., para. 55.
[24] *Nataliya Mikhaylenko* v. *Ukraine*, Application No 49069/11, Judgment of 30 May 2013, para. 38.
[25] *Berisha* v. *Switzerland*, Application No 948/12, Judgment of 30 July 2013, para. 51.
[26] See, Chapter 4 for more discussion of sources of European consensus.

State had acted in the best interest of the child and found no violation. This case is unusual, because if European consensus is established then the Court is likely to find a violation; this is something which did not happen here.

In *A. K. and L. v. Croatia*, the Court considered whether the authorities had violated Article 8 rights by not providing an opportunity for a parent divested of her parental rights to participate in subsequent adoption proceedings. The Court considered laws and practices of 41 Member States[27] and concluded that there was a diversity of approaches. It also pointed out that there was no need to decide whether Croatian law as such complied with the Convention.[28] By doing so, the Court has effectively left this issue in the area of margin of appreciation. However, the Court further considered whether the law at hand offered enough safeguards 'for the protection of the applicants' private and family life'.[29] Since these safeguards were deemed insufficient, the Court found a violation of Article 8.

In *X. and others v. Austria*, the Court came to the rather unusual conclusion that neither European consensus nor lack thereof could be decisively established and that such analysis was not helpful.[30] In this case, the Court considered second-parent adoption by same-sex couples and found that the number of states which allowed single-parent adoption was too small to support any conclusion.

In each of the above-mentioned 13 cases, the Court based its decision on the presence or absence of European consensus on comparative data. In ten of those cases, European consensus or lack thereof directly affected the outcome of the case.

The argument that the Court has begun using a more rigorous 'statistical' approach to comparative law and has clearly identified consensus is not universally accepted. Letsas argues that

> the new Court has moved away from placing decisive weight on the absence of consensus amongst contracting states and from treating it as the ultimate limit on how far it can evolve the meaning and scope of Convention rights. The new Court treats the ECHR as a living instrument by looking for common values and emerging consensus in international law. In doing so, it often raises the human rights standard above what most contracting states currently offer.[31]

---

[27] *A.K. and L. v. Croatia*, Application No 37956/11, Judgment of 8 January 2013, para. 18–33.
[28] Ibid., para. 69–70.   [29] Ibid., para. 70.
[30] *X. and others v. Austria*, Application No 19010/07, Judgment of 19 February 2013, para. 149.
[31] Letsas, 'The ECHR as a Living Instrument', 122–3.

This argument is, undoubtedly, an interesting and provocative one, but unfortunately it does not find much support in the Court's case law. Letsas aims to substantiate his claim by referring to five cases.[32] Some of these cases, for example *Christine Goodwin v. the United Kingdom*, were often considered unusual by the Convention commentators and were criticised for their inconsistent application of consensus.[33] In some other cases mentioned by Letsas, the Court did not even mention European consensus,[34] and it is hard to agree that it had to be mentioned. In the judgment of *Hirst v. the United Kingdom (No 2)*,[35] European consensus was not used consistently with the previous case law, and that was also one of the reasons why this judgment was so fiercely criticised.[36] It seems that it is slightly premature to claim that the idea of European consensus has been abandoned by the Court in favour of an unclear principle of 'common values'.

It is true that, in the past, the ECtHR has not been too concerned with the formal legal nature of a particular legal trend which was used to prove the existence of European consensus, but looked more for the reality of such a trend. Nowadays, such a reality must be clearly substantiated by some traceable developments in the Member States.

3.2.2 European consensus based on international treaties

The second type of consensus is based on the analysis of international treaties which can be perceived by the ECtHR as a sign of existing consensus.[37] Brems suggests that the basis upon which the Court quotes

---

[32] *Hirst v. the United Kingdom (No 2)*, Application No 74025/01, Judgment of 6 October 2005; *Christine Goodwin v. the United Kingdom*, Application No 28957/95, Judgment of 11 July 2002; *E.B. v. France*, Application No 43546/02, Judgment of 22 January 2008; *Demir and Baykara v. Turkey*, Application No 34503/97, Judgment of 12 November 2008; *Rantsev v. Cyprus and Russia*, Application No 25965/04, Judgment of 7 January 2010.

[33] See, R. Sandland, 'Crossing and Not Crossing: Gender, Sexuality and Melancholy in the European Court of Human Rights; *Christine Goodwin v. United Kingdom*', *Feminist Legal Studies*, 11 (2003), 191, 199; J.A. Brauch, 'The Margin of Appreciation and the Jurisprudence of the European Court of Human Rights: Threat to the Rule of Law', *Columbia Journal of European Law*, 11 (2004), 113, 145. Murray mentions *Christine Goodwin v. the United Kingdom* as an example of multiple approaches of the ECtHR to European consensus. He concludes that this difference in approaches is detrimental to the legitimacy of consensus. Murray, 'Consensus: Concordance, or Hegemony of Majority', p. 57.

[34] *Rantsev v. Cyprus and Russia*.   [35] *Hirst v. the United Kingdom (No 2)*.

[36] See, for example, The Backbench Parliamentary Debates, 'Prisoners' Right to Vote', available at www.publications.parliament.uk/pa/cm201011/cmhansrd/cm110210/debt-ext/110210-0002.htm, accessed on 16 June 2013.

[37] See, for example, *Marckx v. Belgium*, Application No 6833/74, Judgment of 13 June 1979, para. 41.

international treaties is the following: 'if a State has underwritten certain detailed obligations in one text [an international treaty], the interpretation of a more general text [the Convention] can be oriented in that sense'.[38]

The Court's treatment of international legal norms is twofold: they can be treated as the facts of the case or as legal arguments. If an international legal norm is treated as a fact, it merely explains the matter at issue and helps the Court to describe the background of the case. In *Slivenko* v. *Latvia*, a case concerning the status of former Soviet citizens in Latvia, the Court quoted the Latvian-Russian treaty on the withdrawal of Russian troops.[39] The Court did not use this treaty to back up its reasoning;[40] the compliance of the provisions of this treaty with the Convention was considered by the judges.[41] Another example is *Prince Hans-Adam II of Liechtenstein* v. *Germany* where the Court quoted international legal provisions. Here again, international law did not form part of a compelling argument but was included to explain the legal regime in which the legal matter at hand had emerged.[42] This type of deployment of international law falls outside the scope of this book as it does not form a legal argument that can influence the reasoning of the Court and it is not going to be analysed in detail.

On the other hand, a treaty, recommendation or convention can be used as a compelling argument in the Court's reasoning and can lead to an identification of consensus. On various occasions, the Court has claimed that it should take into account the evolution of not only

---

[38] E. Brems, *Human Rights: Universality and Diversity* (Springer, 2001), p. 421.
[39] *Slivenko* v. *Latvia*, Application No 48321/99, Judgment of 9 October 2003, para. 64–7.
[40] Ibid., para. 116.
[41] The Court has stated that 'the withdrawal of the armed forces of one independent State from the territory of another, following the dissolution of the State to which they both formerly belonged, constitutes, from the point of view of the Convention, a legitimate means of dealing with the various political, social and economic problems arising from that dissolution. The fact that in the present case the Latvian-Russian treaty provided for the withdrawal of all military officers who after 28 January 1992 had been placed under Russian jurisdiction, including those who had been discharged from the armed forces prior to the entry into force of the treaty (which in this respect therefore had retroactive effect), and that it also obliged their families to leave the country, is not in itself objectionable from the point of view of the Convention and in particular Article 8. Indeed, it can be said that this arrangement respected the family life of the persons concerned in that it did not interfere with the family unit and obliged Russia to accept the whole family within its territory, irrespective of the origin or nationality of the individual family members.' Ibid., para. 116.
[42] *Prince Hans-Adam II of Liechtenstein* v. *Germany*, Application No 42527/98, Judgment of 12 July 2001, para. 23–37.

3.2 TYPOLOGY OF CONSENSUS

domestic but also international law. For instance, in *Marckx* v. *Belgium*, the Court considered the Brussels Convention of 12 September 1962 on the Establishment of Maternal Affiliation of Natural Children and the Convention of 15 October 1975 on the Legal Status of Children Born out of Wedlock. Neither of these conventions had been ratified by Belgium. Despite this, the Court identified a trend in favour of full legal recognition of children born out of wedlock based on these conventions and development in the domestic law of the Contracting Parties.[43]

The Court frequently makes references to the Vienna Convention on the Law of Treaties (VCLT). For example, it mentioned the VCLT in the *Golder* case at a time when the VCLT was not yet in force. The Court explained that

> [t]he Court is prepared to consider ... that it should be guided by Articles 31 to 33 of the Vienna Convention of 23 May 1969 on the Law of Treaties. That Convention has not yet entered into force and it specifies, at Article 4, that it will not be retroactive, but its Articles 31 to 33 [provisions related to treaty interpretation] enunciate in essence generally accepted principles of international law to which the Court has already referred on occasion.[44]

The Court held that the VCLT contains commonly accepted standards in Articles 31–33 and, therefore, it should not have to wait until the Convention comes into force to use it. Drzemczewski points out that the reference to the VCLT in *Golder* was the first attempt to pronounce 'a

---

[43] In *Marckx* v. *Belgium*, the Court stated that '[i]t is true that, at the time when the Convention of 4 November 1950 was drafted, it was regarded as permissible and normal in many European countries to draw a distinction in this area between the "illegitimate" and the "legitimate" family. In the instant case, the Court cannot but be struck by the fact that the domestic law of the great majority of the Member States of the Council of Europe has evolved and is continuing to evolve, in company with the relevant international instruments, towards full juridical recognition of the maxim *"mater semper certa est"*. Admittedly, of the ten States that drew up the Brussels Convention, only eight have signed and only four have ratified it to date. The European Convention of 15 October 1975 on the Legal Status of Children born out of Wedlock has at present been signed by only ten and ratified by only four members of the Council of Europe. However, this state of affairs cannot be relied on in opposition to the evolution noted above. Both the relevant Conventions are in force and there is no reason to attribute the currently small number of Contracting States to a refusal to admit equality between "illegitimate" and "legitimate" children on the point under consideration. In fact, the existence of these two treaties denotes that there is a clear measure of common ground in this area amongst modern societies.' *Marckx* v. *Belgium*, para. 41.

[44] *Golder* v. *the United Kingdom*, Application No 4451/70, Judgment of 21 February 1975, para. 29.

commonly acceptable and authoritative method of interpreting the provisions set out in the Convention'.[45]

The Court has employed various international law materials in its reasoning, including general international treaties,[46] human rights treaties,[47] the Council of Europe regulations and recommendations,[48] EU

---

[45] A. Drzemczewski, 'The Sui Generis Nature of the European Convention on Human Rights', *International and Comparative Law Quarterly*, 29 (1980), 54, 58.

[46] The Court quoted the Vienna Convention of the Law of Treaties (*Golder* v. *the United Kingdom*, para. 29), the UN Convention against Illicit Traffic in Narcotic Drugs and Psychotropic Substances (*Medvedyev and others* v. *France*, Application No 3394/03, Judgment of 29 March 2010, para. 29), the Hague Convention (IV) (*Kononov* v. *Latvia*, Application No 36376/04, Judgment of 17 May 2010, para. 56), the UN Convention on the Law of the Sea (*Medvedyev and others* v. *France*, para. 28) and many others.

[47] The Court, for example, utilised a definition of torture from the UN Convention against Torture and Other Cruel, Inhuman or Degrading Treatment or Punishment (*Selmouni* v. *France*, Application No 25803/94, Judgment of 28 July 1999, para. 97). The Court also used the Universal Declaration of Human Rights (*Al-Adsani* v. *the United Kingdom*, Application No 35763/97, Judgment of 21 November 2001, para. 26; *Saadi* v. *the United Kingdom*, Application No 13229/03, Judgment of 29 January 2008, para. 29-30), International Covenant on Civil and Political Rights (*Makaratzis* v. *Greece*, Application No 50385/99, Judgment of 20 December 2004, para. 28), the Convention on the Rights of the Child (*Sommerfeld* v. *Germany*, Application No 31871/96, Judgment of 8 July 2003, para. 37-9), the Convention on the Elimination of All Forms of Discrimination against Women (*Rantsev* v. *Cyprus and Russia*, para. 147-8) and other human rights treaties adopted within the UN system. The Court has also referred to other regional human rights treaties – the American Convention on Human Rights (*Kurt* v. *Turkey*, Application No 24276/94, Judgment of 25 May 1998, para. 67), Inter-American Convention on the Prevention, Punishment and Eradication of Violence against Women (*Opuz* v. *Turkey*, Application No 33401/02, Judgment of 9 June 2009, para. 86), Inter-American Convention to Prevent and Punish Torture (*Cruz Varas and others* v. *Sweden*, Application No 15576/89, Judgment of 20 March 1991, para. 35). At the same time, the African Charter on Human and Peoples' Rights was mentioned only once in the third party intervention in *Vo* v. *France* (*Vo* v. *France*, Application No 53924/00, Judgment of 8 July 2004, para. 63). The Universal Islamic Declaration of Human Rights was only once mentioned in reported cases; Judge Kovler made a reference to this declaration in his concurring opinion in *Şerife Yiğit* v. *Turkey*, Application No 3976/05, Judgment of 2 November 2011. On a number of occasions, the Court deployed the Council of Europe conventions. The Court used the Framework Convention for the Protection of National Minorities (*D.H. and others* v. *the Czech Republic*, Application No 57325/00, Judgment of 13 November 2007, para. 66), the European Social Charter (*Gustafsson* v. *Sweden*, Application No 18/1995/524/610, Judgment of 25 April 1996, para. 53) and others.

[48] Besides the Council of Europe conventions, the Court has often quoted recommendations and reports from the Council of Europe bodies. In *M.S.S.* v. *Belgium and Greece*, the Court quoted relevant texts of the Council of Europe Commissioner for Human Rights (*M.S.S.* v. *Belgium and Greece*, Application No 30696/09, Judgment of 21 January 2011, para. 87). It also deployed recommendations of the Committee of Ministers (*Enea* v. *Italy*, Application No 74912/01, Judgment of 17 September 2009, para. 48; *Sejdovic* v. *Italy*, Application No 56581/00, Judgment of 1 March 2006, para. 28), the European

law[49] and decisions of international tribunals other than the ECtHR.[50] The Court has also used treaties and decisions from each of these categories to back up its findings about the presence or absence of European consensus.[51]

3.2.3 Internal consensus within the respondent State

The third type of consensus reflects an internal attitude of people in the respondent State to the matter at hand. This type of consensus is not frequently used because it is difficult to identify and verify such attitudes.

<blockquote>
Commission for the Efficiency of Justice (*Scordino* v. *Italy (No 1)*, para. 73-4), the European Committee for the Prevention of Torture and Inhuman or Degrading Treatment or Punishment (*Ramirez Sanchez* v. *France*, Application No 59450/00, Judgment of 4 July 2006, para. 83) and others.

[49] The Court quoted the Treaty on European Union of 1992 (*Bosphorus Hava Yolları Turizm ve Ticaret Anonim Şirketi* v. *Ireland*, Application No 45036/98, Judgment of 30 June 2005, para. 78; *Matthews* v. *the United Kingdom*, Application No 24833/94, Judgment of 18 February 1999, para. 16), the Charter of Fundamental Rights of the European Union (*Bosphorus Hava Yolları Turizm ve Ticaret Anonim Şirketi* v. *Ireland*, para. 80), the European Union Council directives (*Nachova and others* v. *Bulgaria*, Application No 43577/98 and 43579/98, Judgment of 6 July 2005, para. 80; *Stec and others* v. *the United Kingdom*, Application No 65731/01 and 65900/01, Judgment of 12 April 2006, para. 38), the Council regulations (*Anheuser-Busch Inc.* v. *Portugal*, Application No 73049/01, Judgment of 11 January 2007, para. 36), the Council Decisions (*Greens and M.T.* v. *the United Kingdom*, Application No 60041/08 and 60054/08, Judgment of 23 November 2010, para. 52-4) and the resolutions of the European Parliament (*Karner* v. *Austria*, Application No 40016/98, Judgment of 24 July 2003, para. 36).

[50] The Court used judgments of the International Court of Justice (*Cyprus* v. *Turkey*, Application No 25781/94, Judgment of 10 May 2001, para. 86), the Inter-American Court of Human Rights (*Sergey Zolotukhin* v. *Russia*, Application No 14939/03, Judgment of 10 February 2003, para. 40), the Inter-American Commission of Human Rights (*Issa and others* v. *Turkey*, Application No 31821/96, Judgment of 16 November 2004, para. 71), the Human Rights Committee and various bodies of the United Nations (*Folgerø and others* v. *Norway*, Application No 15472/02, Judgment of 29 June 2007, para. 45), the International Military Tribunal in Nuremberg (*Kononov* v. *Latvia*, para. 117-9), the International Criminal Tribunal for Yugoslavia (*Rantsev* v. *Russia and Cyprus*, para. 142-3) and the International Criminal Tribunal for Rwanda (*Ahorugeze* v. *Sweden*, Application No 37075/09, Judgment of 27 October 2011, para. 44-61).

[51] In *Marckx* v. *Belgium*, the Court established European consensus in favour of equal treatment of children born out of wedlock and 'legitimate' children based on the Brussels Convention of 12 September 1962 on the Establishment of Maternal Affiliation of Natural Children and the European Convention of 15 October 1975 on the Legal Status of Children Born out of Wedlock. *Marckx* v. *Belgium*, para. 41. However, in *Chapman* v. *the United Kingdom*, the Court stated that the Framework Convention for the Protection of National Minorities was not concrete enough to indicate a consensus. *Chapman* v. *the United Kingdom*, Application No 27238/95, Judgment of 18 January 2001, para. 94.
</blockquote>

There are a limited number of sources that the ECtHR can use to substantiate such internal consensus.

First, the Court uses declarations of national parliaments and developments in national law as a source of internal consensus. In *Stafford v. the United Kingdom*, the matter at issue was the English tariff system for prisoners serving life sentences. In this case, the Court repeated its formula that it should follow its previous judgments for the sake of legal certainty unless changing conditions in the Contracting States were established.[52] The ECtHR stated that '[s]imilar considerations apply as regards the changing conditions and any emerging consensus discernible within the domestic legal order of the respondent Contracting State'.[53] The Court then analysed domestic English law and came to the conclusion that developments in national law that constituted an 'internal consensus' could justify an evolutive interpretation of the Convention.

In some cases, approval by the national Parliament was considered as a sign of consensus of this type. In *Borgers v. Belgium*, the Court examined whether the *procureur général*'s opinions could be regarded as neutral. The Court stated that

> [n]o one questions the objectivity with which the procureur général's department at the Court of Cassation discharges its functions. This is shown by the consensus which has existed in Belgium in relation to it since its inception and by its approval by Parliament on various occasions. Nevertheless, the opinion of the procureur général's department cannot be regarded as neutral from the point of view of the parties to the cassation proceedings. By recommending that an accused's appeal be allowed or dismissed, the official of the procureur général's department becomes objectively speaking his ally or his opponent. In the latter event, Article 6 para. 1 requires that the rights of the defence and the principle of equality of arms be respected.[54]

In this case, the Court had not accepted a solution supported by internal consensus, but in theory this method can lead to a paradoxical situation. A law which has been passed by a parliament can be held to be non-compliant with the Convention.[55] However, the internal consensus approach as outlined in *Borgers* allows the Court to consider motions

---

[52] *Stafford v. the United Kingdom*, Application No 46295/99, Judgment of 28 May 2002, para. 68.
[53] Ibid., para. 69.
[54] *Borgers v. Belgium*, Application No 12005/86, Judgment of 30 October 1991, para. 26.
[55] Ibid.

passed by the same Parliament to determine consensus, and these motions, therefore, can influence the interpretation of the Convention rights in question. This is perhaps one of the reasons why the Court uses this approach sparingly.

Second, the Court sometimes discusses perceived internal consensus if it was argued by the respondent State. The internal consensus argument was deployed by the UK government in *Tyrer* v. *the United Kingdom*.[56] *Tyrer* concerned the long-standing practice of sentencing people to 'birching' in criminal trials in the Isle of Man.[57] The applicant in this case – a juvenile who had been subjected to this punishment – claimed that it contravened Article 3 of the Convention. However, the UK claimed that corporal punishment 'did not outrage public opinion in the Island'[58] and ought to be saved from Convention incompatibility on that basis. The government did not produce any hard proof of the existence of such consensus in their submissions. In this case, the Court rejected the argument of the government, holding that

> even assuming that local public opinion can have an incidence on the interpretation of the concept of 'degrading punishment' appearing in Article 3, the Court does not regard it as established that judicial corporal punishment is not considered degrading by those members of the Manx population who favour its retention: it might well be that one of the reasons why they view the penalty as an effective deterrent is precisely the element of degradation which it involves. As regards their belief that judicial corporal punishment deters criminals, it must be pointed out that a punishment does not lose its degrading character just because it is believed to be, or actually is, an effective deterrent or aid to crime control. Above all, as the Court must emphasise, it is never permissible to have recourse to punishments which are contrary to Article 3 . . . whatever their deterrent effect may be.[59]

In this case, even if internal consensus existed, which the Court doubted, it seems that it could not justify interference with Article 3 of the Convention. A similar situation arose in the case of *Dudgeon* v. *the United Kingdom*.[60] The applicant claimed that existence of 'the

---

[56] *Tyrer* v. *the United Kingdom*.
[57] Birching was a statutorily regulated form of corporal punishment conducted by police officers (Summary Jurisdiction Act 1960, section 10). Regulation of this punishment was so precise that the size and weight of the cane to be used was specified in the Directive of the Lieutenant-Governor of 30 May 1960.
[58] *Tyrer* v. *the United Kingdom*, para. 31.   [59] Ibid.
[60] *Dudgeon* v. *the United Kingdom*, Application No 7525/76, Judgment of 23 September 1981.

abominable crime of buggery', as prohibited by sections 61 and 62 of the Offences against the Person Act 1861, was a violation of the Convention. The UK argued that continued criminalisation of male homosexual sex in Northern Ireland did not contravene the Convention based on what it claimed was 'the strength of feeling in Northern Ireland against the proposed change and, in particular, the strength of the view that it would be seriously damaging to the moral fabric of Northern Irish society' to decriminalise such acts.[61] The UK further argued that Northern Ireland was a particularly conservative society that placed greater emphasis than most Convention States on religion, and this also applied to heterosexual conduct.[62] Although the Court accepted that these claims were relevant to the matter at hand, it did not agree that internal consensus with such a weak evidential foundation could justify the limitation of rights prescribed by the Convention:

> As compared with the era when that legislation was enacted, there is now a better understanding, and in consequence an increased tolerance, of homosexual behaviour to the extent that in the great majority of the member States of the Council of Europe it is no longer considered to be necessary or appropriate to treat homosexual practices of the kind now in question as in themselves a matter to which the sanctions of the criminal law should be applied; the Court cannot overlook the marked changes which have occurred in this regard in the domestic law of the member States.[63]

Neither *Tyrer* nor *Dudgeon* categorically ruled out the possibility that an internal consensus could exist, but in neither case was the claim successful.

Third, the ECtHR uses the results of referendums to substantiate its claims about the presence of internal consensus. While this source seems the most credible, it can also misrepresent public opinion on the issue. The Court used the internal consensus argument in *A., B. and C. v. Ireland*, which was concerned with the extremely restrictive abortion regime in place in Ireland. Although abortion is permitted under the Irish constitution where the life of the mother is at risk[64] (including from suicide[65]), no legislation has ever been introduced regulating the mechanism by which medical professionals can determine whether or not a woman's life is endangered and certify that an abortion is

---

[61] Ibid., para. 46. [62] Ibid., para. 56. [63] Ibid., para. 60.
[64] Art 40.3.3, *Bunreacht na hÉireann* (Constitution of Ireland).
[65] *Attorney General v. X* [1992] 1 IR 1 (Supreme Court of Ireland, 5 March 1992).

3.2 TYPOLOGY OF CONSENSUS 53

constitutionally permissible.[66] Furthermore, serious risk to the life (as opposed to the health) of the mother is the only situation in which an abortion can be legally acquired in Ireland, although travel to another jurisdiction in order to procure an abortion is permitted and information relating to abortion is freely available.[67] The claimants in *A., B. and C.* challenged this abortion regime. The Court deployed internal consensus which aimed to reflect the 'profound moral views'[68] of the Irish people. This conclusion was based on the argument proposed by the Irish government that the results of three constitutional referendums on abortion,[69] together with public demands for guarantees about abortion in the Maastricht[70] and Lisbon[71] referendums,[72] evidenced an internal consensus of a profound nature. De Londras and Dzehtsiarou argue that the methodology of identification of internal consensus in *A., B. and C.* was questionable.[73] It might well be that Irish people were simply

---

[66] See, generally, J. Schweppe (ed.), *The Unborn Child, Article 40.3.3° and Abortion in Ireland: 25 Years of Protection?* (Liffey Press, 2008).

[67] Regulation of Information (Services outside the State for Termination of Pregnancies) Act 1995.

[68] *A., B. and C. v. Ireland*, para. 126.

[69] Abortion referendums were held in 1983 (introducing the 8th Amendment to the Constitution (protecting the life of the unborn with equal protection to the life of the mother)), 1992 (introducing the 13th Amendment to the Constitution (allowing for freedom to travel for the purposes of abortion) and 14th Amendment to the Constitution (allowing for the provision of information relating to abortion), but rejecting a proposed amendment to preclude abortion where the life of the mother was endangered by the risk of suicide), and 2002 (rejecting a proposal to preclude abortion where the life of the mother is endangered by suicide). For a comprehensive outline, see, for example, G. Hogan and G. Whyte, *Kelly: The Irish Constitution*, 4th edn (Tottel, 2003).

[70] Concerns about abortion becoming more available in Ireland through EU intervention resulted in Protocol 17 of the Maastricht Treaty, which provides '[n]othing in the Treaty on European Union, or in the Treaties establishing the European Communities, or in the Treaties or Acts modifying or supplementing those Treaties, shall affect the application in Ireland of Art 40.3.3 of the Constitution of Ireland'.

[71] In advance of the second referendum on the Lisbon Treaty, the European Council (Heads of Government) adopted a Decision including, in Section A, a guarantee that '[n]othing in the Treaty of Lisbon attributing legal status to the Charter of Fundamental Rights of the European Union, or in the provisions of that Treaty in the area of Freedom, Security and Justice affects in any way the scope and applicability of the protection of the right to life in Art 40.3.1, 40.3.2 and 40.3.3 ... [of] the Constitution of Ireland'.

[72] Changes to the founding treaties of the European Union that alter the 'essential scope or objectives' of the European Union can only be ratified by Ireland if approved by constitutional referendum: *Crotty v. An Taoiseach* [1987] IR 713 (Supreme Court of Ireland, 9 April 1987).

[73] F. de Londras and K. Dzehtsiarou, 'Grand Chamber of the European Court of Human Rights, *A., B. and C. v. Ireland*, Decision of 17 December 2010', *International and Comparative Law Quarterly* 62 (2013), 250.

unsatisfied with the wording of proposals that were submitted to them by the government. Some people voted against the proposal because they considered that it went too far. However, one can plausibly suggest that some people voted against these proposals because they did not go far enough.[74]

The situation in *A., B. and C.*, where extensive statistical data from the referendums were available, is exceptional. Nevertheless, even these comparatively reliable statistical data were reasonably contested by applicants[75] and legal scholars.[76] In other cases, the claim that a particular solution is supported by the general public is even harder to substantiate.

Some commentators point out that the Court should take into account the opinion of the general public. Mahoney argues that the judgments of the Court should be based on internal consensus and should not be social experiments. He states that

> [t]he international machinery of human rights protection under the Convention should not act as an undue brake on social and economic experimentation. Where societal values are still the subject of debate and controversy at national level, they should not easily be converted by the Court into protected Convention values allowing for only one approach.[77]

It may well be that the persuasiveness of a judgment would increase if the solution was supported by a societal majority within a State. At the same time, the Court cannot simply follow public opinion because human rights are typically seen as guarantees against the tyranny of the majority.[78] Moreover, given the difficulties associated with the identification of internal consensus, it may well happen that the Court would not take into account a prevailing view of the majority, since data from referendums, as in the case of *A., B. and C.*, are rarely available, but actually a view of the active and influential minority, elites or lobby groups. In reality, internal consensus is rarely used because it is highly challenging to identify it.

One can argue that European consensus as well as national consensus can be seen as an assault on the counter-majoritarian nature of human rights. Having said that, European consensus is a comparative analysis of laws of the Contracting Parties that, presumably, were adopted with

---

[74] See, ibid. for a more detailed discussion.   [75] *A., B. and C. v. Ireland*, para. 177.
[76] De Londras and Dzehtsiarou, '*A., B. and C. v. Ireland*'.
[77] P. Mahoney, 'Marvellous Richness of Diversity or Invidious Cultural Relativism?' *Human Rights Law Journal*, 17 (1998), 1, 3.
[78] R. Dworkin, *Taking Rights Seriously* (Harvard University Press, 1977), p. 194.

3.2 TYPOLOGY OF CONSENSUS

European human rights law in mind. Moreover, the nature of European consensus as a *rebuttable* presumption mitigates threats of the tyranny of the majority. In contrast, internal consensus operates at national level and has a number of attendant difficulties. The citizens of a State are not full subjects of international law. They cannot undertake international obligations in the same manner as States do. This type of analysis, therefore, cannot lay claim to the same level of normative legitimacy as those other types of consensus previously discussed.

3.2.4 Consensus among experts

The fourth type of consensus is consensus among experts. The Court typically uses this type of consensus when it has to assess scientific developments in Europe and worldwide. For instance, in *L. and V. v. Austria*, the applicants challenged Article 209 of the Austrian Criminal Code, which provided for a higher minimum age for consensual homosexual intercourse than for heterosexual intercourse. The Court affirmed the decision of the commission in *Sutherland v. the United Kingdom*.[79] This referred to 'recent research according to which sexual orientation is usually established before puberty in both boys and girls and to the fact that the majority of Member States of the Council of Europe have recognised equal ages of consent'. It explicitly stated that it was 'opportune to reconsider its earlier case-law in the light of these modern developments'.[80]

Another example is *B. v. France*, where the Court, in considering the rights of transgender people, quoted an expert opinion:

> in the light of the relevant studies carried out and work done by experts in this field, that there still remains some uncertainty as to the essential nature of transsexualism and that the legitimacy of surgical intervention in such cases is sometimes questioned.[81]

This issue was further discussed in *Christine Goodwin v. the United Kingdom*.[82] The Court confirmed that there were significant disagreements in this area but stated that this could not provide any determining

---

[79] *Sutherland v. the United Kingdom*, Application No 25186/94, Decision of 1 July 1997.
[80] *L. and V. v. Austria*, Application No 39392/98 and 39829/98, Judgment of 9 January 2003, para. 47.
[81] *B. v. France*, Application No 13343/87, Judgment of 25 March 1992, para. 48.
[82] *Christine Goodwin v. the United Kingdom*.

argument as regards the legal recognition of transsexuals.[83] In short, the Court uses expert opinions in order to resolve highly complicated and specialist issues. However, such evidence is treated as supplementary and technical rather than decisive.[84] The nature of expert evidence, whereby different experts promote different views, makes the attainment of such consensus difficult, if not impossible, in most cases.

3.3 Interactions between different types of consensus

The Court has often employed different types of consensus in a single case. On various occasions, the Court used two[85] or even three[86] different types of consensus. There is no need for the Court to weigh the different types if they support the same solution in the case. In *Micallef* v. *Malta*, the Court used the laws of the Contracting Parties and international law to support its findings in favour of evolutive interpretation. In this case, the Court extended the application of Article 6 to interim procedures. The Court stated that

> there is widespread consensus among Council of Europe member States, which either implicitly or explicitly provide [sic] for the applicability of Article 6 guarantees to interim measures, including injunction

---

[83] Ibid., para. 81–3.
[84] Some parallels here can be drawn with the impact of epistemic communities on the decision-making process. Epistemic communities were defined by Haas as 'a network of professionals with recognised expertise and competence in a particular domain and an authoritative claim to policy-relevant knowledge within that domain or issue-area'. P.M. Haas, 'Introduction: Epistemic Communities and International Policy Coordination', *International Organization*, 46 (1992), 1, 3. The commentators positively regard influence of epistemic communities on the decision-making process. See, for example, Ibid.; A.R. Zito, 'Epistemic Communities, European Union Governance and the Public Voice', *Science and Public Policy*, 28 (2001), 465. However, it is not suggested that the impact of epistemic communities is unlimited. Some commentators emphasised that if epistemic communities are involved, then a decision is affected by a limited elitist group. See, for example, L. Susskind, *Environmental Diplomacy: Negotiating More Effective Global Agreements* (Oxford University Press, 1994). Limited effect of the epistemic communities is also determined by possibly different tasks the decision-making institute pursues to the ones the epistemic communities pursue. See, P. Sabatier, 'The Advocacy Coalition Framework: Revisions and Relevance for Europe', *Journal of European Public Policy*, 5 (1998), 98; A. Jordan and J. Greenaway, 'Shifting Agendas, Changing Regulatory Structures and the "New" Politics of Environmental Pollution: British Coastal Water Policy, 1955–1995', *Public Administration*, 76 (1998), 669.
[85] See, for example, *Micallef* v. *Malta*, Application No 17056/06, Judgment of 15 October 2009.
[86] See, for example, *Christine Goodwin* v. *the United Kingdom*.

3.3 DIFFERENT TYPES OF CONSENSUS

proceedings. Similarly, as can be seen from its case-law, the Court of Justice of the European Communities considers that provisional measures must be subject to the guarantees of a fair trial, particularly to the right to be heard.[87]

The Court deployed two concurrent types of consensus to strengthen the solution selected. However, the Court has to weigh the different types of consensus in cases where they support conflicting solutions.

3.3.1 Interaction between European consensus based on comparative law and European consensus based on international treaties

The Court should clarify its methodology for deciding between consensus based on international treaties, which usually represents consensus at the level of principles, as discussed in Chapter 2, and European consensus based on a comparative analysis of laws and practices of the Contracting Parties, which often deals with rules. These two types of consensus can point in different directions. In *Kafkaris* v. *Cyprus*, the Court considered whether the Cypriot legal regime of managing the release of those sentenced to life imprisonment complied with the Convention. The Court pointed out that there were no uniform standards in relation to life imprisonment, its review and adjustments in Europe.[88] The majority of the Court also claimed that 'no clear tendency can be ascertained with regard to the system and procedures implemented in respect of early release'.[89] Therefore, the Court decided that the legal regime in Cyprus did not violate Article 3 of the Convention. Dissenting Judges Tulkens, Cabral Barreto, Fura-Sandström, Spielmann and Jebens refocused the analysis from the laws of the Contracting Parties to international law documents. They stated that

> [f]or more than thirty years the Committee of Ministers and the Parliamentary Assembly have repeatedly concerned themselves with matters relating to long-term sentences and have expressly called on member States to 'introduce conditional release in their legislation if it does not already provide for this measure' (Committee of Ministers Recommendation (2003) 22 of 23 September 2003 on conditional release). The same Recommendation further acknowledges that conditional release – which is not a form of leniency or of lighter punishment but a

---
[87] *Micallef* v. *Malta*, para. 78.
[88] *Kafkaris* v. *Cyprus*, Application No 21906/04, Judgment of 12 February 2008, para. 104.
[89] Ibid.

means of sentence implementation – 'is one of the most effective and constructive means of preventing reoffending and promoting resettlement'. The European Prison Rules adopted by the Committee of Ministers on 11 January 2006 (Recommendation (2006)2), reflecting the existing European consensus in this field, also refers to the question of release of sentenced prisoners: 'In the case of those prisoners with longer sentences in particular, steps shall be taken to ensure a gradual return to life in free society.' And very recently, in a statement of 12 November 2007, the Council of Europe's Commissioner for Human Rights firmly asserted that 'the use of life sentences should be questioned'. He added that if release was denied persistently until the end of a detainee's life, this would amount to de facto life imprisonment.[90]

In this case, the minority judges argued in favour of consensus based on international treaties, while the majority focused on the lack of consensus based on comparative law. It has to be noted that the majority did not substantiate its findings of a lack of European consensus in their judgment. A similar but not identical complaint was recently adjudicated by the ECtHR in the case of *Vinter and others v. the United Kingdom*. The applicants in this case argued that a life sentence without parole violated Article 3 of the ECHR. The Court concluded that 'there is ... now clear support in European and international law for the principle that all prisoners, including those serving life sentences, be offered the possibility of rehabilitation and the prospect of release if that rehabilitation is achieved'.[91] This includes both consensus based on comparative law and consensus based on international law.

In *Kafkaris*, a lack of European consensus prevailed over an emerging trend in international law. This case poses two challenging questions: first, whether lack of consensus should have as much impact on the outcome of the case as a present European consensus does; second, whether consensus based on international law can trump a lack of European consensus. It is nearly impossible to answer both of these questions in the abstract. The Court should enquire into the reasons behind a lack of consensus and determine whether international law captures the most recent developments in the regulation of the issue. If so, it seems that under limited circumstances the Court can give priority to international law as it did in *D. H. v. the Czech Republic*. In this case, the Czech government argued that there was a lack of

---

[90] Ibid., Dissenting Opinion of Judges Tulkens, Cabral Barreto, Fura-Sandström, Spielmann and Jebens, para. 4.
[91] *Vinter and others v. the United Kingdom*, para. 114.

3.3 DIFFERENT TYPES OF CONSENSUS   59

consensus of the first type while the majority deployed the consensus of the second type. The case concerned segregation of Roma children from other children at school. The government argued that no European standard or consensus existed regarding the criteria to be used to determine whether children should be placed in special schools or how children with special learning needs should be educated, and that the special school was one of the possible and acceptable solutions to the problem.[92] The majority of the Court stated that there was an emerging international consensus amongst the Contracting States of the Council of Europe that recognised the special needs of minorities and an obligation to protect their security, identity and lifestyle, not only for the purpose of safeguarding the interests of the minorities themselves but also to preserve a cultural diversity of value to the whole community.[93] The Court deployed relevant international mechanisms in its reasoning.[94] Dissenting Judge Jungwiert, however, pointed out that the majority of the recommendations, reports and other documents cited by the Court in this case were relatively vague, and largely theoretical.[95] Nevertheless, the Court held that there was a violation of Article 14 in conjunction with Article 2 of Protocol 1.

It is not immediately clear why the Court preferred international consensus in *D.H. v. the Czech Republic* and a lack of European consensus in *Kafkaris* v. *Cyprus*. One can argue that these two cases dealt with crucially different factual scenarios. However, the Court must explain in which circumstances international consensus can prevail over a lack of European consensus. It seems that, in doing so, the Court does not merely choose between international and domestic laws; the ECtHR has to choose between consensus of principles, which is often represented by international consensus,[96] and consensus (or lack thereof) of rules, which is usually identified through a comparison of the laws of the Contracting Parties.[97] It is not suggested that the Court should establish fixed and inflexible rules in order to find a balance between these two types of consensus. However, the reasons for preferring one over the other should be clearly articulated in the judgment. These reasons may depend on the facts and context of the case, clarity of the trend of rules and applicability of the principles to the case.

---

[92] *D.H. and others v. the Czech Republic*, para. 155.   [93] Ibid., para. 181.
[94] Ibid., para. 182, 184, 187.   [95] Ibid., Dissenting Opinion of Judge Jungwiert.
[96] See, *Chapman v. the United Kingdom*; *D.H. and others v. the Czech Republic*; *Marckx v. Belgium*.
[97] *Micallef* v. *Malta*; *Ünal Tekeli* v. *Turkey*.

3.3.2 Interaction between European consensus and internal consensus

The interactions between European and internal consensus pose questions of normative legitimacy if the commonly accepted standards represented by European consensus are confronted by the standards adopted in a particular Contracting Party represented by internal consensus. As noted in *Tyrer v. the United Kingdom*, the Court questioned the Isle of Man attorney general's argument that corporal punishment did not outrage public opinion on the island.[98] At the same time, the Court relied on the developments and commonly accepted standards in the penal policy of the Member States of the Council of Europe in this field.[99]

De Londras and Dzehtsiarou have recently examined the situation where the Court chooses internal consensus over European one and have called this phenomenon 'trumping consensus'.[100] The Court agreed to 'trump' European consensus only on one occasion, in *A., B. and C. v. Ireland*. The Court considered the results of referendums in Ireland and agreed with the government that there was internal consensus in relation to abortion in Ireland.[101] At the same time, the Court came to the conclusion that there was European consensus in favour of allowing abortion on broader grounds than accorded under Irish law.[102] The majority of the Court avoided juxtaposing European consensus and internal consensus explicitly and, instead, drew them apart on two different issues by comparing European consensus on the matter of abortion and the lack of European consensus on the matter of when life begins:

> In the present case, and contrary to the Government's submission, the Court considers that there is indeed a consensus amongst a substantial majority of the Contracting States of the Council of Europe towards allowing abortion on broader grounds than accorded under Irish law. In particular, the Court notes that the first and second applicants could have obtained an abortion on request (according to certain criteria including gestational limits) in some 30 such States. The first applicant could have obtained an abortion justified on health and well-being grounds in approximately 40 Contracting States and the second applicant could have obtained an abortion justified on well-being grounds in some 35 Contracting States. Only 3 States have more restrictive access to abortion services than in Ireland namely, a prohibition on abortion regardless of the risk to the woman's life ... However, the Court does not consider that

---

[98] *Tyrer v. the United Kingdom*, para. 31.   [99] Ibid.
[100] De Londras and Dzehtsiarou, '*A., B. and C. v. Ireland*'.
[101] *A, B and C v. Ireland*, para. 226.   [102] Ibid., para. 235.

3.3 DIFFERENT TYPES OF CONSENSUS

this consensus decisively narrows the broad margin of appreciation of the State. Of central importance is the finding in the above-cited *Vo* case that the question of when the right to life begins came within the States' margin of appreciation because there was no European consensus on the scientific and legal definition of the beginning of life, so that it was impossible to answer the question whether the unborn was a person to be protected for the purposes of Article 2. Since the rights claimed on behalf of the foetus and those of the mother are inextricably interconnected, the margin of appreciation accorded to a State's protection of the unborn necessarily translates into a margin of appreciation for that State as to how it balances the conflicting rights of the mother. It follows that, even if it appears from the national laws referred to that most Contracting Parties may in their legislation have resolved those conflicting rights and interests in favour of greater legal access to abortion, this consensus cannot be a decisive factor in the Court's examination of whether the impugned prohibition on abortion in Ireland for health and well-being reasons struck a fair balance between the conflicting rights and interests, notwithstanding an evolutive interpretation of the Convention.[103]

The Court, therefore, was not choosing between internal and European consensus explicitly. Despite these two types of consensus being discussed in different parts of the judgment[104] it has been argued that internal consensus outweighed European consensus.[105] Dissenting judges Rozakis, Tulkens, Fura, Hirvelä, Malinverni and Poalelungi expressed their opinion on the issue of balancing the different types of consensus:

> it is the first time that the Court has disregarded the existence of a European consensus on the basis of 'profound moral views'. Even assuming that these profound moral views are still well embedded in the conscience of the majority of Irish people, to consider that this can override the European consensus, which tends in a completely different direction, is a real and dangerous new departure in the Court's case-law.[106]

In concurring with the dissenting judges in *A., B. and C.*, it is worth mentioning that a justification based on internal consensus seems questionable and can lead to negative consequences for the substantive

---

[103] Ibid., para. 235–7.
[104] Internal consensus was analysed in the part of the judgment concerned with the legitimate aim of interference; European consensus was considered in the part of the judgment where the Court analysed necessity of interference in democratic society.
[105] S. McAvoy, 'Profound Moral Values?', available at www.humanrights.ie/index.php/2011/01/04/profound-moral-values-mcavoy-on-a-b-c-v-ireland, accessed on 24 February 2011. See also, de Londras and Dzehtsiarou, '*A., B. and C. v. Ireland*'.
[106] *A., B. and C. v. Ireland*, Dissenting Opinion of Judges Rozakis, Tulkens, Fura, Hirvelä, Malinverni and Poalelungi, para. 9.

legitimacy of the rulings of the ECtHR. It is widely accepted that the ECtHR is becoming a constitutionalist court.[107] In order to ensure compliance with its judgments, the Court has to be legitimate, and it is central to this book to argue that European consensus is capable of enhancing the legitimacy of the ECtHR.[108] Trumping internal consensus has the potential to undermine the positive impact on legitimacy that European consensus might have. De Londras and Dzehtsiarou argue that there are at least two serious threats to the legitimacy of the ECtHR if it allows the trumping of internal consensus:

> First of all it may act to 'fudge' the question of what a particular provision of the Convention requires of states and of whether (and, if so, under what circumstances) a State can provide a level of protection lower than that apparently required but still remain within the bounds of the Convention. In other words, States may wonder what exactly it is that the Convention requires of them and whether they can themselves construct a compelling enough case for an internal consensus that would allow for them to 'trump' the general European position. Furthermore, a State that currently forms part of the European consensus as identified by the Court may in fact have in place a certain legal or regulatory regime precisely because it considered that to be required in order to be Convention compliant, even if it was not particularly desired. In other words, there may be situations where the Convention has had precisely the exogenous force on domestic legal and regulatory systems that was desired (i.e. it has resulted in domestic legal change 'upwards' even without a judgment against the State), but the identification of a trumping internal consensus in one State may either foster resentment in other States *or* result in other States recalibrating laws 'downwards' on the basis of a self-declared trumping internal consensus. That is arguably more likely to happen in relation to matters of particular moral and social controversy – such as

---

[107] S. Hennette-Vauchez, 'Reformatory Rationales Mismatch the Plural Paths of Legitimacy of ECHR Law' in J. Christoffersen and M.R. Madsen (eds.), *The European Court of Human Rights between Law and Politics* (Oxford University Press, 2011); L. Wildhaber, 'Rethinking the European Court of Human Rights' in J. Christoffersen and M.R. Madsen (eds.), *The European Court of Human Rights between Law and Politics* (Oxford University Press, 2011); L. Wildhaber, 'A Constitutional Future for the ECHR', *Human Rights Law Journal*, 5 (2002), 161. Some argue the Court is in fact a constitutional court. See A. Stone Sweet, *A Europe of Rights: The Impact of the ECHR on National Legal Systems* (Oxford University Press, 2008); A. Stone Sweet, 'On the Constitutionalisation of the Convention: The European Court of Human Rights as a Constitutional Court', *Revue Trimestrielle des Droits de l'Homme*, 80 (2009), 923; K. Dzehtsiarou and A. Greene, 'Restructuring the European Court of Human Rights: Preserving the Right of Individual Petition and Promoting Constitutionalism', *Public Law* (2013), 710.

[108] See, Chapter 6 for more details.

3.3 DIFFERENT TYPES OF CONSENSUS

abortion – where campaigners on a particular side of the debate might argue that in fact the Convention does not require as liberal a legal regime as exists and in fact that further restricting individual freedoms would be permissible based on the case in which a trumping internal consensus was established. Second, the notion that European consensus might be subordinate to internal consensus within any particular State might bolster broader arguments that the Convention ought to be subordinate to decisions taken at the national level. This would likely undermine the effectiveness and harmonising capacity of judgments emanating from the Strasbourg Court. As its core, an argument of trumping internal consensus is one that makes the nature and content of an international legal obligation subject to public sentiment and public acceptance of obligations within the contracting party, notwithstanding the fact that individuals are not full subjects of international law. This adds to the counterintuitive nature of the proposition that commonly accepted minimal human rights standards would be subordinate to public sentiment within a respondent State.[109]

The argument that the Contracting Parties will use internal consensus to question the Court's rulings can be substantiated by reference to the hostile reaction of the British media and politicians to the Court's decisions in *Hirst (No 2)* v. *the United Kingdom* and *Greens and M. T.* v. *the United Kingdom*. The Court ruled that a blanket ban on prisoner voting which existed in the UK violated Article 3 of Protocol 1. It is worth noting that the Court's deployment of consensus in this case was questionable, and there was no overwhelming consensus as in *A., B. and C.* Nevertheless, in *Hirst*, the Court accepted that

> although there is some disagreement about the legal position in certain States, it is undisputed that the United Kingdom is not alone among Convention countries in depriving all convicted prisoners of the right to vote. It may also be said that the law in the United Kingdom is less far-reaching than in certain other States. Not only are exceptions made for persons committed to prison for contempt of court or for default in paying fines, but unlike the position in some countries, the legal incapacity to vote is removed as soon as the person ceases to be detained. However, the fact remains that it is a minority of Contracting States in which a blanket restriction on the right of convicted prisoners to vote is imposed or in which there is no provision allowing prisoners to vote. Even according to the Government's own figures, the number of such States does not exceed thirteen.[110]

---

[109] De Londras and Dzehtsiarou, '*A., B. and C.* v. *Ireland*', 259.
[110] *Hirst* v. *the United Kingdom (No 2)*, para. 81.

Despite this quite substantial divergence in opinions, the Court found a violation in this case, and this ruling could be executed only through the amendment of relevant British law. However, the UK back bench parliamentarians adopted a motion rejecting amendments to legislation proposed by the governments following the Strasbourg ruling.[111]

The parliamentarians used an internal consensus-related argument, namely that if a particular law enjoys national support then the ECtHR cannot legitimately interfere. David Davis, a Member of the British Parliament, stated that '[o]ne of the points about laws in a democracy is that they exist, at the very least, with the acquiescence – the consent, we hope – of everybody in that democracy. Between 75% and 90% of the population cannot understand what we are doing in even considering this proposal [to allow prisoners to vote].'[112] Jack Straw pointed out that

> [a] ban on convicted prisoners voting while in jail has existed in this country at least since 1970. Post-war, the question has been considered under a Labour Administration in 1968, a Conservative Administration in 1983 and a Labour Administration in 1999–2000. On each occasion, the position was confirmed by an overwhelming cross-party consensus. On each occasion, amendments could easily have been moved in the House by those who supported an end to the ban, and voted on. On none of those occasions, and on no other occasion that I can recall, has this ever been a matter of active pursuit for Members of any party in this House.

Philip Hollobone stated that '[i]t is the settled view of the British people, through their elected representatives in the British Parliament, that prisoners should not have the right to vote, and it has been that way since 1870'.[113] Finally, he questioned the legitimacy of the ECtHR by asking '[h]ow has it come about that we, in a sovereign Parliament, have let these decisions be taken by a kangaroo court in Strasbourg, the judgments of which do not enjoy the respect of our constituents?'[114] Setting aside the hostile attitude of the British MPs towards the ECtHR, these arguments tend to place internal legitimacy over European. Analysis of internal consensus by the British MPs vaguely resembles

---

[111] I. White and V. Miller, 'Prisoners' Voting Rights. Summary of the Debate', available at www.parliament.uk/documents/commons/lib/research/briefings/snpc-01764.pdf, accessed on 2 July 2011; see also E. Bates, 'Controversy over Prisoners' Right to Vote in UK', available at http://echrblog.blogspot.com/2011/02/controversy-over-prisoners-right-to.html, accessed on 25 February 2011; C. Murray, 'The Backlash against Prisoner Voting Reform in the UK', available at http://www.humanrights.ie/index.php/2011/01/28/the-backlash-against-prisoner-voting-rights-in-the-uk, accessed on 25 February 2011.
[112] The Backbench Parliamentary Debates, 'Prisoners' Right to Vote'. [113] Ibid.
[114] Ibid.

3.3 DIFFERENT TYPES OF CONSENSUS

the one conducted by the ECtHR itself in *A., B. and C. v. Ireland*. In *A., B. and C.*, the matter at issue was arguably more morally sensitive than in *Hirst* and *Greens and M. T.*[115] However, it is another reason for heeding the warning that the dissenting judges articulated, namely that the Court undertook a dangerous departure from its case law.[116]

3.3.3 European consensus and international trends

International trend has not been listed as one of the types of consensus as it has only been used by the ECtHR once, in *Christine Goodwin v. the United Kingdom*, and it cannot be technically called a consensus. International trend means a development in the laws of States which are not members of the Council of Europe. The Court often quotes legal provisions or case law of the highest courts of the United States,[117] Canada,[118] Australia,[119] New Zealand,[120] South Africa[121] and other countries. Detailed analysis of these references falls outside the scope of this book. This section will only consider cases where foreign laws contradict European consensus or lack thereof.

In *Christine Goodwin*, the ECtHR used the international trend in transsexual rights protection to support its decision to overrule its previous judgment. The Grand Chamber of the Court delivered its judgment in *Christine Goodwin* only four years after it considered an almost identical issue in *Sheffield and Horsham v. the United Kingdom*.[122] In the latter case, the Court confirmed that there was no consensus in Europe over 'the problems created by the recognition in law of post-operative gender status'.[123] In 2002, in *Christine Goodwin*, the ECtHR noted that nothing had changed in Europe, and therefore the Court

---

[115] *Greens and M.T. v. the United Kingdom*; *Hirst v. the United Kingdom (No 2)*.
[116] *A., B. and C. v. Ireland*, Joint Partly Dissenting Opinion of Judges Rozakis, Tulkens, Fura, Hirvelä, Malinverni and Poalelungi, para. 9.
[117] *Appleby and others v. the United Kingdom*, Application No 44306/98, Judgment of 6 May 2003, para. 25–30.
[118] *Hirst v. the United Kingdom (No 2)*, para. 35–7.
[119] *Neulinger and Shuruk v. Switzerland*, Application No 41615/07, Judgment of 6 July 2010, para. 72.
[120] *Gas and Dubois v. France*, Application No 25951/07, Judgment of 15 March 2012, para. 56.
[121] *Hirst v. the United Kingdom (No 2)*, para. 38–9.
[122] *Sheffield and Horsham v. the United Kingdom*, Application No 22985/93 and 23390/94, Judgment of 30 July 1998.
[123] Ibid., para. 57.

decided to justify evolutive interpretation by reference to an international trend.[124]

The Court deployed international trend to substantiate its claim that external circumstances had changed since its judgment in *Sheffield and Horsham*.[125] However, the hardly identifiable, vague concept of international trend may undermine the legitimacy of the judgments and negatively affect the legitimacy of European consensus.[126]

This section argues that the Court's reliance on an international trend in *Christine Goodwin* was far-fetched. Moreover, deployment of international trend brings serious legitimacy concerns for the individual judgment and the role of European consensus. It is not argued here that the Court had to decide this case differently on its merits, especially given that the violation of the Convention should have been found four years earlier in *Sheffield and Horsham*; however, the methods of interpretation deployed in this case are open to criticism.

In *Christine Goodwin*, the ECtHR confirmed the lack of a European consensus regarding transsexual rights but identified a 'continuing international trend' in this area.[127] Moreover, the ECtHR stated that there was 'clear and uncontested evidence' of this trend.[128] The Court mentioned the following jurisdictions to substantiate its claim of the existence of an international trend that recognised transsexual rights: Singapore, Canada, South Africa, Israel, Australia, New Zealand and all except two of the states of the United States of America.

Taken literally, the phrase 'continuing international trend' is less demanding than European consensus in terms of the quantity of the comparators.[129] Legal development in six predominantly common-law jurisdictions led the Court to conclude that the international trend was present. This approach can face serious legitimacy challenges. First, the conclusion about the presence of the 'continuing international trend' was based on the *amicus curiae* brief submitted by the human rights NGO called Liberty. The Court did not consider laws of those countries which were not listed by Liberty. Second, the international trend was a reason to disregard the lack of European consensus. One can suggest that in

---

[124] *Christine Goodwin v. the United Kingdom*, paras. 84–5.   [125] Ibid., para. 84.
[126] J.L. Murray, 'The Influence of the European Convention on Fundamental Rights on Community Law', *Fordham International Law Journal*, 33 (2010), 1388, 1405.
[127] *Christine Goodwin v. the United Kingdom*.   [128] Ibid., para. 84.
[129] If 'consensus' is understood literally, it requires total unanimity among the Contracting Parties. The term trend suggests development in a particular direction. See, Chapter 2 for more details.

3.3 DIFFERENT TYPES OF CONSENSUS 67

Christine Goodwin the ECtHR attached more weight to international trend than to legal developments within the Contracting Parties. This can undermine the legitimacy of European consensus, since the ECtHR makes it subordinate to a vague concept of 'international trend'. Finally, if European consensus has a legitimising potential as it is an implicit consent of the Contracting Parties and a sign of a dialogue between the ECtHR and the Contracting Parties,[130] then the legitimising potential of the 'international trend' is doubtful, since the Contracting Parties have never consented to be constrained by the ECHR rights as they are understood in the United States, New Zealand or Australia.

The Court did not define what it meant by 'continuing international trend'. If this trend can be established when only one or few jurisdictions amended their laws in a particular direction, then the trend did exist in *Christine Goodwin* in the material time. However, if this is the case, then arguably any legal development outside the Council of Europe can allow the Court to disregard European consensus or lack thereof. If an international trend requires more substantial change, then the Court should have considered how transsexual rights are protected in the jurisdictions other than those listed by 'Liberty'.

While the Court took into account developments in some democratic States, it did not insist that it should deal solely with the 'continuing international trend among democratic nations'. Therefore, the following outline of how transsexual rights are recognised worldwide and not only among democratic States seems relevant. This section examines sample laws related to the status of transsexuals to show that the Court could equally establish an 'international trend' that restricted transsexual rights. For example, in Islamic law, which is widespread in Asia, Africa and some parts of Europe, transsexual rights are not recognised. Islam permits only hermaphrodites to undergo a sex change operation so that the person can be either a female or a male.[131] However, Islam forbids males to behave like females in terms of cross-dressing, wearing make-up, injecting hormones to enlarge their breasts and undergoing sex change operations.[132] Despite this, in Turkey, which is a Member of the

---

[130] For a more detailed discussion of the legitimacy of European consensus, see Chapter 6.
[131] B. Dupret, 'Sexual Morality at the Egyptian Bar: Female Circumcision, Sex Change Operations, and Motives for Suing', *Islamic Law and Society*, 9 (2002), 42, 51.
[132] Y.K. Teh, 'The Male To Female Transsexuals in Malaysia: What Should We Do with Them?' (Fourth International Malaysian Studies Conference 2004), available at www.cpiasia.net/v3/index.php/social/173-gender/630-the-male-to-female-transsexuals-in-malaysia-what-should-we-do-with-them, accessed on 28 June 2011.

Council of Europe and where the majority of the population is Muslim, a transsexual person may obtain a new identity card that specifies his or her post-operative sex.[133] In the majority of the non-European countries with a dominating Muslim population, gender reassignment surgery is legally forbidden.

In a similar way to Islamic law, Chinese legislation and practice cannot be considered to be a tolerant one towards gender reassignment surgery. It is nearly impossible to obtain permission to perform transsexual surgery. The problem is not a lack of appropriate surgical techniques and facilities. If permission were given, transsexual surgery could be performed with little difficulty in most large hospitals. The problem is perceptual and ideological.[134]

In India, there is no recognition of the rights of transsexuals in law.[135] Traditional prejudices influence the legal framework in this area.[136] In India and Bangladesh, there are a few groups that identify themselves as an intermediary sex between male and female. They are not protected by law; their transgressive sexuality, which is hostile to heterosexist norms of society, is circumscribed by experiences of shame, dishonour and violence.[137]

Most of the African States hold intolerant attitudes towards transsexuals. Transsexual rights are not recognised; transsexuals, for instance, are deprived of the right to marry. The South African Law Reform Commission published a report on domestic partnerships, and this contains facts about intolerance towards transsexuals in Zimbabwean, Kenyan, Nigerian and Namibian law and practice.[138]

The lack of recognition of transsexual rights in the Muslim world, in China and India and in many African countries makes the Court findings that establish a 'continuing international trend' less credible. The methodology used by the Court can be described as 'choosing friends in a crowd': considering the jurisdictions which support the necessary

---

[133] A. Polat, 'Family Attitudes toward Transgendered People in Turkey: Experience from a Secular Islamic Country', *International Journal of Psychiatry in Medicine*, 35 (2005), 383.
[134] F.-F. Ruan, *Sex in China* (Springer, 1991), p. 156.
[135] Report of People's Union for Civil Liberties, 'Human Rights Violations against Sexual Minorities in India' (2001).
[136] See R.P. Goldman, 'Transsexualism, Gender, and Anxiety in Traditional India', *Journal of the American Oriental Society*, 113 (1993), 374.
[137] People's Union for Civil Liberties, 'Human Rights Violations against Sexual Minorities in India'.
[138] South African Law Reform Commission, 'Report on Domestic Partnerships', available at www.doj.gov.za/salrc/reports/r_prj118_2006march.pdf, accessed on 4 July 2011.

3.3 DIFFERENT TYPES OF CONSENSUS 69

outcome while disregarding the others.[139] Sunstein observes that 'assessment of international practice may turn out to be opportunistic rather than objective – a matter of looking for friendly precedents, rather than some kind of consensus'.[140] Arguably, that is what happened in *Christine Goodwin* v. *the United Kingdom*.

Even if one agrees that an international trend existed in *Christine Goodwin*, the mere fact of deployment of the 'continuing international trend' poses some legitimacy concerns. One can wonder to what extent international trend can legitimately be deployed as a compelling argument in the reasoning of the ECtHR. There are at least two challenges the Court's deployment of international trends can face: normative and procedural.

From the normative point of view, one should consider if the Court can deploy foreign law when the issue at matter has been regulated by the Contracting Parties to the Convention. It is common for national and international courts to deploy foreign laws in their judgments,[141] but these laws only have persuasive value and do not normally trump national law. Discussion about deployment of foreign law is especially heated in relation to the jurisprudence of the US Supreme Court. In some cases it relies on consensus amongst the US states in its reasoning.[142] This practice is controversial enough,[143] but the US Supreme Court's reliance on foreign laws has attracted even greater criticism. The dissenting opinion of Justice Scalia in *Lawrence* v. *Texas* illustrates the main patterns of such critique. In this case, the US Supreme Court was asked to decide whether Texas laws criminalising homosexual behaviour violated the US

---

[139] *Roper* v. *Simmons*, 543 US 551, 617 (2005) (Scalia J., dissenting). For more detailed discussion of the case selection in comparative law, see, R. Hirschl, 'The Question of Case Selection in Comparative Constitutional Law', *American Journal of Comparative Law*, 53 (2005), 125; S. Kentridge, 'Comparative Law in Constitutional Adjudication: The South African Experience', *Tulane Law Review*, 80 (2006), 245, 251.

[140] C.R. Sunstein, *A Constitution of Many Minds* (Princeton University Press, 2009), p. 192.

[141] See, B. Flanagan and S. Ahern, 'Judicial Decision-Making and Transnational Law: A Survey of Common Law Supreme Court Judges', *International and Comparative Law Quarterly*, 60 (2011), 1; K. Dzehtsiarou and C. O'Mahony, 'Evolutive Interpretation of Rights Provisions: A Comparison of the European Court of Human Rights and the US Supreme Court', *Columbia Human Rights Law Review*, 44 (2013), 309; I. Cram, 'Resort to Foreign Constitutional Norms in Domestic Human Rights Jurisprudence with Reference to Terrorism Cases', *Cambridge Law Journal*, 68 (2009), 118.

[142] See, for example, *Roper* v. *Simmons*.

[143] See, T. Jacoby, 'The Subtle Unraveling of Federalism: The Illogic of Using State Legislation as Evidence of an Evolving National Consensus', *North Carolina Law Review*, 84 (2006), 1089; 'State Law as "Other Law": Our Fifty Sovereigns in the Federal Constitutional Canon', *Harvard Law Review*, 120 (2007), 1670.

constitution.[144] Justice Scalia first emphasised that the Supreme Court was selective in its assessment of foreign laws, deploying only laws that supported its position. He also pointed out that '[t]he Court's discussion of these foreign views (ignoring, of course, the many countries that have retained criminal prohibitions on sodomy) is therefore meaningless dicta. Dangerous dicta, however, since this Court ... should not impose foreign moods, fads, or fashions on Americans.'[145] The ECtHR is more open to foreign views than the US Supreme Court. However, this does not mean that these views should prevail over European consensus. Chapter 6 will argue that European consensus enhances the legitimacy of the Court because it can be conceptualised as an implicit consent of the Contracting Parties and a mode of dialogue between the ECtHR and the Contracting Parties. Reliance on foreign laws can achieve neither of these.

The second challenge that reliance on international trends may face is a procedural one, namely that such reliance undermines the predictability of the Court's case law. Brauch correctly points out that the ECtHR

> does not tell individuals or governments when a State action becomes a Convention violation. In these cases [*Sheffield and Horsham*], the Court essentially told the United Kingdom: 'You may rely on your birth certificate record system for now, but at some undetermined time in the future, there will be a consensus. And then you must stop.' Yet the United Kingdom had no guidance on when that would be or how such a consensus would be reached – or even identified. Even worse, in the end, the United Kingdom was waiting for the wrong thing. When the Court finally arrived at the I. and Goodwin decisions, finding the United Kingdom's system to violate Article 8, it did so upon a totally different basis. Not a consensus. A 'trend'. And not even a European trend, but an 'international trend'. Apparently, the United Kingdom and other countries within the Council of Europe should have been monitoring legal trends in Australia and New Zealand to determine their obligations under the European Convention.[146]

Unpredictability of the 'continuing international trend' is also pointed out by Sandland: 'the Court seems almost to endorse a chaos theory version of jurisprudence, where developments and "trends" bounce around the globe in unpredictable ways'.[147] In examining *Christine Goodwin*, Murray comes to the conclusion that European consensus is

---

[144] *Lawrence v. Texas*, 539 US 558 (2003). [145] Ibid.
[146] Brauch, 'The Margin of Appreciation', 145.
[147] Sandland, 'Crossing and Not Crossing'.

not an objective criterion in the Court's reasoning.[148] This observation suggests that the Court's decision to overrule a lack of European consensus on the basis of an international trend poses serious questions of legitimacy. This section argues that if such a vague, intangible and potentially conflicting notion of an international trend is used, then the potential predictability flowing from consensus ceases to exist. *Christine Goodwin* is the only case where the 'continuing international trend' concept has been deployed. If the Court applies this concept again, it should clearly articulate how it should be identified and treated, especially when compared to European consensus.

3.4 Conclusion

Four types of consensus have been deployed by the ECtHR. The first type is based on the analysis of national laws of the Contracting Parties. The second type of consensus is based on international treaties. The third type of consensus is internal consensus, which apparently reflects the public sentiments in a particular Member State. The fourth type is consensus among the experts, which is rarely used by the Court as it is deployed only in cases that require special scientific or technical knowledge.

The Court sometimes deploys two or even more types of consensus in the same judgment. In some cases, these types of consensus can contradict each other. Therefore, finding a balance between different types is particularly important. If the Court is choosing between the first and second types of consensus, it can be flexible but should clearly state the reasons for basing its judgments on a particular type. If European consensus is allowed to be trumped by internal consensus, then the Court is risking its legitimacy, because it confirms that internal interests can prevail over European ones. Finally, foreign laws can be used by the Court for persuasive purposes. However, they cannot claim the same level of legitimacy as European consensus.

---

[148] Murray mentions *Christine Goodwin* v. *the United Kingdom* as an example of multiple approaches of the ECtHR to European consensus. He concludes that '[t]hese differences in the approach of the Court to the determinative value of consensus and the somewhat lax approach to the objective indicia used to determine consensus'. Murray, 'Consensus: Concordance, or Hegemony of Majority', p. 57.

4

Behind the scenes

Comparative analysis within the Court

4.1 Introduction

The European consensus argument is applied by the European Court of Human Rights (ECtHR or Court) to almost all Convention rights. Once deployed, this argument creates a presumption that is not easily rebutted.[1] The Court will follow a solution supported by the majority of the Contracting Parties unless strong justification is available to the contrary. In these circumstances, the Court should base its conclusion as to the presence or absence of European consensus on sound comparative legal research. Otherwise, the consensus argument loses its bite and undermines the credibility of the ECtHR. Carozza states that

> [t]he Court's haphazard and overly casual assertions of similarities or divergences in national laws constitute a serious weakness that undermines the legitimacy of the Court by rationalizing its crucial turns in justification on little more than hunches about European commonality and patterns of legal, social, and moral development.[2]

Some commentators see European consensus as an entirely unacceptable method of interpretation of the European Convention on Human Rights (ECHR or Convention).[3] For these commentators, it makes little difference whether consensus is based on proper comparative analysis or not. However, there is a larger group of critics who see value in the European consensus argument but maintain that the way it is identified

---

The author is grateful to Montserrat Enrich-Mas, the Head of the Research and Library Division of the Court, for providing information about the working methods of the Research Division.

[1] E. Brems, *Human Rights: Universality and Diversity* (Springer, 2001), p. 420.

[2] P.G. Carozza, 'Uses and Misuses of Comparative Law in International Human Rights: Some Reflections on the Jurisprudence of the European Court of Human Rights', *Notre Dame Law Review*, 73 (1997–1998), 1217, 1225.

[3] See, for example, G. Letsas, *A Theory of Interpretation of the European Convention on Human Rights* (Oxford University Press, 2009), p. 3.

can be improved.[4] This chapter discusses the latter criticism and argues that the Court's comparative legal research has evolved substantially during the last 10–15 years. The Court has come a long way from basing its findings on *ad hoc* comparative data and knowledge of the judges[5] to much more professionally prepared comparative reports. This chapter offers a snapshot of how comparative data are collected and presented in the judgments of the Court. It argues that the Court's efforts in professionalising comparative research should be welcomed because they increase the credibility of European consensus.

This chapter first examines how comparative research fits the Court's own vision of a successful regional human rights tribunal. It argues that presenting the results of comparative law makes the judgments more convincing, even for those Contracting Parties that were not respondents in the case. It also suggests that the Court uses comparative law for the purposes of persuasion and information. Section 4.3 considers the reasons why many commentators are concerned about the way comparative law is collected and presented by the Court. The Court's practice is described in Section 4.4, which also addresses some points raised in Section 4.3. This chapter also offers analyses of the key challenges that the Court faces and suggests the following solutions. First, in order to be comprehensive, comparative research should summarise the relevant laws of all 47 Contracting Parties, as well as incorporate a summary that integrates comparative research into the text of the judgment. Second, the Court should take into account the relevant national context in which the norm being scrutinised operates. Third, the subject matter of comparison and the questions asked to the Research Division should be carefully considered and discussed by the judges of the Chamber or the Grand Chamber. Finally, the Court should carefully approach the translation of legal terms and the comparison of functionally equivalent laws. It is suggested that if the ECtHR follows these rules, a conclusion about the presence or absence of European consensus based on comparative analysis will become clearer and more consistent. In this manner, the Court can fully utilise the legitimising potential of European consensus.

---

[4] See, for example, L.R. Helfer, 'Consensus, Coherence and the European Convention on Human Rights', *Cornell International Law Journal*, 23 (1993), 133, 164.
[5] L. Wildhaber, A. Hjartarson and S. Donnelly, 'No Consensus on Consensus? The Practice of the European Court of Human Rights', *Human Rights Law Journal*, 33 (2013), 248, 257.

4.2 Purposes of comparative law

The ECtHR invests resources in producing comparative law reports, and it seems that these resources are well spent. This section examines how comparative law fits the vision of the ECtHR as an influential regional human rights court. Of central importance for this section is the argument that rigorous comparative research is needed to support the Court's role as an institution capable of shaping the European public order and influencing the development of human rights worldwide. This section continues by pointing out that comparative law is not only produced by the Court for the purposes of persuasion but can also be used for information purposes only.

4.2.1 Fit and vision

The ECtHR is not only the Court that adjudicates human rights disputes between individuals and States, but it is also an institution that inspires human rights protection across the world.[6] This broader mission of the ECtHR is twofold: on the one hand, the Court is there to shape European public order; on the other hand, it contributes to the development of international human rights standards.

The Court's involvement in European public order[7] often means an involvement in 'public policy', as understood by courts in the

---

[6] For analysis of the application of European consensus in Europe, see, H. Keller and A. Stone Sweet (eds.), *A Europe of Rights: The Impact of the ECHR on National Legal Systems* (Oxford University Press, 2008); A. Bodnar, 'Res Interpretata: Legal Effect of the European Court of Human Rights' Judgments for Other States Than Those Which Were Party to the Proceedings' in Y. Haeck and E. Brems (eds.), *Human Rights and Civil Liberties in the 21st Century* (Springer, 2014). The Court has also been quoted by the Inter-American Court of Human Rights and the UN Human Rights Committee; see J.G. Merrills, *The Development of International Law by the European Court of Human Rights* (Manchester University Press, 1993), pp. 17–21. National supreme and constitutional courts also often refer to the ECtHR jurisprudence. See, for example, the US Supreme Court quoting with approval the ECtHR case of *Dudgeon v. the United Kingdom* in *Lawrence v. Texas*, 539 US 558, 570, 583–84 (2003).

[7] See, for example, *Loizidou v. Turkey (Preliminary Objections)*, Application No 15318/89, Judgment of 23 March 1995, para. 93, where the Court emphasised 'the special character of the Convention as an instrument of European public order (*ordre public*) for the protection of individual human beings'; *Banković and others v. Belgium et al.*, Application No 52207/99, Decision of 12 December 2001, para. 80; C. Eckes and T. Konstadinides, 'Introduction' in C. Eckes and T. Konstadinides (eds.), *Crime within the Area of Freedom, Security and Justice* (Cambridge University Press, 2011), p. 3.

4.2 PURPOSES OF COMPARATIVE LAW

common-law countries.[8] Forde states that '[i]n civil law countries *ordre public* also connotes legislative provisions which are peremptory or *jus cogens*, i.e. provisions which cannot be contracted out of or otherwise undercut'.[9] For the purposes of this chapter, the notion of European public order is taken to consist of a set of shared rules and principles among European nations which are so fundamental that they form the foundation of European society. For example, democracy is one of these principles.[10] While broader examination of European public order clearly falls outside the scope of this book, it is sufficient to say that its principles should not be seen to have been picked arbitrarily by the ECtHR and should indeed be shared by European nations.[11] Lord Hoffmann, writing extrajudicially, offers a powerful critique of what he considers inadequate representation of European public order. While discussing the concurring opinion of Judge Zupančič in *von Hannover* v. *Germany*,[12] Lord Hoffmann states that

> [w]hat legislative power the judicial representative of Slovenia can wield from his chambers in Strasbourg. Out with this pernicious American influence. What do their courts or Founding Fathers know of human rights? It is we in Strasbourg who decree the European public order. Let the balance be struck differently, I say, and all the courts of Europe must jump to attention.[13]

---

[8] See M. Forde, 'The "*Ordre Public*" Exception and Adjudicative Jurisdiction Conventions', *International and Comparative Law Quarterly*, 29 (1980), 259; W.E. Holder, 'Public Policy and National Preferences, The Exclusion of Foreign law in English Private International Law', *International and Comparative Law Quarterly*, 17 (1968), 926.

[9] Forde, 'The "*Ordre Public*" Exception', 259.

[10] In *Yumak and Sadak* v. *Turkey*, the Court pointed out that '[d]emocracy constitutes a fundamental element of the "European public order"'. *Yumak and Sadak* v. *Turkey*, Application No 10226/03, Judgment of 8 July 2008, para. 105.

[11] Mahoney argues that the ECHR is 'above all about law in society'. He points out that such a society consists of ECHR Contracting Parties taken individually and collectively as well as broader international community. P. Mahoney, 'The Comparative Method in Judgments of the European Court of Human Rights: Reference Back to National Law' in G. Canivet, M. Andenas and D. Fairgrieve (eds.), *Comparative Law before the Courts* (The British Institute of International and Comparative Law, 2004), p. 137.

[12] Especially the following paragraphs: 'The German private-law doctrine of Persönlichkeitsrecht testifies to a broader concentric circle of protected privacy. Moreover, I believe that the courts have to some extent and under American influence made a fetish of the freedom of the press. The Persönlichkeitsrecht doctrine imparts a higher level of civilised interpersonal deportment. It is time that the pendulum swung back to a different kind of balance between what is private and secluded and what is public and unshielded.' *Von Hannover* v. *Germany*, Application No 59320/00, Judgment of 24 June 2004, Concurring Opinion of Judge Zupančič.

[13] L. Hoffmann, 'The Universality of Human Rights', *Law Quarterly Review*, 125 (2009), 416, 429.

Setting aside the emotional aspect of this statement, the main point of Lord Hoffmann's critique is that the key principles should not be stated so blatantly by the ECtHR but should be strongly justified by the fact that they are shared and supported by the Contracting Parties. In this way, comparative law can help the Court to demonstrate the level of acceptance of a particular rule or principle. If European consensus based on rigorous comparative legal analysis supports the Court's findings, it appears to be a powerful tool the Court can use to gain the support of the stakeholders. This approach to comparative law is generally shared by judges; former ECtHR Judge Caflisch pointed out that comparative analysis keeps 'the ECtHR firmly on a level of reality'.[14] A judge of the Supreme Court of Israel, Aaron Barak, observed that comparative law 'grants comfort to the judge and gives him the feeling that he is treading on safe ground, and it also gives legitimacy to the chosen solution'.[15]

The Court's impact does not stop at the borders of the Council of Europe. The ECtHR has a worldwide mission of promoting human rights; its judgments are quoted in many countries outside the immediate signatories, and the ECtHR is treated as an example for other regional and national courts that deal with human rights issues. The judges of the Court understand this mission. Judge Tulkens states that

> it is necessary for the international bodies concerned to engage in a continuing and permanent dialogue on fundamental rights – a dialogue that should contribute to the development of a true 'common law' of human rights. This can be achieved by a process of interaction, as the different international courts learn from and assimilate each other's case law.[16]

If the ECtHR aspires to develop its worldwide mission, it needs to continue to build up its comparative legal research. Flanagan and Ahern conducted a survey of 43 judges from the British House of Lords, the Caribbean Court of Justice, the High Court of Australia, the Constitutional Court of South Africa, and the Supreme Courts of Ireland, India, Israel, Canada, New Zealand and the United States.[17] They

---

[14] K. Dzehtsiarou, *Interview with Judge Lucius Caflisch* (European Court of Human Rights, Strasbourg, 2008).

[15] A. Barak, 'Constitutional Human Rights and Private Law', *Review of Constitutional Studies*, 3 (1996), 218, 242.

[16] F. Tulkens, 'Introduction: Fifty Years of the European Court of Human Rights Viewed by Its Fellow International Courts' (Strasbourg, 30 January 2009).

[17] B. Flanagan and S. Ahern, 'Judicial Decision-Making and Transnational Law: A Survey of Common Law Supreme Court Judges', *International and Comparative Law Quarterly*, 60 (2011), 1.

4.2 PURPOSES OF COMPARATIVE LAW

established a link between deployment results of comparative studies and the concern of the judges for their judgments to be internationally recognised. They state that

> [t]he hypothesis [transnational judicial acceptance] is also consistent with the large proportion of judges for whom foreign judges form part of their judgment audience (47 percent), and the fact that half of those judges noted their responsiveness to their audience's attitude towards the use of comparative material.[18]

It seems that judges are of the opinion that if they employ comparative materials, then their judgments may seem more legitimate, not only within their jurisdiction but also to the outside world. It seems that the comparative law method fits well with the ECtHR's mission to explain and apply principles of European public order and helps to export them worldwide.

4.2.2 Information and persuasion

Available comparative legal data are normally deployed by the ECtHR in its reasoning. Dzehtsiarou and Lukashevich describe two channels for comparative law to impact the outcome of the case: for informational purposes and for the purpose of persuasion.[19] If comparative data are mentioned in the judgment but they are not explicitly used in the reasoning of the Court, then they have been used for informational purposes only. It is quite unusual for comparative data to be mentioned in the judgment without leading the Court to establish European consensus or lack thereof. The article by Dzehtsiarou and Lukashevich was published in 2012, and there have been new examples of comparative law deployed for informational purposes since then.

In *Söderman* v. *Sweden*, the Grand Chamber considered whether Swedish law provided sufficient remedies to protect a minor girl whose stepfather attempted covertly to film her naked. The Court quoted comparative law materials extensively in the judgment in relation to three relevant issues: first, the Court established that child pornography had been criminalised in all Contracting Parties included in the survey;[20]

---

[18] Ibid., p. 19.
[19] K. Dzehtsiarou and V. Lukashevich, 'Informed Decision-Making: the Comparative Endeavours of the Strasbourg Court', *Netherlands Quarterly of Human Rights*, 30 (2012), 272.
[20] *Söderman* v. *Sweden*, Application No 5786/08, Judgment of 12 November 2013, para. 53.

second, the Court confirmed that an overwhelming majority of these States had criminalised covert filming of a child for sexual purposes;[21] and third, a majority of States had criminalised covert filming of an individual for non-sexual purposes.[22] However, these comparative data were not explicitly mentioned by the Court in its reasoning, despite the fact that it discussed the margin of appreciation of the Contracting Party.[23] The ECtHR often discusses comparative law in the part of the judgment dealing with the scope of the margin of appreciation afforded to the Contracting Parties. The breadth of the margin of appreciation often depends on the degree of convergence of legal standards in Europe; a broader acceptance of a particular standard narrows down the margin of appreciation. In this case, the Court did not use comparative law to determine the scope of the margin of appreciation but nevertheless found a violation.

In *Lashin* v. *Russia*, the applicant complained that his legal incapacitation due to a mental illness was not in compliance with the Convention as such incapacitation was not reassessed periodically. The Court quoted comparative law on the issue of access to marriage for persons with mental disabilities and found that there was no consensus on the issue.[24] However, this comparative law did not feature in the Court's reasoning. Moreover, the Court did not specifically discuss the issue of marriage in its judgment.[25] It can therefore be concluded that comparative law was used for purely informational purposes in this case.

If it serves a persuasive purpose, then comparative law is likely to be the ground for establishing European consensus or lack thereof. This chapter is equally applicable to comparative research, irrespective of whether it leads to a finding of European consensus or not.

4.3 What is wrong with comparison? Criticism of comparative legal research conducted by the Court

It has been argued that '[c]omparativism is inherent in the ECHR system of protection'.[26] Having said that, the ECtHR has been criticised for not

---

[21] Ibid., para. 54. [22] Ibid., para. 55. [23] Ibid., para. 79.
[24] *Lashin* v. *Russia*, Application No 33117/02, Judgment of 22 January 2013, para. 67.
[25] Ibid., para. 124.
[26] E. Örücü, 'Whither Comparativism in Human Rights Cases?' in E. Örücü (ed.), *Judicial Comparativism in Human Rights Cases* (United Kingdom National Committee of Comparative Law, 2003), p. 238. See also, Mahoney, 'The Comparative Method', 135; W.J. Ganshof van der Meersch, 'Reliance, in the Case-Law of the European Court of Human Rights, on the Domestic Law of the States', *Human Rights Law Journal*, 1 (1980), 13, 15–6.

4.3 WHAT IS WRONG WITH COMPARISON?

following a rigorous methodology in its comparative analysis. The Court's use of comparative law has been criticised as insufficiently systematic to extract a rigorous 'common European denominator'.[27] Furthermore, the Court's conclusions about the presence or absence of European consensus have been deemed unsubstantiated,[28] and the Court's methodology has been called *ad hoc* and incoherent.[29] Arai-Takahashi states that

> [w]hile reliance on the comparative method is crucial for the complementary development of both national and international human rights jurisprudence, the Strasbourg organs need to be well prepared and informed about both national and international human rights jurisprudence. Vague references to emerging national standards, which are not empirically verifiable, undermine their credibility and sow the seed of suspicion that that they are engaged in an unfounded judicial activism.[30]

This frustration has been mirrored by the judges of the ECtHR on a number of occasions.[31] For example, in some cases, the Court could not deploy comparative data because they were incomplete, as illustrated by Judge Tulkens:

> in the famous *Lautsi* Chamber case we asked for comparative analysis. We received this comparative analysis but it was difficult for us to use this comparative analysis because this was a comparative analysis of fifteen or seventeen countries ... [W]e had these 17 countries with different situations from one country to another. But at the end of the day, we decided not to use this comparative analysis in the Chamber judgment. And, indeed, how can we use it if there are only 17 out of 47. It is not representative enough.[32]

---

[27] M. Delmas-Marty, *The European Convention for the Protection of Human Rights. International Protection versus National Restrictions* (Kluwer Academic Publishers, 1992), p. 305.

[28] H.C. Yourow, *The Margin of Appreciation Doctrine in the Dynamics of European Human Rights Jurisprudence* (Martinus Nijhoff Publishers, 1995), p. 195.

[29] Helfer, 'Consensus, Coherence and the European Convention on Human Rights', 133, 133–41.

[30] Y. Arai-Takahashi, *The Margin of Appreciation Doctrine and the Principle of Proportionality in the Jurisprudence of the ECHR* (Intersentia, 2002), pp. 192–3. See also Mahoney, 'The Comparative Method', 149; Carozza, 'Uses and Misuses of Comparative Law', 1225.

[31] K. Dzehtsiarou, *Interview with Judge Françoise Tulkens* (European Court of Human Rights, Strasbourg, 2010); somewhat similar opinions were expressed in the following interviews: K. Dzehtsiarou, *Interview with Judge Lech Garlicki* (European Court of Human Rights, Strasbourg, 2009); K. Dzehtsiarou, *Interview with Judge Renate Jaeger* (European Court of Human Rights, Strasbourg, 2010).

[32] Dzehtsiarou, *Interview with Françoise Tulkens*.

In their dissenting opinions, the ECtHR judges do not normally criticise the comparative law method deployed by the Court. That said, sometimes they express concerns about how comparative law has been interpreted by the majority of the judges in a particular case. The dissenters can argue that the majority did not take into account the context in which a legal provision under question operated in the Member States[33] or the subject matter of comparison was not chosen properly.[34]

These concerns about the lack of a rigorous methodology in comparative research are not unanimously shared by all commentators. Legg, for instance, lists three reasons why 'it is not desirable for the Tribunals [the ECtHR, the Inter-American Court of Human Rights (IACtHR) and the United Nations Human Rights Committee (UN HRC)] to calculate the current practice of States with precision and the concerns about ambiguity are overstated'.[35] These reasons are now discussed in turn.

First, Legg suggests that European consensus is only one of the considerations the Court takes into account in adjudicating cases, and, depending on the importance of comparative law in a particular case, 'the amount of information about state consensus will rightly vary'.[36] It is true that comparative law can be deployed for different purposes and hence the value of comparative research can vary. This study identifies at least two purposes: persuasion and information. However, this does not justify the Court's practice of deploying incomplete or misleading comparative information. The Court's legitimacy arguably depends on its ability to base its decisions on a verified and objective account of events. Moreover, at the moment, when comparative research is requested, it is unclear how important comparative law will eventually become in a particular case.

Second, Legg points out that it is not possible to determine a precise level of conformity between States in order to establish consensus.[37] He argues that, '[g]iven the huge diversity of case scenarios and issues, it is better to leave to the judgment and discretion of the Tribunals what

---

[33] *J.A. Pye (Oxford) Ltd and J.A. Pye (Oxford) Land Ltd v. the United Kingdom*, Application No 44302/02, Judgment of 30 August 2007. Dissenting Opinion of Judge Loucaides Joined by Judge Kovler.

[34] *Leyla Şahin v. Turkey*, Application No 44774/98, Judgment of 10 November 2005. Dissenting Opinion of Judge Tulkens. *Lautsi and others v. Italy*, Application No 30814/06, Judgment of 18 March 2011. Dissenting Opinion of Judge Malinverni Joined by Judge Kalaydjieva, para. 1.

[35] A. Legg, *The Margin of Appreciation in International Human Rights Law* (Oxford University Press, 2012), p. 127.

[36] Ibid.   [37] Ibid.

4.3 WHAT IS WRONG WITH COMPARISON?

criteria are needed for an appropriate consensus from case to case'.[38] This is exactly the reason why the Court has been criticised for resorting to arbitrary and political decision-making.[39] Zwart argues that the Court should adopt a protocol that would clarify the rules related to the number of States required to establish consensus and it would 'keep it [the ECtHR] from relying too often on the practice in certain States, while ignoring the practice in others'.[40] Indeed, arbitrary decision-making suggested by Legg can amount to an assault on the rule of law as manifested in the ECHR system of protection.

Finally, Legg states that

> [l]imiting the amount of information given in the judgment about the methodology for reaching consensus provides the Tribunals with a mechanism for balancing what might otherwise appear to be apologist or utopian reasoning. Finding some sort of trend amongst states that goes against the respondent state might make a controversial decision appear more palatable. Similarly, finding a lack of consensus or practice favouring the state might make a decision that appears overly conservative or apologist appear prudent.[41]

In other words, it is suggested that the Court should not clearly indicate how it has arrived at a particular solution but provide a smokescreen to cover its motives. It is very doubtful that such a strategy can be sustainable in the long run. Such reasoning is open for criticism from a wide range of stakeholders, for not presenting clear evidence supporting the judgment. One can argue that transparent and fair examination of comprehensive comparative data would increase trust in the Court's rulings.

This section has pointed out why a number of commentators have been concerned with the way comparative analysis has been conducted by the Court. It also argues that these concerns should be taken seriously. The following section shows that some of them have been taken seriously by the ECtHR.

---

[38] Ibid., p. 128.
[39] J.A. Brauch, 'The Margin of Appreciation and the Jurisprudence of the European Court of Human Rights: Threat to the Rule of Law', *Columbia Journal of European Law*, 11 (2004), 113, 129.
[40] T. Zwart, 'More Human Rights Than Court: Why the Legitimacy of the European Court of Human Rights Is in Need of Repair and How It Can Be Done' in S. Flogaitis, T. Zwart and J. Fraser (eds.), *The European Court of Human Rights and Its Discontents* (Edward Elgar, 2013), p. 90.
[41] Legg, *The Margin of Appreciation*, p. 128.

4.4 Evolution of comparative legal research

The ECtHR uses various sources of comparative data to back up its findings for the presence or absence of European consensus. This section outlines four ways of identifying European consensus. First, it can be the case that the Court does not specify evidence supporting its findings concerning the presence or absence of European consensus. Second, some judgments refer to the cases previously decided by the ECtHR. Third, the Court itself produces independent comparative analysis and summarises it in the text of the judgment. Fourth, in some cases, especially in the past, the Court has relied on data provided by third parties. It is safe to suggest that the Court has recently professionalised comparative research and now mostly relies on comparative law reports that it prepares for itself.

On a number of occasions, the Court has used comparative data from a variety of different sources in a single judgment. This section analyses all four ways of identification of consensus and argues that while in-house produced comparative research is the most reliable source of information, the combination of materials obtained from a variety of sources can help the Court to establish the most up-to-date and accurate account of the law in force in the Contracting Parties.

4.4.1 Limited factual justification

In some cases, the Court has established the existence or lack of European consensus without including relevant comparative data in the text of the judgment. In *Tyrer v. the United Kingdom*, the Court stated that there was a consensus in Europe against judicial corporal punishment.[42] However, the Court did not provide any comparative data to support this statement. This lack of foundation for the European consensus argument was recognised as a serious pitfall and was criticised by commentators.[43] Former ECtHR judge Lech Garlicki states that, in the early years of the Court, consensus could have been identified without a comparative study since judges from all Contracting Parties were sitting on the case and they could point out whether legal provisions in their respective countries departed from the European trend.[44] McCrudden observes that the

---

[42] *Tyrer v. the United Kingdom*, Application No 5856/72, Judgment of 25 April 1978, para. 31.
[43] Brauch, 'The Margin of Appreciation', 128.
[44] Judge Garlicki observes that consensus was identified by 'maybe using the general knowledge of the judges or even without the unit [Research Division] it was possible to arrange

ECtHR 'often relied on individual judges' own knowledge'.[45] Currently, this practice is becoming more and more problematic because of the variety and complexity of legal systems of the Contracting Parties to the Convention.[46] Moreover, in the past, judges elected in respect of all Contracting Parties had to sit on a single case. Since the Council of Europe has now grown in numbers, this is no longer possible.[47]

In more recent cases, the Court has also resorted to seemingly groundless findings of European consensus although this happens less and less often. In *Appleby and others v. the United Kingdom*, the Court identified lack of consensus without providing any references to the laws of the Contracting Parties. In this case, the applicants set about collecting signatures for a petition. They tried to set up a stall and canvass views in The Galleries, a shopping mall in Washington (England), which had effectively become the town centre. However, the applicants were prevented from doing so by Postel, a private company which had bought most of the shopping mall and, under domestic law, had the power to exclude anyone conducting unauthorised activities on its land. No reference to the laws of the Contracting Parties was made in this case. This did not, however, prevent the Court from stating that

> [a]uthorities from the individual States show a variety of approaches to the public- and private-law issues that have arisen in widely differing factual situations. It cannot be said that there is as yet any emerging consensus that could assist the Court in its examination in this case concerning Article 10 of the Convention.[48]

Similarly, in *Fretté v. France*, the Court deployed European consensus in relation to adoption by a homosexual person. The Court stated that

> [i]t is indisputable that there is no common ground on the question. Although most of the Contracting States do not expressly prohibit

---

research by the case lawyer ... Basically, the research division is better because it is more reliable, you can believe that if they inform you that something is the case, then it really is.' Dzehtsiarou, *Interview with Lech Garlicki*.

[45] C. McCrudden, 'Using Comparative Reasoning in Human Rights Adjudication: The Court of Justice of the European Union and the European Court of Human Rights Compared', *Cambridge Yearbook of European Legal Studies*, 15 (2012–2013), 383, 391.

[46] There are 47 Contracting Parties to the Convention among which common law, civil law and some transitional law countries are present.

[47] Pursuant to the Convention, the highest formation of the Court is the Grand Chamber. It comprises only 17 judges and they cannot possess knowledge about legal regulations in all 47 Contracting Parties.

[48] *Appleby and others v. the United Kingdom*, Application No 44306/98, Judgment of 6 May 2003, para. 46.

homosexuals from adopting where single persons may adopt, it is not possible to find in the legal and social orders of the Contracting States uniform principles on these social issues on which opinions within a democratic society may reasonably differ widely.[49]

The Court did not specify the Contracting Parties where adoption by homosexuals was explicitly prohibited. This does not necessarily mean that comparative analysis was not in the case file in the above-mentioned cases. However, such analysis was not integrated into the text of the judgments, which is problematic because it makes the Court's findings appear groundless.

In some cases, comparative analysis is suggested but it is not clearly articulated in the text of the judgment. For example, in the Chamber case of *Shofman v. Russia*, the ECtHR dealt with the issue of whether certain time limits for challenging paternity were compatible with the Convention. The Court stated that

> [a] comparative examination of the Contracting States' legislation on the institution of paternity actions reveals that there is no universally adopted standard. With the notable exception of the small number of States that have no statutory time-limit for bringing proceedings contesting paternity, a limitation period exists which is usually of six months or a year, but may be as long as two years.[50]

The Court, however, did not provide any details of the various laws in the Contracting Parties. This approach is at odds with the Court's practice of at least stating briefly the most representative examples in the comparative law section of the judgments.[51] Such a brief description of comparative data adds credibility to the Court's claims about the presence or absence of consensus.

4.4.2 Recourse to previous findings

In some cases, the ECtHR has made reference to previously decided cases in order to establish European consensus. This approach seems to be in line with the usual practice of relying on precedents in adjudicating cases.[52] However, it is only justifiable if the referred cases do indeed

---

[49] *Fretté v. France*, Application No 36515/97, Judgment of 26 February 2002, para. 41.
[50] *Shofman v. Russia*, Application No 74826/01, Judgment of 24 November 2005, para. 37.
[51] See, for example, *Van der Heijden v. the Netherlands*, Application No 42857/05, Judgment of 3 April 2012, para. 31–6.
[52] While previously decided cases do not have *de jure* precedential value for the ECtHR, it does not depart from its own previous judgments without a good reason.

contain relevant comparative legal data and if these data are still up to date.

An example of good practice is the case of *Christine Goodwin v. the United Kingdom*, where the ECtHR considered the question of recognition of the reassigned gender of transsexuals in birth certificates and other official documents. The Court explored the state of European law at the time and referred to the previously decided case of *Sheffield and Horsham v. the United Kingdom*:

> Already at the time of the Sheffield and Horsham case, there was an emerging consensus within Contracting States in the Council of Europe on providing legal recognition following gender re-assignment.[53]

In *Sheffield and Horsham*, the ECtHR extensively quoted comparative law data submitted by the third-party intervener in the text of the judgment.[54] In contrast to *Sheffield and Horsham*, sometimes previously decided cases do not contain comparative data which could substantiate the Court's findings about European consensus. In *Dickson v. the United Kingdom*, the Grand Chamber of the ECtHR delivered a judgment concerning prohibition of artificial insemination in prison. The applicants challenged the decision of the Secretary of State disallowing conjugal visits and claimed that the State was in breach of Articles 8 and 12 of the Convention. The Court did not quote any comparative data in the judgments and simply stated that more than half of the Contracting States allowed for conjugal visits for prisoners (subject to a variety of different restrictions).[55] After this statement, the Court referred to *Aliev v. Ukraine*.[56] However, *Aliev* does not contain an analysis of national laws in relation to conjugal visits. In *Aliev*, the Court merely stated that

> [w]hilst noting with approval the reform movements in several European countries to improve prison conditions by facilitating conjugal visits, the Court considers that the refusal of such visits may for the present time be regarded as justified for the prevention of disorder and crime within the meaning of the second paragraph of Article 8 of the Convention.[57]

---

[53] *Christine Goodwin v. the United Kingdom*, Application No 28957/95, Judgment of 11 July 2002, para. 84.
[54] *Sheffield and Horsham v. the United Kingdom*, Application No 22985/93 and 23390/94, Judgment of 30 July 1998, para. 35.
[55] *Dickson v. the United Kingdom*, Application No 44362/04, Judgment of 4 December 2007, para. 81.
[56] *Aliev v. Ukraine*, 7 August 2003, Application No 41220/98, Judgment of 29 April 2003, para. 81.
[57] Ibid.

Similarly, in *L. and V. v. Austria* and *S.L. v. Austria*, the Court considered whether the law which prescribed different ages of consent for homosexual and heterosexual sexual intercourse was in compliance with the ECHR. The Court stated that

> there is an ever growing European consensus to apply equal ages of consent for heterosexual, lesbian and homosexual relations. Similarly, the Commission observed in *Sutherland v. the United Kingdom* that 'equality of treatment in respect of the age of consent is now recognised by the great majority of Member States of the Council of Europe'.[58]

However, in *Sutherland*, the commission did not describe the state of law in Europe in relation to the age of consent for homosexual intercourse.[59] This issue was picked up by the dissenting judges who argued that the commission did not substantiate its findings. The dissenters argued that

> [a] number of States parties to the Convention still maintain different minimum ages for homosexual and heterosexual relations, sometimes as far as four years apart. According to the majority of the Commission 'equality of treatment in respect of age for consent is now recognised by the great majority of Member States of the Council of Europe' ... Does that statement really reflect the present situation?[60]

This section suggests that the Court can justifiably rely on its findings in previous cases. However, the Court's references to previous cases that contain no comparative data can undermine the credibility of such references and put the court's reasoning under question.

4.4.3 *Comparative law research prepared by the ECtHR*

The ECtHR often refers to its in-house comparative research. Currently, comparative law reports are prepared in the majority of Grand Chamber cases[61] as well as in some cases dealt with by the Chambers. Research is carried out upon a request from the judge-rapporteur[62] by the Research

---

[58] *L. and V. v. Austria*, Application No 39392/98 and 39829/98, Judgment of 9 January 2003, para. 50.
[59] *Sutherland v. the United Kingdom*, Application No 25186/94, Decision of 1 July 1997.
[60] Ibid., Dissenting Opinion of M.M.K. Herndl and I. Békés.
[61] See, statistical analysis of the Grand Chamber cases below.
[62] The judge-rapporteur is a judge appointed by the section president according to Rule 49 which provides that where an application is made under Article 34 of the Convention and its examination by a chamber or a committee seems justified, the president of the section to which the case has been assigned will designate a judge as judge-rapporteur, who will examine the application.

4.4 EVOLUTION OF COMPARATIVE LEGAL RESEARCH

Division of the Court, which operates within the Court's Registry. In some cases, the judge-rapporteur can contact the lawyers of the Research Division before sending the request and inquire whether there might be a consensus in relation to a matter at issue. This does not mean that this protocol is always followed or even strictly required. If the judge-rapporteur decides that comparative research would be helpful, a special research request form has to be filled out. It is normally done by the lawyer of the Registry who is preparing the case file. Among other details, such as the name of the case and the name of the judge-rapporteur, this form indicates what type of research is required from the Research Division. The form provides for four options:

1. case law of the ECtHR,
2. comparative law,
3. international law, and
4. EU law.

The form allows the requesting lawyer to select one, a few or all of these options. The requesting lawyer should also describe the scope of research and frame the questions that the Research Division is expected to answer. The form also includes an indicative deadline.

This research request form is then submitted to the Grand Chamber Registrar if the case will be dealt with by the Grand Chamber or to the section registrar if it will be adjudicated by the Chamber. After being approved by the registrar, the form is transferred to the Research Division, which then compiles a report on the issue. The comparative law section of the Research Division report consists of country reports, namely a summary of relevant laws and practices of the Contracting Parties. Some of these country reports are prepared by the lawyers of the Research Division when they can understand the language of these countries and are familiar with their legal systems.[63] If the lawyers of the Research Division cannot cover some Contracting Parties themselves, they send requests to national lawyers working at the Registry. Each of these lawyers prepares a report summarising relevant law and practice in their respective countries. They usually have 15 days to do this. Each national report is then signed by the judge of the ECtHR elected in respect of the country concerned. Afterwards, the national reports are compiled by the Research Division in a composite report, which is then

---

[63] The head of the Research and Library Division informed the author that now the lawyers of the division can cover about 15 legal systems of the Contracting Parties.

sent back to the judge-rapporteur and other judges of the Chamber or Grand Chamber, respectively. These reports are confidential and not accessible to the general public.

This formalised way of requesting comparative research is relatively new. However, there were lawyers dealing with comparative legal research even before 1998, when Protocol 11 significantly reformed the Strasbourg system of human rights protection. Before 1998, both the ECtHR and the European Commission of Human Rights had a lawyer responsible for research and publications. However, at that time, these lawyers were mainly dealing with indexing of the case law and preparation of the Court's publications. From 2000–2001, the Court began investing more resources into the Research Division. The number of lawyers in the Research Division has increased considerably, and judges have started sending more requests for comparative research. In 2013, there were ten full-time lawyers working at the Research Division. Despite this significant increase in numbers, the lawyers of the Research Division still have a heavy workload, as they not only deal with comparative research reports but also prepare the online guidelines for the applicants;[64] sometimes, they draft the Grand Chamber judgments and are involved in other activities of the Court. That said, the more advanced Research Division has clearly affected the structure and content of the ECtHR judgments.

A summary of comparative research is almost always included in the judgment and is entitled either 'law in Contracting States',[65] 'comparative and international law'[66] or 'relevant comparative law and material'.[67] By means of an example, in the *A., B., and C. v. Ireland* case, the ECtHR stated that

> [a]bortion is available on request (according to certain criteria including gestational limits) in some 30 Contracting States. An abortion justified on health grounds is available in some 40 Contracting States and justified on well-being grounds in some 35 such States. Three Contracting States prohibit abortion in all circumstances (Andorra, Malta and San Marino). In recent years, certain States have extended the grounds on

---

[64] See, for example, *Practical Guide on Admissibility Criteria* (Council of Europe, 2011), available at www.echr.coe.int/Documents/Admissibility_guide_ENG.pdf, accessed on 20 August 2014.
[65] *A., B. and C. v. Ireland*, Application No 25579/05, Judgment of 16 December 2010, para. 112.
[66] *Stoll v. Switzerland*, Application No 69698/01, Judgment of 10 December 2007, para. 44.
[67] *Burden v. United Kingdom*, Application No 13378/05, Judgment of 29 April 2008, para. 25–6.

4.4 EVOLUTION OF COMPARATIVE LEGAL RESEARCH

which abortion can be obtained (Monaco, Montenegro, Portugal and Spain).[68]

Based on these findings, the ECtHR managed to establish that there was indeed European consensus in favour of 'allowing abortion on broader grounds than accorded under Irish law'.[69]

Likewise, the Court also quotes comparative data to support its findings in cases where there is no consensus. The Court provides examples of a variety of possible solutions to the matter at issue. For example, in *Murphy* v. *Ireland*, the Court examined laws prohibiting religious advertisements in the media. The Court stated that

> there appears to be no clear consensus between the Contracting States as to the manner in which to legislate for the broadcasting of religious advertisements. Certain States have similar prohibitions (for example, Greece, Switzerland and Portugal), certain prohibit religious advertisements considered offensive (for example, Spain and see also Council Directive 89/552/EEC) and certain have no legislative restriction (the Netherlands). There appears to be no uniform conception of the requirements of the protection of the rights of others in the context of the legislative regulation of the broadcasting of religious advertising.[70]

The Court is not in a position to quote in full a comparative report prepared by the Research Division.[71] However, even a short comment such as the one outlined above shows that the Court is making an informed decision.

It should be noted that the Court's engagement in comparative research opens it up to some criticism. The first is that it can be argued that it is not for the Court to actively seek evidence that would support its judgments. In an adversarial process, it is up to the parties to present comparative law when it is beneficial for their case.[72] In an inquisitorial process, the Court's involvement in comparative law or other fact-finding missions seems more justifiable.

While the ECtHR mainly relies on evidence provided by the parties, in some cases it actively seeks to establish facts through fact-finding

---

[68] *A., B. and C.* v. *Ireland*, para. 112. [69] Ibid., para. 235.
[70] *Murphy* v. *Ireland*, Application No 44179/98, Judgment of 10 July 2003, para. 81.
[71] Dzehtsiarou, *Interview with Judge Tulkens*. The Research Division of the Court is a department within the Court's Registry which is responsible for compiling comparative reports on the Court's request.
[72] In adversarial process, judicial officers 'are to serve as neutral umpires and thus have no independent knowledge of the facts'. A.D. Kessler, 'Our Inquisitorial Tradition: Equity Procedure, Due Process, and the Search for an Alternative to the Adversarial', *Cornell Law Review*, 90 (2004–2005), 1181, 1183.

missions,[73] in-house research,[74] requesting documents and explanations.[75] It can be argued that the fact that the Court engages in fact-finding does not necessarily mean that it ought to do so. This argument, however, can be rebutted by legal and normative accounts of the nature of the ECtHR. From the legal perspective, the ECHR authorises the Court to conduct investigations of human rights violations. Pursuant to Article 38, the Court can 'undertake an investigation, for the effective conduct of which the High Contracting Parties concerned shall furnish all necessary facilities'.[76]

If this formally legal justification is not satisfactory, there is a normative argument in favour of research conducted by the Court. It seems that in order to prove that the Court should be able to help parties in acquiring evidence and arguments, it has to be established that the parties have unequal means of securing such evidence and that the judgment of the Court might have implications beyond an immediate effect on the parties.

The parties in the cases before the ECtHR are substantively unequal in their means of securing evidence.[77] The States have a machinery of various institutions designed to collect evidence and conduct fact-finding missions. In contrast, the applicants are clearly lacking such institutional and financial capacities. Furthermore, it is naïve to expect the applicants to provide the Court with comprehensive comparative analysis even if such analysis would strengthen their case, due to the complexity of the task and specific expertise required. Therefore, it seems justifiable for the Court to actively engage in finding evidence that can prove or disprove an applicant's allegations.

The judgments of the ECtHR not only affect the parties to the case but can also create novel human rights standards for Europe.[78] Moreover, it is an ongoing debate whether the judgments of the Court should have an *erga omnes* effect.[79] If so, they may influence not only individuals other

---

[73] See, *Ilaşcu and others v. Moldova and Russia*, Application No 48787/99, Judgment of 8 July 2004.
[74] See, *A., B. and C. v. Ireland*.
[75] See, *Janowiec and others v. Russia*, Application No 55508/07 and 29520/09, Judgment of 16 April 2012.
[76] Article 38 of the ECHR.   [77] Unless it is an inter-state complaint.
[78] For example, the ECtHR has developed the right to access to court under Article 6 of the Convention in the case of *Golder v. the United Kingdom*, Application No 4451/70, Judgment of 21 February 1975.
[79] The Interlaken Declaration added some clarity to the ongoing debate about the *erga omnes* effect of the judgments of the ECtHR. Greer points out that '[a]lthough there may

4.4 EVOLUTION OF COMPARATIVE LEGAL RESEARCH

than the applicant but also States other than the respondent State. In such circumstances, the Court should not rely solely on the arguments presented by the Contracting Parties. It is an obligation of the ECtHR to try to examine the matter at issue from all possible angles, especially in difficult and novel cases. Therefore, it seems reasonable to expect the Court to invest its resources in comparative law research which can provide valuable data for such examination.

The second possible criticism is that lawyers and judges of the ECtHR are not necessarily experts in the particular areas of law that are under review. As such, there may be circumstances where this lack of specific expert knowledge might lead the lawyers to form an account of national law which is not up to date or which does not take into consideration certain aspects of national legal regulations.

One of the judges interviewed for this book points out that, in an ideal situation, the reasons for adopting a particular solution by the States could assist the Court in coming to the most adequate and appropriate decision. In particular, an inquiry into the reasons as to the absence of relevant legislation in a particular field could be enlightening in appraising the reasons for a lack of consensus.[80] Judge Tulkens has identified another difficulty; she states that, 'we ask the lawyer to see in the literature what the position of national law is. However, it is very hard for the

---

be room for debate about whether or not "the principle of solidarity" is in fact embodied in the Convention, and whether or not it suggests an erga omnes effect ... Since the final, authoritative, interpretation of these rights and freedoms lies with the Court, if the Court finds a certain practice in a certain state to be contrary to the Convention, it would be very difficult for another state to argue that precisely the same practice did not constitute a breach of its obligations.' S. Greer, *The European Convention on Human Rights. Achievements, Problems and Prospects* (Cambridge University Press, 2006), p. 280. Ress points out that '[n]ormally, judgments of the Court do not have an erga omnes effect, but they have an orientation effect'. G. Ress, 'The Effect of Decisions and Judgments of the European Court of Human Rights in the Domestic Legal Order', *Texas International Law Journal*, 40 (2005), 359, 374. Helfer also argues that '[t]here is no obligation, however, for government decision-makers to give ECHR judgments this *erga omnes* effect'. L.R. Helfer, 'Redesigning the European Court of Human Rights: Embeddedness as a Deep Structural Principle of the European Human Rights Regime', *European Journal of International Law*, 19 (2008), 125, 136. For more general debate about *erga omnes* obligations in international law, see, M. Ragazzi, *The Concept of International Obligations Erga Omnes* (Oxford University Press, 2000); T. Meron, 'State Responsibility for Violations of Human Rights', *Proceedings of the Annual Meeting (American Society of International Law)*, 83 (1989), 372; E.B. Weiss, 'Invoking State Responsibility in the Twenty-First Century', *American Journal of International Law*, 96 (2002), 798.

[80] K. Dzehtsiarou, *Interview with Judge 18* (European Court of Human Rights, Strasbourg).

lawyer to be aware of all the recent developments.'[81] Therefore, the Court's practice of combining in-house comparative reports with other sources of comparative data, such as third-party submissions, should be welcomed, as, collectively, they can provide a multifaceted description of a given legal issue.[82]

Third, due to the heavy workload of the 'filtering' lawyers[83] and the judges of the Court,[84] it is extremely burdensome for the lawyers to engage in lengthy and detailed research on a particular legal topic. That said, the Court's engagement in comparative research makes it possible for it to base its decision on more reliable data. Therefore, arguably the benefits to the Court's reliability and credibility should outweigh certain workload burdens. This conclusion appears to be shared by the ECtHR, and, therefore, since 1998, when Protocol 11 was used to reshape the Strasbourg system,[85] the Court has been deploying comparative data more and more often in its judgments. The following statistical survey of the Grand Chamber judgments[86] aims to substantiate this claim.

For this survey, all judgments of the Grand Chamber of the ECtHR delivered between 1998 and 2013 inclusive[87] have been analysed with a view to identifying those cases where the ECtHR has used comparative research. In the course of conducting this research, the following methodological questions had to be answered. First, it had to be decided

---

[81] Dzehtsiarou, *Interview with Judge Tulkens*.
[82] Umbricht argues that 'in any decision-making process, the greater the amount of information and views considered, the greater the chance for a good outcome'. G.C. Umbricht, 'An *"Amicus Curiae* Brief" on *Amicus Curiae* Briefs at the WTO', *Journal of International Economic Law*, 4 (2001), 773, 774.
[83] Those lawyers who deal with the applications submitted to the Court before they are communicated to the government. These lawyers usually prepare reports which are subsequently incorporated in the report of the Research Division.
[84] The Court's backlog in 2013 was roughly 99,900 pending applications. *Annual Report 2013 of the ECtHR* (Strasbourg, 2014), p. 193.
[85] The most significant changes of Protocol 11 were that the European Commission on Human Rights was abolished and the ECtHR became permanent.
[86] Only Grand Chamber judgments are taken into account for a number of reasons. First, the Grand Chamber normally deals with the most complex issues, and comparative analysis might help the judges to make an informed decision. Second, especially before Protocol 14 empowered the committees to deliver judgments on merits, the Chambers of the Court delivered a lot of judgments in repetitive 'clone' cases which did not require any interpretation of the Convention and could be decided on the basis of previously decided cases. Finally, the sheer number of chamber cases would make those cases where comparative law has been deployed marginal. Moreover, researching such a large number of cases would prove to be disproportionately difficult.
[87] Altogether, there are 302 judgments.

4.4 EVOLUTION OF COMPARATIVE LEGAL RESEARCH

whether references to international legal instruments other than the ECHR could be considered comparative law for the purposes of this survey. Since the results of the survey would be significantly different depending on the answer to this question, it was decided to run two tests: one including references to international law and another excluding them. Second, the majority of the cases where comparative law was deployed contained comparative data prepared by the Registry.[88] Having said that, in cases such as *Sheffield and Horsham v. the United Kingdom*,[89] *Christine Goodwin v. the United Kingdom*,[90] *Sanoma Uitgevers B.V. v. the Netherlands*,[91] *Animal Defenders International v. the United Kingdom*[92] and *Del Río Prada v. Spain*,[93] the ECtHR used comparative data submitted by non-governmental organisations (NGOs) or international organisations. Each of these submissions is referred to in the judgments but the length and depth of these references vary. In *Animal Defenders International v. the United Kingdom*, for example, the ECtHR referred to the survey conducted by the European Platform of Regulatory Authorities. This reference lists the States analysed, and there is a relatively detailed description of how the matter at issue is regulated in these States.[94] In contrast, in *Del Río Prada v. Spain*, the Court simply pointed out that

> [i]n support of its argument that the principle of non-retroactivity should apply to procedural rules or rules governing the execution of sentences which seriously affected the rights of the accused or convicted person, the International Commission of Jurists referred to various sources of international and comparative law (statutes and rules of procedure of international criminal courts, Portuguese, French and Netherlands legislation and case-law).[95]

The benefits of outsourcing comparative law to NGOs are discussed in the following section. It was decided to include the cases containing comparative data submitted by NGOs in the list of cases in which

---

[88] It is assumed that if the Court does not make a reference to any particular source of comparative legal data, it means that this research is done by the Court itself.
[89] *Sheffield and Horsham v. the United Kingdom*.
[90] *Christine Goodwin v. the United Kingdom*.
[91] *Sanoma Uitgevers B.V. v. the Netherlands*, Application No 38224/03, Judgment of 14 September 2010.
[92] *Animal Defenders International v. the United Kingdom*, Application No 48876/08, Judgment of 22 April 2013.
[93] *Del Río Prada v. Spain*, Application No 42750/09, Judgment of 21 October 2013.
[94] *Animal Defenders International v. the United Kingdom*, para. 65–9.
[95] *Del Río Prada v. Spain*, para. 76.

comparative law was deployed. This approach is justified by the fact that there is a very small number of such cases and that it is safe to assume that the Court has taken these comparative surveys into account.

Finally, some judgments delivered by the Grand Chamber of the ECtHR are identical in terms of facts, reasoning and outcomes although they are considered by the Court as separate cases.[96] Therefore, comparative law used in one of these cases will be copy-pasted into the rest of them. This could influence the findings because the same comparative research may be counted twice or more. Having said that, it was decided to follow the Court's approach to these cases and consider them separately.[97]

The following analysis shows that the number of judgments in which comparative law has been mentioned continues to increase. In 1998, comparative data were used in only one Grand Chamber case,[98] and they were submitted to the Court by third-party interveners. In 1999, only two identical judgments contained comparative data,[99] and in 2000 and 2001, none of the Grand Chamber judgments referred to comparative law. In contrast, in 2010 nine judgments (50 per cent of all judgments delivered), in 2011 eight (62 per cent), in 2012 eight (30 per cent) and in 2013 eight (67 per cent) contained a summary of domestic legal provisions of the Contracting Parties other than the respondent State. Figure 4.1 illustrates the dynamic of the Court's deployment of comparative law (as percentages of the overall number of judgments).

The graph shows an increase in the overall proportion of judgments where comparative law has been deployed, from 0 per cent in 2000 and 2001 to more than 50 per cent in 2011 and 2013. One can observe a similar tendency if both references to international and comparative law

---

[96] See, for example, *Chapman v. the United Kingdom*, Application No 27238/95, Judgment of 18 January 2001; *Lee v. the United Kingdom*, Application No 25289/94, Judgment of 18 January 2001; *Jane Smith v. the United Kingdom*, Application No 25154/94, Judgment of 18 January 2001; *Beard v. the United Kingdom*, Application No 24882/94, Judgment of 18 January 2001; *Coster v. the United Kingdom*, Application No 24876/94, Judgment of 18 January 2001.

[97] There were only four instances of this situation: in 1999, two cases containing international law materials and two cases containing comparative data could have been adjoined; in 2001, five cases also containing international law and practice could have been adjoined; in 2002, two; and in 2006, nine cases.

[98] *Sheffield and Horsham v. the United Kingdom*.

[99] *T. v. the United Kingdom*, Application No 24724/94, Judgment of 16 December 1999; *V. v. the United Kingdom*, Application No 24888/94, Judgment of 16 December 1999.

4.4 EVOLUTION OF COMPARATIVE LEGAL RESEARCH   95

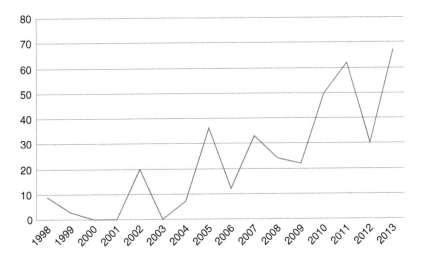

Figure 4.1   Judgments of the Grand Chamber in which comparative law materials were deployed (1998–2013).

are considered. In 1998, only two judgments (18 per cent) fell into this category; in 1999, there were six (10 per cent); and in 2000, there were four (18 per cent). In contrast, in 2011 and in 2013, all judgments delivered by the ECtHR had references to some international and comparative law materials. Figure 4.2 shows the dynamic of the Court's deployment of international or comparative law (as percentages of the overall number of judgments).

Figure 4.3 also illustrates that international law was deployed by the Court in a considerably higher number of cases.[100]

The fact that 'comparative or international law' was used in a significantly higher number of cases can perhaps be explained by the complexity of comparative law. Most international instruments are easily accessible and do not require specialist skills to find them. At the same time, comparative law analysis is a complex exercise that requires familiarity with the national legal systems of the Contracting Parties and a comprehensive knowledge of languages. While the lawyers of the Registry can find relevant international law materials themselves, they would certainly require assistance in collecting comparative law data.

---

[100] The Court rarely deploys only comparative law. In the majority of cases where comparative law has been used, international law has also been quoted.

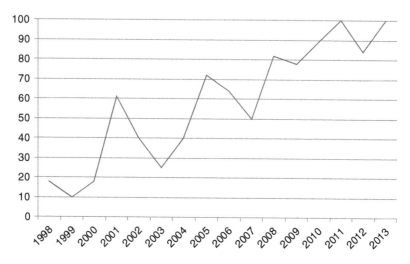

Figure 4.2 Judgments of the Grand Chamber in which comparative or international law materials were deployed (1998–2013).

Comparative analysis is complicated and time consuming.[101] Çalı, Koch and Bruch point out that the reasonable length of proceedings in the ECtHR is considered by the stakeholders as an important legitimising factor.[102] However, European consensus will not seriously affect the length of proceedings since it is usually deployed in 'hard cases'.[103] The main reason for the excessive length of procedures in the ECtHR is an overwhelming amount of repetitive meritorious and inadmissible cases.[104] Moreover, comparative research is typically requested when a case is relinquished or referred to the Grand Chamber of the Court,[105] which normally deals with no more than 25 cases per year.[106] Therefore,

[101] K. Dzehtsiarou, *Interview with Michael O'Boyle* (European Court of Human Rights, Strasbourg, 2009).
[102] B. Çalı, A. Koch and N. Bruch, 'The Legitimacy of the European Court of Human Rights: The View from the Ground' (2011), available at http://ecthrproject.files.wordpress.com/2011/04/ecthrlegitimacyreport.pdf, accessed on 23 July 2014, p. 13.
[103] Tamanaha argues that '[w]hat jurists refer to as "hard cases" usually fall into one of the two ... categories: cases involving gaps, conflicts, or ambiguities in the law, and cases involving bad rules or bad results'. B.Z. Tamanaha, *Beyond the Formalist-Realist Divide* (Princeton University Press, 2009), p. 192.
[104] See Interlaken Declaration adopted on 19 February 2010, Izmir Declaration adopted on 27 April 2011 and Brighton Declaration adopted on 20 April 2012.
[105] K. Dzehtsiarou, *Interview with Judge Ján Šikuta* (European Court of Human Rights, Strasbourg, 2010).
[106] ECtHR HUDOC database search.

4.4 EVOLUTION OF COMPARATIVE LEGAL RESEARCH 97

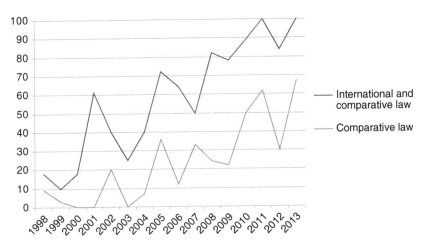

Figure 4.3 Judgments of the Grand Chamber in which comparative law materials were deployed and where both comparative and international law materials were deployed (1998–2013).

the lawyers of the Registry dealing with Grand Chamber cases can spend more time on in-depth research on the matter at hand. Even despite the fact that the Court has used comparative law more often in recent years, this number is still very low. Thus, they cannot substantively affect the length of procedure at the ECtHR.

4.4.4 Comparative research conducted by third parties

Occasionally, the Court summarises comparative analysis provided by third parties and deploys it in its reasoning.[107] Most of the judges interviewed indicated a positive appreciation of third-party reports. One of the judges, for example, pointed out that '[w]e rely more on our Research Division. But if what the Research Division report provides is confirmed by NGOs then it is very important.'[108] As outlined in the previous section, various sources of information can mitigate the possible limits of the research conducted by the Court.

---

[107] In some cases, not only third parties but also the applicant or the respondent State rely on European consensus or lack thereof in their arguments. See, for example, *Hirst v. the United Kingdom (No 2)*, Application No 74025/01, Judgment of 6 October 2005.
[108] Dzehtsiarou, *Interview with Judge 18*.

The Court has used external expertise in deciding a number of cases; these include third-party interventions from NGOs,[109] universities[110] and non-respondent governments[111] and international organisations.[112] Most often, however, the Court deploys comparative analysis from *amicus curiae* briefs prepared by NGOs.[113]

The judges who were interviewed attached different values to the *amicus curiae* briefs submitted by NGOs. Most of them pointed out that such briefs reflected the biases of the NGOs that drafted them.[114] In an interview conducted for this book, former Judge Jaeger was of the opinion that quoting an NGO's *amicus curiae* brief 'is nothing more than a matter of politeness. The Court tries to strengthen human rights NGOs in their role and, therefore, it acknowledges their reports in the judgments. However, the main role of NGOs is on the implementation stage.'[115] However, the opinion of Judge Jaeger is unrepresentative of the majority of the judges interviewed.

---

[109] *K.U.* v. *Finland*, Application No 2872/02, Judgment of 2 December 2008, para. 33–4.

[110] Dzehtsiarou, *Interview with Françoise Tulkens*. See also *Z and others* v. *the United Kingdom*, Application No 29392/95, Judgment of 10 May 2001, para. 7; *Stübing* v. *Germany*, Application No 43547/08, Judgment of 12 April 2012, para. 30; *Babar Ahmad and others* v. *the United Kingdom*, Application No 24027/07, 11949/08, 36742/08, 66911/09 and 67354/09, Judgment of 10 April 2012, para. 138; *Harkins and Edwards* v. *the United Kingdom*, Application No 9146/07 and 32650/07, Judgment of 17 January 2012, para. 66; *Konstantin Markin* v. *Russia*, Application No 30078/06, Judgment of 22 March 2012, para. 119.

[111] *Lautsi* v. *Italy*, para. 47–9.

[112] See, *Kiyutin* v. *Russia*, Application No 2700/10, Judgment of 10 March 2011, para. 36–8; *Evans* v. *the United Kingdom*, Application No 6339/05, Judgment of 10 April 2007, para. 39–42; *Stoll* v. *Switzerland*, para. 44.

[113] Former Judge of the ECtHR Myjer, writing extrajudicially, points out that '[p]arties and third parties interveners often submit to the Court all kind of documents with information on comparative law, international documents, academic writing and expert reports'. E. Myjer, 'Pierter Van Dijk and His Favourite Strasbourg Judgment' in M. van Roosmalen et al. (eds.), *Fundamental Rights and Principles* (Intersentia, 2013), p. 69.

[114] Judge Myjer stated that judges were aware that the data provided by the parties might sometimes be one-sided and for that reason the conclusion of European consensus based on these data might not illustrate the real legal position in Europe. Therefore, Judge Myjer said that it was very wise for the Court to have its own Research Division. K. Dzehtsiarou, *Interview with Judge Egbert Myjer* (European Court of Human Rights, Strasbourg, 2009). Judge Tulkens pointed out that human rights NGOs are agenda driven and the judges take into account the bias of their reports. Dzehtsiarou, *Interview with Judge Tulkens*. O'Boyle mentioned that sometimes the ECtHR could not use the NGO reports because their submissions were one-sided. Dzehtsiarou, *Interview with Michael O'Boyle*.

[115] Dzehtsiarou, *Interview with Judge Renate Jaeger*.

4.4 EVOLUTION OF COMPARATIVE LEGAL RESEARCH 99

The practice of NGOs becoming involved in the activities of international organisations is quite common.[116] An advantage of NGOs is that they are focused on a particular legal issue and can be considered experts in the area of their activity. Furthermore, they are not subordinate to the Contracting Parties and for that reason they can independently assess national laws.[117] That said, NGOs are agenda driven, and, therefore, their assessment can be affected by the aims they are striving to achieve.[118] Moreover, some NGOs may operate only within one jurisdiction and may not have sufficient awareness of foreign legal systems. This can lead to inadequate conclusions.

Alternatively, the ECtHR might request comparative analysis from universities. The Court has not used this theoretically available possibility thus far. However, on a few occasions, the Court has accepted third-party interventions from universities which were initiated by these universities.[119] Among the advantages gained by this method of conducting comparative research are experience, independence, methodological adequacy, consistency and flexibility.[120] However, considering the specific

---

[116] NGOs are involved in the decision-making of the WTO. See, Umbricht, 'An *"Amicus Curiae* Brief"'; P. Van den Bossche, 'NGO Involvement in the WTO: A Comparative Perspective', *Journal of International Economic Law*, 11 (2008), 717. The Court of Justice of the European Union also accepts *amicus curiae* briefs from NGOs. See J. Peel, 'Giving the Public Voice in the Protection of the Global Environment: Avenues for Participation by NGOs in Dispute Resolution at the European Court of Justice and World Trade Organization', *Colorado Journal of International Environmental Law and Policy*, 12 (2001), 47. NGO reports are accepted by the UN institutions. See, K. Martens, *NGOs and the United Nations: Institutionalization, Professionalization and Adaptation* (Palgrave Macmillan, 2005).

[117] Some commentators argue that NGO involvement in the decision-making process increases the transparency and accountability of the institutions; it allows for participation of civil society in the decision-making process. All this positively affects the legitimacy of an international institution. See, Umbricht, 'An *"Amicus Curiae* Brief"', 773. For a more detailed discussion of the NGOs' role in international law see, A.-K. Lindblom, *Non-Governmental Organisations in International Law* (Cambridge University Press, 2006); J.E. Alvarez, *International Organizations as Law-Makers* (Oxford University Press, 2006).

[118] Dzehtsiarou, *Interview with Judge Myjer*; Dzehtsiarou, *Interview with Judge Tulkens*.

[119] See, Dzehtsiarou, *Interview with Judge Tulkens*. See, also *Z. and others v. the United Kingdom*, para. 7.

[120] Deployment of comparative law in the decision-making process is a recent development. Kiekbaev points out that '[c]omparative law for a long time seemed an object of purely scientific research and not directly connected with daily life. Substantial upheavals in the political and legal climate were undoubtedly brought about by the processes of European integration and of globalization.' D.I. Kiekbaev, 'Comparative Law: Method, Science or Educational Discipline?', *Electronic Journal of Comparative Law*, available at www.ejcl.org/73/art73-2.html, accessed on 5 July 2011. Even a few

nature of the requests from the ECtHR, a university or any other research institution will have to put in place a rigid supervision and control mechanism; this might not be too welcome in an institution based on free and unrestrained discussion. Moreover, a university willing to handle research requests from the ECtHR could face a complicated balancing act, where it would have to weigh the amount of valuable academic resources to be invested against potential reputational risks (if research does not live up to the highest standards).

Finally, one potential source of comparative information would be a Court's request about the state of law in a particular Contracting Party from the national authorities of the Contracting Party itself. This could later be incorporated into the report on a particular legal matter prepared by the Research Division of the ECtHR. The mechanics of such a scheme would be fundamentally different from the ready-made comparative law reports submitted by NGOs or universities. The authorities of the Contracting Parties would instead be asked to present an updated account of the regulation of a specific question in a respective jurisdiction. Within such a scheme, it would still be the ECtHR which is responsible for the comparison, and, thus, the risk of undue influence on the Court would be mitigated.

An obstacle to this way of collecting comparative data is the absence of a clear legal basis in the Convention for such requests, an issue which was not foreseen by the drafters of the Convention. A potential solution can be found in Article 38, which places a duty on the Contracting Parties concerned to furnish all necessary facilities for the Court to conduct an investigation. Also, other Contracting Parties may have to provide reports on the state of national law in respect to a particular legal matter. Rule 44A of the Rules of Court provides that

> [t]he parties have a duty to cooperate fully in the conduct of the proceedings and, in particular, to take such action within their power as the Court considers necessary for the proper administration of justice. This duty

decades ago, comparative law was a part of legal theory 'not immediately relevant to the daily life of the law'. T. Koopmans, 'Comparative Law and the Courts', *International and Comparative Law Quarterly*, 45 (1996), 545, 545. It was not used by legal practitioners. See, W.J. Kamba, 'Comparative Law: A Theoretical Framework', *International and Comparative Law Quarterly*, 23 (1974), 485, 489. Universities were the birthplace of comparative law. It seems therefore logical that at least some universities have well-established traditions of conducting sound comparative research.

shall also apply to a Contracting Party not party to the proceedings where such cooperation is necessary.[121]

Another challenging aspect of this proposal is the time frame. The national reports will have to be prepared within a relatively short period of time.[122] This may make it difficult for the Contracting Parties to respond on time, especially if the States receive a substantial number of such requests.

Among the advantages of this way of carrying out comparative research is that the authority in the Contracting Party would be very well aware of the state of national law in respect of a particular legal issue.

4.5 Key challenges

Section 4.2 of this chapter argued that comparative law research fits the vision of the ECtHR and that the Court has gone a long way towards professionalising its comparative legal research. This section will explore key challenges in conducting comparative studies and will discuss possible solutions. It is argued here that the ECtHR can further improve its comparative legal analysis if it manages to overcome four major challenges discussed below.

Four key challenges are analysed in this section. First, it is examined whether laws of all Contracting Parties should be considered for the purposes of comparative law. This section argues that in order for comparative legal research to achieve its persuasive purpose, it should take into account the law and practice of all or nearly all Contracting Parties. Smaller samples can be misleading and do not represent the real state of law in Europe. Second, the law of the Contracting Parties should not be taken out of its national context. If so, the results of comparative analysis can provide inadequate advice for the Court to follow. Third, the Court should carefully consider the subject matter of comparative analysis. It should be discussed by the judges to avoid manipulations of the results of the comparative research. Finally, this section examines the

---

[121] Rules of Court, Rule 44A. While it seems that requests of the Court to the national authorities fall within the ambit of the mentioned rule, one can argue that the uncommon nature of these requests requires a specific rule to be added to the Rules of Court. However, it is hard to foresee any major objections from the Contracting Parties to any such proposed scheme, since it would bring greater transparency to the proceedings within the Court. See, for example, *A., B. and C. v. Ireland*, para. 175.

[122] The head of the Research Division, Montserrat Enrich Mas, stated that these reports should be normally finalised within a two-month period.

challenge of translating legal terms. Sometimes, similar terms may have a different meaning in different languages. These challenges should be taken seriously by the ECtHR.

4.5.1 Comprehensive comparative research

Comparative law materials are compiled in the report by the Research Division, and this is made available to the judges before the hearings. This section argues that such a report should contain a summary of the relevant laws of all or nearly all Contracting Parties. If the ECtHR allowed a subset of the 47 Contracting States to the ECHR to be established for the purpose of assessing the level of consensus on the issue at hand, it would open it up to inconsistencies at best and accusations of manipulation at worst. By defining the subset of States 'for whom the issue exists' either broadly or narrowly, the number of States necessary to establish a consensus can be artificially increased or decreased. One obvious danger to be avoided is that judges define the subset in a way that favours the end result they would personally prefer to see.[123]

Even if judges do not give in to the temptation of manipulating the subset to favour a particular result, there is a more basic reason for including all States in the analysis: the decision reached in the case will have a bearing on all States and not just on those whose position was considered by the Court.

This suggestion can be substantiated by reference to the *erga omnes* effect of the judgments of the ECtHR.[124] Consequently, the judgments of the Court should be taken into account by all Contracting Parties and not only by the respondent Party to the case.[125] If a non-respondent Contracting Party has a regulation or practice similar to the one which was held to be in violation of the ECHR, such a regulation and practice should therefore be amended.[126] In a situation where the judgments of the Court should be implemented by all 47 Member States, one would

---

[123] See, K. Dzehtsiarou and C. O'Mahony, 'Evolutive Interpretation of Rights Provisions: A Comparison of the European Court of Human Rights and the US Supreme Court', *Columbia Human Rights Law Review*, 44 (2013), 309, 342–3.

[124] In the Interlaken Declaration, the Contracting Parties were called upon to commit themselves to 'taking into account the Court's developing case-law, also with a view to considering the conclusions to be drawn from a judgment finding a violation of the Convention by another State, where the same problem of principle exists within their own legal system'. Interlaken Declaration adopted on 19 February 2010, para. 4.

[125] Dzehtsiarou, *Interview with Dean Spielmann*.   [126] See, *supra* Note 79.

expect the laws of all Member States to have been considered when the Court identifies European consensus. In other words, if a judgment affects all Contracting Parties, all of them should be able to influence a judgment through European consensus.

A further point is that considering only a subset of States might lead, in a sufficiently narrow case, to a situation where the position adopted in just a handful of States could ultimately determine the issue for all States. Since the ultimate decision will have consequences for all 47 Contracting States to the ECHR, it makes sense for consensus analysis to factor in all of these States. Otherwise, a majority of perhaps no more than seven States out of ten 'for whom the issue exists' could lead to an interpretation being adopted that applied to 37 other States whose positions were not even considered.[127]

However, it is sometimes impossible to compare the laws of all Contracting Parties. Some of these are underlined in the following statement by Judge Bîrsan:

> They [lawyers of the Research Division] do not always have all 47 countries in the comparative law reports. We can have two kinds of explanations: the institution does not exist in all countries; information is not always available.[128]

If comparative analysis of all Contracting Parties is impossible, the Court should state clearly that it has taken into account the omission of some Contracting Parties and whether or not the trend is sufficiently established without considering the laws of the absent Contracting Parties. Some States may have no position on the issue at hand because they have genuinely not considered it. These should not make up a part of the group on one side of the issue or the other, but a third group should be established. However, the figure necessary to constitute a majority should only be calculated from the total number entitled to have a say.

If this suggestion is followed, the ECtHR will not face the so-called cherry-picking criticism attached to comparative law.[129] Commentators

---

[127] Wildhaber, Hjartarson and Donnelly argue that '[i]t would seem self-evident that in a Court with 47 member States comparative research should be as comprehensive as possible. Where judgments rely on only half or less of all legal orders, the consensus argument is bound to lose in strength and credibility.' Wildhaber, Hjartarson and Donnelly, 'No Consensus on Consensus?', 258.

[128] K. Dzehtsiarou, *Interview with Judge Corneliu Bîrsan* (European Court of Human Rights, Strasbourg, 2010).

[129] See, for example, C. Saunders, 'Judicial Engagement with Comparative Law' in T. Ginsburg and R. Nixon (eds.), *Comparative Constitutional Law* (Edward Elgar, 2011), p. 587.

have pointed out that results of comparative law can be substantially diverse if different Contracting Parties are compared.[130] McCrudden has criticised cherry-picking in the courts' selection of legislation to which they refer, arguing that courts are more likely to quote foreign judgments or include comparative materials which support their own convictions.[131]

In order to minimise these concerns, the ECtHR should be proactive by exploring the laws and practices of all Contracting Parties. If a 'blanket comparison'[132] is not possible, the Court should put forward a criterion for the selection of the Member States that justifies such a selection.

In any case, even when the Court explores the laws of all 47 Member States, this is not always clearly outlined in the text of the judgment. In recent cases, the Court has mentioned the number of Contracting Parties that were considered for comparative research.[133] Wildhaber, Hjartarson and Donnelly argue that comparative analysis is representative if more than 60 per cent of the Contracting Parties are considered.[134] This approach seems reasonable but the Court should aspire to cover as many Contracting Parties as possible, in every case where a comparative law report has been prepared.[135]

This section argues that properly identified European consensus should be based on comprehensive comparative research that aims to explore relevant laws of all the Contracting Parties. Such comparative research should be summarised in the text of the judgments with a brief

---

[130] Kamba, 'Comparative Law: A Theoretical Framework', 485, 510; O. Kahn-Freund, 'Comparative Law as an Academic Subject', *Law Quarterly Review*, 82 (1966), 40.
[131] C. McCrudden, 'A Common Law of Human Rights?: Transnational Judicial Conversations on Constitutional Rights', *Oxford Journal of Legal Studies*, 4 (2000), 499, 507. See also, Örücü, 'Whither Comparativism in Human Rights Cases?', p. 231.
[132] Comparison of the laws of all Contracting Parties to the Convention.
[133] For example, in *Söderman v. Sweden*, the Court pointed out that '[f]rom the information available to the Court, including a survey of thirty-nine Council of Europe member States, it would appear that child pornography is criminalised in all of those States'. *Söderman v. Sweden*, para. 53.
[134] Wildhaber, Hjartarson and Donnelly, 'No Consensus on Consensus?', 258.
[135] Wildhaber, Hjartarson and Donnelly offer the following statistical information on how many Contracting Parties have been covered for the purposes of comparative law in its case law: 'We have explored how many legal orders of member States the Court analyses in actual practice and can report that: in about 56% of post-1998 judgments which discuss consensus in the 47 European member States, the number of legal orders may be qualified as representative; in about 12.3% roughly half of all States are taken into consideration (and are indicated separately); in about 7% the comparative research is less than representative; and in about 24.6% the "new" Court remains content to follow the example of the "old" Court, indicating that it recognizes or fails to recognize consensus, without any further details or simply speaking of a "majority of States".' Ibid.

note of which States were compared and what the results of the comparisons were. Such a summary should highlight different or conflicting practices; if a trend is identifiable, the Court should nevertheless outline if there are any diverging laws.

The lack of a transparent outline of comparative law can lead to several drawbacks, namely the inability of the parties to foresee the Court's findings,[136] frustration amongst the general public and commentators given that the established consensus can affect the meaning of the Convention rights and an inability to examine the judgments of the Court in terms of the accuracy of the comparative research.

4.5.2 Legal provisions in context

In order for comparative research to be adequate, it should not simply describe the laws of the Contracting Parties but should also take into account the relevant national context in which a norm operates, including practical, social and legal contexts. This section welcomes the current approach of the ECtHR to comparative law and suggests that the Court could go further and consider various sources of information to achieve a higher standard of comparative research.

It has been acknowledged that a norm-centred comparison does not provide adequate results.[137] This type of comparison is one that focuses

---

[136] Argumentative transparency of the judicial decisions is deemed important for ethical and pragmatic reasons. Komarek summarised the legal debate in relation to transparency of the arguments in the following terms: according to Dworkin, a judge 'must propose and justify his (necessarily personal) interpretive choices in terms of how they best promote a coherent and principled treatment of all of society's members. Unlike those of Dworkin, Llewellyn's concerns were pragmatic and not ethical: these were to provide true reasons motivating the judge in taking the decision in order to achieve predictability and, consequently, to adopt better rules, which would reflect the true reality in the courts.' J. Komarek, 'Questioning Judicial Deliberations', *Oxford Journal of Legal Studies*, 29 (2009), 805, 817. Stranieri correctly observes that 'a representation of legal reasoning ... can ... lead to greater transparency and clarity'. A. Stranieri, 'An Explicit Representation of Judicial Reasoning to Enhance Transparency and Consistency without Sacrificing Discretion', available at www.njca.com.au/Professional%20Development/programs%20by%20year/2009/Judic%20Reas%20papers/stranieri.pdf, accessed on 20 July 2011.

[137] D.J. Gerber, 'System Dynamics: Toward a Language of Comparative Law?', *American Journal of Comparative Law*, 46 (1998), 719, 721. In some countries, the law as expressed in textbooks is quite different to the law under which people live. J.C. Reitz, 'How to Do Comparative Law', *American Journal of Comparative Law*, 46 (1998), 617, 630; W. Ewald, 'The Jurisprudential Approach to Comparative Law: A Field Guide to "Rats"', *American Journal of Comparative Law*, 46 (1998), 701, 702. Hoecke and Warrington argue that if the

on black-letter law without taking into account the context in which laws operate. Stone argues that an objective comparative survey should be interdisciplinary: 'We must study the history, the politics, the economics, the cultural background in literature and the arts, the religion, beliefs and practices, the philosophies, if we are to reach sound conclusions as to what is and what is not common.'[138] However, this idealistic approach has been criticised, notably by De Cruz, who regards it as impractical because a comparativist can hardly be a specialist in all these areas and it is not always necessary to consider such details.[139] Mahoney has suggested a more balanced approach to comparative legal research which focuses on the context of rules compared: 'national rules cannot simply be compared in isolation but have above all to be understood in their local context, in relation to the national legal system concerned and their operation in practice'.[140]

This point can be illustrated by a simple example. In *Shofman* v. *Russia*,[141] the Court used comparative law to determine whether there was a commonly accepted standard in respect of time limits for bringing proceedings contesting paternity. The Court came to the conclusion that there was no such standard. However, the Court stated that it was not enough to compare the periods of time which different legal systems left for this kind of legal action; it was also important to compare the point at which these terms began:

> the difference between the various legal systems that is relevant to the present case is not only the length of the limitation period as such, but also its *dies a quo*. In some States the period is calculated from the moment the putative father knew or should have known that he had been registered as the child's father. The other States, which are approximately equal in number, accept as the starting point the date he learnt or should have learnt of circumstances casting doubt on the child's legitimacy. Many States in the latter category have introduced a second time-limit, making it possible to disclaim paternity only when the child is still young. A few States in which time starts to run from the child's birth, irrespective of the father's awareness of any other facts, also fall into the latter category.[142]

cultural parameters are not taken into account, one might find much more similarities than there are in reality. M.V. Hoecke and M. Warrington, 'Legal Cultures, Legal Paradigms and Legal Doctrine: Towards a New Model for Comparative Law', *International and Comparative Law Quarterly*, 47 (1998), 495, 511.

[138] F.F. Stone, 'The End to Be Served by Comparative Law', *Tulane Law Review*, 25 (1951), 325, 332.
[139] P. De Cruz, *Comparative Law in a Changing World* (Routledge-Cavendish, 1999), p. 236.
[140] Mahoney, 'The Comparative Method', p. 146.   [141] *Shofman* v. *Russia*.
[142] Ibid., para. 38.

4.5 KEY CHALLENGES

The same numerical periods of time might lead to completely different outcomes for the claimant if they begin from the moment of a child's birth or from the moment of the father's awareness of the circumstances. This is an obvious example; however, sometimes these differences are hidden from researchers and can only be identified through examination of legal practice adopted in the particular State.

The judges of the ECtHR have also pointed out that legal norms should be approached in the context in which they operate. Judge Tulkens maintains that

> it is very difficult to do an accurate comparative law not only in the text but also in reality. When they [lawyers of the Research Division of the Court] ask to conduct a comparative research they ask all judges here to confirm it. And it is very sensitive to have a report with a situation with the law today.[143]

The Research Division's comparative report is compiled on the basis of reports prepared by the national lawyers that are approved by the national judge. This arrangement presumes that the Court will consider national law within the national context.[144] Judge Jaeger pointed out that reports of the state of national laws are prepared by the national lawyers who are aware of the local context in which a law is operating. For that reason, the report of the Research Division is very useful for the Court.[145] In some judgments, the Court has expressed its awareness about the way laws operate in a national context.

An example of this is the case of *Tănase and Chirtoacă* v. *Moldova*, where the Court explored Member State legislation regarding dual citizenship. The Court stated that '[i]n some of the countries which ban double nationality, in practice the provisions aimed at preventing multiple nationalities have remained a dead letter (for instance Estonia)'.[146] If the Court had relied on the black-letter Estonian law and laws of other

---

[143] Dzehtsiarou, *Interview with Judge Tulkens*.
[144] It can be argued that the national lawyers would not document certain local aspects of domestic legal practice because it seems a commonplace to them. However, the lawyers of the ECtHR work and live outside their home country (with the exception of the French lawyers) and they often know what can be considered unusual in their domestic legal systems. This problem can be partially rectified by the detailed description of the matter at issue as argued below because the national lawyers will be better aware of what kind of information is expected from them.
[145] Dzehtsiarou, *Interview with Judge Jaeger*.
[146] *Tănase and Chirtoacă* v. *Moldova*, Application No 7/08, Judgment of 18 November 2008, para. 49.

countries with a similar practice, then such reliance would have incorrectly affected the outcomes of the comparative survey.

In other cases, the Court has explored a legal issue which is in the process of being developed in some countries. In *Odièvre* v. *France*, the Court considered whether the Contracting Parties provided for the right to give birth anonymously. The Court stated that

> [i]t is relatively rare for mothers to be entitled to give birth anonymously under European domestic legislation, as Italy and Luxembourg stand alone in not imposing a statutory obligation on the natural parents to register a newborn child or to state their identity when registering it. Conversely, many countries make it obligatory to provide the names, not only of the mother, to whom the child is automatically linked, but also of the father ... The current trend in certain countries is towards the acceptance, if not of a right to give birth anonymously, then at least of a right to give birth 'discreetly'. An example of this is provided by Belgium, where a debate has begun, largely as a result of the large number of women crossing the border to give birth anonymously in France. In an opinion delivered on 12 January 1998 the Consultative Committee on Bioethics set out the two lines of argument that were defensible from an ethical standpoint: the first considered it unacceptable for children to be brought into the world without parents; for that reason its proponents proposed that facilities for 'giving birth discreetly' should be provided, without completely closing the door on all attempts to trace the parents.[147]

Such a substantive analysis of the laws of the Contracting Parties is relatively rare. More often than not, a judgment contains a brief outline of the current state of relevant laws.[148]

NGO *amicus curiae* briefs[149] and reports of international supervisory bodies sometimes contain information about the real-life application of a relevant law which the Court may avail itself of in its assessment of the laws of the Contracting Parties. In *Nachova and others* v. *Bulgaria*, for example, the Court dealt with the prohibition of discrimination of people of Roma origin. The ECtHR quoted the report of the European Commission against Racism and Intolerance. The report provided that the Framework Programme for Equal Integration of Roma in Bulgarian Society had been adopted by the Bulgarian authorities; '[t]here is, however, a unanimous feeling within the Roma community and among

---

[147] *Odièvre* v. *France*, Application No 42326/98, Judgment of 13 February 2003, para. 19.
[148] See, for example, *Perdigão* v. *Portugal*, Application No 24768/06, Judgment of 16 November 2010, para. 47–50; *Anheuser-Busch Inc.* v. *Portugal*, Application No 73049/01, Judgment of 11 January 2007, para. 39–40.
[149] *Christine Goodwin* v. *the United Kingdom*, para. 55–7.

non-governmental organisations, that, apart from the few initiatives mentioned in this report, the programme has remained a dead letter'.[150] This observation seems to suggest that multiple sources inform the Court about the environment in which the laws are operating better; they provide varying viewpoints, experiences and knowledge on the matter at issue.

The Court's practice of conducting independent research in conjunction with the consideration of other sources of information should be welcomed. In an interview for this book, Judge Rozakis pointed out that

> [a]lthough admittedly national lawyers are not experts in all aspects of domestic law still we do not rely only on that. We also rely on independent research done by the Division itself. They try to find out not only what the law is but also how the law is interpreted by national courts. Now we have Internet and it is easier to do this research. Step by step they try to find out what the law is in reality and only after that they send the findings to the national lawyers for the further comments and then to the national judge for confirmation.[151]

This section argues that, for comparative legal research to be adequate, it should take into account relevant national laws in the context of the national legal system. The fact that the Research Division requests legal reports from the national lawyers and considers comparative data from various sources can to some extent satisfy this requirement.

4.5.3 Subject matter of comparison

The subject of comparative law should be thoroughly considered.[152] Otherwise, comparative research can lead to inadequate conclusions. This challenge in identifying European consensus was emphasised by the dissenting judge in *Leyla Şahin v. Turkey*. In this case, the ECtHR assessed the compliance of the Turkish legal prohibition on the wearing of the Islamic headscarf in universities with the Convention. The Court conducted comparative research and noted that certain European countries had placed bans on the wearing of religious signs in schools. However, only Azerbaijan, Turkey and Albania had introduced

---

[150] *Nachova and others v. Bulgaria*, Application No 43577/98 and 43579/98, Judgment of 6 July 2005, para. 58.
[151] K. Dzehtsiarou, *Interview with Judge Christos Rozakis* (European Court of Human Rights, Strasbourg, 2010).
[152] Dzehtsiarou, *Interview with Judge Tulkens*.

regulations on wearing the Islamic headscarf in universities.[153] Nevertheless, the Court stated that there was no uniform approach towards regulation of this issue in educational establishments. The Court indicated the 'diversity of the approaches taken by national authorities on the issue'.[154] This conclusion was made on the basis of comparing the legislation regulating wearing religious symbols at both schools and universities.

The ECtHR has chosen not to distinguish between legal regulations on wearing religious signs at schools of primary and secondary level and at universities, which are the third-level institutions. However, university students need much less paternalistic treatment from the State than do pupils at school. This point was highlighted by Judge Tulkens in her dissenting opinion. She stated that

> [t]he comparative-law materials do not allow for such a conclusion [of a lack of European consensus], as in none of the Member States has the ban on wearing religious symbols extended to university education, which is intended for young adults, who are less amenable to pressure.[155]

In this case, the choice of the subject of comparison crucially affected the Court's conclusion about European consensus.

The choice of comparators and the subject of comparison depends on the questions the judge-rapporteurs ask the Research Division of the ECtHR in their requests.[156] These questions are crucial for the usability of the comparative analysis and its impact on the final judgment of the Court. It seems appropriate that the questions can be proposed by the judge-rapporteur but they should be discussed by the Chamber or the Grand Chamber before the request to conduct comparative research is sent to the Research Division. Thorough consideration and discussion of the question put before the Research Division can increase the effectiveness of comparative data as all judges involved in the decision-making will be able to request information they consider relevant.

The Court can legitimately deploy the European consensus argument based on comparative analysis if such analysis is comprehensive and based on a rigorous methodology. Otherwise, the Court's conclusion about the presence or absence of European consensus can be challenged as ill informed.

---

[153] *Leyla Şahin v. Turkey*, para. 55–65.   [154] Ibid., para. 109.
[155] Ibid., Dissenting Opinion of Judge Tulkens.
[156] Currently, the judge-rapporteur himself or herself decides what questions should be put before the Research Division.

4.5 KEY CHALLENGES

4.5.4 *Translation of legal terms*

The Court should determine the subject of comparison carefully. However, even if the right comparators are selected, the Court can face a further issue relating to the translation of legal terms; this has been regarded as a serious challenge in comparative law. It is suggested here that the Court is well equipped to handle this challenge as it deals with legal translation on a daily basis. That said, translation of legal terms for comparative research has some specific features. In order to engage in comparative law effectively, the lawyers should be well informed of the matter at issue. Therefore, this section will show that the lawyers of the Court who prepare reports for the Research Division should be informed about the context and circumstances of the case in order to prepare an adequate outline of the state of the law in his or her national State.

Some commentators argue that absolutely equivalent translation is impossible.[157] Kamba points out that

> even in English speaking countries, homonyms may have different meanings. Hence, if the basic legal concepts are similar, different terms may be utilised so as to create an impression of divergence, and this may even occur within the same legal family.[158]

It is even more problematic if legal terms need to be translated into English or French.

If exact translation is impossible, then the terms should be compared based on their functional equivalency which is understood here as the comparison of legal provisions that can have a different literal translation

---

[157] Schroth argues that '[a]ll translation is compromise. It is usually better in legal translation to make the audience aware of the difficulties than artfully to disguise them. Legal translation in practice usually involves the additional difficulty that neither the lawyers nor the professional translators combine the necessary qualifications in one person. When all of those qualifications are found somewhere in a team, satisfactory results are often possible given a clear understanding of the problem. An alternative approach in some circumstances is avoidance, or at least reduction, of the problem by specifying the governing language, legal system or court.' P.W. Schroth, 'Legal Translation', *American Journal of Comparative Law*, 34 (1986), 47, 65. Rotman also points out that '[a]lthough legal translation demands precision and certainty, it is bound to use abstractions, whose meanings derive from particular changing cultural and social contexts. These contexts generate a certain degree of ambiguity, which increases when the legal cultures and systems are vastly different from each other.' E. Rotman, 'The Inherent Problems of Legal Translation Theoretical Aspects', *Indiana International and Comparative Law Review*, 6 (1996), 187, 189.

[158] Kamba, 'Comparative Law: A Theoretical Framework', 505.

but fulfil a similar function in the legal system.[159] In some cases, the Court has confirmed this approach and that it is prepared to compare similar but not identical terms. In *J. A. Pye (Oxford) Ltd and J. A. Pye (Oxford) Land Ltd* v. *the United Kingdom*, the Court stated that

> [i]t is plain from the comparative material submitted by the parties that a large number of Member States possesses some form of mechanism for transferring title in accordance with principles similar to adverse possession in the common law systems, and that such transfer is effected without the payment of compensation to the original owner.[160]

The Court was not in a position to compare procedures that were exactly the same as those in the case at hand; however, it seems to have compared legal procedures that were functionally similar. Reitz argues that good comparative analysis should describe the degree to which there are equivalents in the national systems of the Member States.[161] In order to describe the equivalents, the national lawyer should be knowledgeable about the subject of comparison, namely the legal issue under scrutiny.

The specific nature of the ECtHR as an international tribunal suggests that it constantly faces the challenge of legal terms' translation.[162] There

---

[159] The same terms can describe different legal phenomena in different legal systems. Kamba notes that '[t]he term possession, for example, has a juridical meaning in French law different from that under English law'. Ibid., 222. For that reason, the terms should be compared according to the function they fulfil in the national legal system. Zweigert and Kötz argue that functionality is a basic principle of comparative law: '[t]he basic methodological principle of all comparative law is that of functionality. From this basic principle stem all the other rules which determine the choice of laws to compare, the scope of the undertaking, the creation of a system of comparative law ... in law, the only things which are comparable are those which fulfil the same function.' K. Zweigert and H. Kötz, *An Introduction to Comparative Law* (Clarendon Press, 1998), p. 34. See also, J. Hill, 'Comparative Law, Law Reform and Legal Theory', *Oxford Journal of Legal Studies*, 9 (1989), 101. It is worth mentioning that functionalism is the topic of an ongoing academic debate. Michaels, for example, argues that '[t]he functional method has become both the mantra and the *bête noire* of comparative law. For its proponents, functionalism offers the most, perhaps the only, fruitful method; to its opponents, it represents everything bad about mainstream comparative law.' R. Michaels, 'The Functionalist Method of Comparative Law' in M. Reimann and R. Zimmermann (eds.), *The Oxford Handbook of Comparative Law* (Oxford University Press, 2006), p. 340. See also, A. Riles, 'Wigmore's Treasure Box: Comparative Law in the Era of Information', *Harvard International Law Journal*, 40 (1999), 221. Some commentators call for 'more methodologically aware functionalism'. Michaels, 'The Functionalist Method of Comparative Law', p. 340.

[160] *J.A. Pye (Oxford) Ltd and J.A. Pye (Oxford) Land Ltd* v. *the United Kingdom*, para. 72.

[161] Reitz, 'How to Do Comparative Law', 621.

[162] For only a minority of the judges, English or French – official languages of the ECtHR – are mother tongues. The majority of the judges are working in a foreign language.

4.5 KEY CHALLENGES

are 47 Contracting Parties to the Convention; each of them has at least one national language. All necessary legal terms are translated by the lawyers of the Registry, who are trained national lawyers and have excellent linguistic skills. However, preparing comparative research is more complicated than the everyday practice of the Court. If comparative research is requested, the lawyer who is preparing this research should be familiar with the relevant laws of his national State. He or she should be able to translate it into English or French, and, furthermore, the lawyer should understand the function of the legal provision under scrutiny in the case at hand.

In order to ensure that the comparative analysis focuses on functional equivalents, lawyers dealing with requests from the Research Division should be informed in as much detail as possible about the functioning of the laws or practices which are to be scrutinised by the Court in the case at hand. Currently, the request from the Research Division contains only questions that the lawyer should answer, often without a detailed explanation of the matter at issue.[163] This substantially limits the capacity of the national lawyer to carry out effective research relevant to the substantive issues within the case.[164] It can be noted that the lawyers dealing with requests can access more detailed information in certain situations.

The ECtHR possesses unique resources in terms of comparative research. As noted, such research can be carried out by the national lawyers employed by the Court who are fluent in both English and

---

Therefore, they have to constantly translate legal terms. This issue can be found in the other European court, and De Cruz made the following observation in the context of the European Union about the specific nature of the decision-making of the European Court of Justice (ECJ): 'By virtue of their legal background and origins, judges of the ECJ are bound to draw upon their own experience as lawyers within the Member States. The Court seeks to evaluate and possibly utilise solutions provided by the legal systems from which the judges are drawn.' De Cruz, *Comparative Law*, p. 21. This observation also seems correct in relation to the ECtHR.

[163] Such requests are confidential, and their content cannot be accessed by the general public. The author appeared to be aware of the usual content of the requests from the interviews with the members of the Registry of the Court and his experience as a trainee lawyer at the Court.

[164] This statement requires qualification. As has been mentioned earlier, the comparative studies are normally prepared in the Grand Chamber cases. If the case was referred to the Grand Chamber pursuant to Article 43 of the ECHR, the lawyer who prepares the national report might access the Chamber judgment in the case at hand that would contain more detailed information about the case. In case of relinquishment of the case to the Grand Chamber pursuant to Article 30 of the ECHR, the Chamber judgment is unavailable. In this case, the Research Division requests occasionally contain the rapporteur's note with some relevant information on the case.

French. However, this potential would not be fully utilised if the lawyers were not to know the nature and the context of the matter at issue. It is proposed to include a more detailed explanation of the matter at issue within the request of the Research Division. This would make the lawyers better aware of the subject of comparison, and this would subsequently lead to a more comprehensive and adequate basis for determining the existence and nature of European consensus.

4.6 Conclusion

This section has examined how comparative law data are collected and deployed by the ECtHR. It is important because comparative law provides a foundation for the Court's decision about the presence or absence of European consensus. Central for this chapter is the argument that deployment of comparative law fits the vision of the ECtHR as a strong and influential regional human rights court capable of setting human rights standards not only in Europe but also worldwide. In order to support this vision, comparative law should be based on sound methodology and provide results that reflect reality. Otherwise, the positive effect of comparative law can vanish. This chapter has examined a number of challenges that have to be addressed by those involved in comparative law: translation of legal terms, national context, comprehensive coverage and subject matter of comparison.

This chapter has also established that the ECtHR deploys comparative and international law more and more often in its judgments, especially in the Grand Chamber cases. The Court more often relies on in-house comparative law reports. This is a sign of the professionalisation of comparative law deployed by the Court. The Court's reliance on in-house comparative law is a positive trend in the Court's practice.

5

Criticism of European consensus

5.1 Introduction

This chapter opens the discussion on the normative value of European consensus. While Chapters 2–4 explained the technicalities of identification and application of European consensus, Chapters 5–7 will examine whether deployment of European consensus is appropriate in human rights adjudication. This chapter deals with the criticism of the concept and offers some counter-arguments to this criticism. Chapter 6 then analyses why European consensus is capable of enhancing the legitimacy of the European Court of Human Rights (ECtHR or Court) and its judgments. Finally, Chapter 7 explores whether the judges of the ECtHR consider this tool to be legitimate and appropriate. These three chapters aim to show that some substantive criticisms of European consensus are far-fetched.

It has been argued that criticism of European consensus can be divided into procedural and substantive.[1] The key target of procedural criticism is the method, namely how consensus is identified and applied in the reasoning. Substantive criticism attacks the normative value of European consensus and its appropriateness in human rights adjudication. The main argument here is that human rights are substantively anti-majoritarian; they protect individuals from the dictates of the majority. In contrast, European consensus can be conceptualised as a majoritarian decision-making approach. The second section of this chapter explains and analyses the anti-majoritarian argument against consensus, which is most pressing in the cases dealing with minority rights.[2] The third section

---

[1] K. Dzehtsiarou, 'Does Consensus Matter? Legitimacy of European Consensus in the Case Law of the European Court of Human Rights', *Public Law* (2011), 534, 539–41.
[2] Ethnic minorities: *Chapman* v. *the United Kingdom*, Application No 27238/95, Judgment of 18 January 2001; LGBT: *Dudgeon* v. *the United Kingdom*, Application No 7525/76, Judgment of 23 September 1981, etc.

of this chapter argues that application of European consensus does not endanger these rights. It is also argued here that this threat is overestimated in Europe. However, the deployment of consensus decision-making by other regional human rights tribunals or in the worldwide context might prove to be more problematic.

Section 5.4 of this chapter argues that some criticism of European consensus is associated with criticism primarily directed towards the margin of appreciation or evolutive interpretation. This part analyses criticism of these two doctrines and suggests that these methods lack some clarity of scope and application. It is suggested that, if applied systematically, European consensus can add such clarity.

5.2 'Anti-majoritarian argument' against consensus

Commentators such as Letsas,[3] Murray[4] and Benvenisti[5] challenge European consensus as a concept. Letsas questions the normative legitimacy of European consensus and claims that human rights adjudication should be based on the moral prevalence of human rights. For him, the moral value of rights, not the number of States supporting a particular standard, legitimises the judgments of the ECtHR. He argues that deployment of European consensus is not normatively legitimate since consensus links rights to what the majority of the Contracting Parties has decided. Such linkage ultimately undermines the universal moral superiority of rights.[6] I shall call this approach the 'anti-majoritarian argument' because it suggests that human rights adjudication should not rely upon the will of the majority of the Contracting Parties. Letsas explains that

---

[3] See, G. Letsas, *A Theory of Interpretation of the European Convention on Human Rights* (Oxford University Press, 2009), pp. 120–31; G. Letsas, 'The Truth in Autonomous Concepts: How to Interpret the ECHR', *European Journal of International Law*, 15 (2004), 279.

[4] J.L. Murray, 'Consensus: Concordance, or Hegemony of Majority' in *Dialogues between Judges* (Council of Europe, 2008).

[5] E. Benvenisti, 'Margin of Appreciation, Consensus, and Universal Standards', *Journal of International Law and Politics*, 31 (1999), 843.

[6] Letsas argues that '[p]iecemeal evolution of the ECHR standards according to how many States have abandoned moralistic preferences in different areas of national law deeply offends the values of legality and equality'. Letsas, *A Theory of Interpretation*, p. 124. Brauch similarly points out that '[i]ronically, in the name of protecting human rights, the Court adopts a standard that actually threatens human rights'. J.A. Brauch, 'The Margin of Appreciation and the Jurisprudence of the European Court of Human Rights: Threat to the Rule of Law', *Columbia Journal of European Law*, 11 (2004), 113, 146.

[h]uman rights are not criteria concepts whose meaning is exhausted by their common usage across Contracting States. They are meant to express a moral commitment to objective principles of liberal democracy. It follows that the European Court of Human Rights does not exercise illegitimate judicial discretion in looking for and allying these principles to unforeseen and controversial cases.[7]

According to Letsas, the ECtHR itself should base its judgments on the moral foundations of rights, and he insists that national courts should also use methods of interpretation that are justifiable from the point of view of abstract values of political morality: pluralism, tolerance and broad-mindedness.[8] Nevertheless, he admits that the moral foundations of human rights are controversial.[9] Therefore, he seems to suggest that the ECtHR should base its judgments mainly on controversial and abstract values.

Abstract moral values could act as a solid base in human rights adjudication if there was no disagreement on how these values should apply, especially in certain borderline, controversial or 'hard' cases. Rational people can disagree about the application of rights even if they agree that rights are valuable as such.[10] Hence, the application of abstract moral principles should be independently legitimate.[11] In many hard cases, these abstract moral principles provide insufficient guidance. From this perspective, the 'anti-majoritarian argument' seems to lose touch

---

[7] Letsas, *A Theory of Interpretation*, p. 3.   [8] Ibid.   [9] Ibid., p. 18.
[10] J. Waldron, 'Deliberation, Disagreement and Voting' in H.H. Koh and R.C. Slye (eds.), *Deliberative Democracy and Human Right* (Yale University Press, 1999), pp. 210–26. Waldron argues that 'there is substantial dissensus as to what rights there are and what they amount to. Some of these disagreements are apparent at a philosophical level (e.g., whether socioeconomic rights should be included in the Bill of Rights), some become apparent when we try to relate abstract principles of right to particular legislative proposals (e.g., whether the free exercise of religion demands exemptions from otherwise generally applicable laws), and some become apparent only in the context of hard individual cases (e.g., how much tolerance for dissident speech there should be in a time of national emergency).' J. Waldron, 'The Core of the Case against Judicial Review', *Yale Law Journal*, 115 (2006), 1346, 1366–7.
[11] A. Stone, 'Judicial Review without Rights: Some Problems for the Democratic Legitimacy of Structural Judicial Review', *Oxford Journal of Legal Studies*, 28 (2008), 1, 7. In the interview, Judge Myjer discussed *E.B. v. France*, where the Court considered whether homosexuals had a right to adopt under the Convention. Judge Myjer pointed out that 'if there is a general principle – that there should be the possibility of homosexuals adopting – a lot of difficulties can arise from the implementation of this principle. In a situation such as this, yes, I think that consensus might assist the Court.' K. Dzehtsiarou, *Interview with Judge Egbert Myjer* (European Court of Human Rights, Strasbourg, 2009).

with reality.[12] If courts base their judgments solely on abstract moral values, they are likely to be accused of making arbitrary or political judgments.[13] These accusations can be detrimental to the effectiveness and legitimacy of the decision-making body.

Having said this, it can be accepted that the moral value of human rights makes them normatively legitimate.[14] Greer, for example, observes that moral principles act as primary principles of interpretation.[15] However, it does not seem appropriate to justify every judgment delivered by the ECtHR by reference to the abstract moral values of human rights.[16] A more precise legitimacy-conferring model is required. It is argued here that European consensus can provide such a model. Moreover, European consensus does not negate the moral value of human rights. Judge Garlicki points out that there should be a presumption that the Contracting Parties take the values enshrined in the European Convention on Human Rights (ECHR or Convention) into account when they adopt particular legal solutions.[17] Indeed, some Contracting Parties put in place systems for checking compatibility

---

[12] Judge Caflisch points out that 'it [European consensus] stays firmly on a level of reality. And there is no point in seeing unity where there is no ... The Court has to deliver its judgments on the basis of reality maybe with a bit of incremental idealism but not total.' K. Dzehtsiarou, *Interview with Judge Lucius Caflisch* (European University Institute, Florence, 2008).

[13] In relation to the US Supreme Court, Posner points out that '[c]onstitutional cases in the open area are aptly regarded as "political" because the Constitution is about politics and because cases in the open area are not susceptible of confident evaluation on the basis of professional legal norms. They can be decided only on the basis of a political judgment, and a political judgment cannot be called right or wrong by reference to legal norms.' R.A. Posner, 'The Supreme Court, 2004 Term – Foreword: A Political Court', *Harvard Law Review*, 119 (2005), 31, 40.

[14] See, J. Donnelly, 'Human Rights: A New Standard of Civilization?', *International Affairs*, 74 (1998), 1, 20; Letsas, *A Theory of Interpretation*, p. 121; N. Stammers, 'A Critique of Social Approaches to Human Rights', *Human Rights Quarterly*, 17 (1995), 488, 492.

[15] S. Greer, *The European Convention on Human Rights. Achievements, Problems and Prospects* (Cambridge University Press, 2006), pp. 195–213.

[16] Lord Hoffmann questions this broad exploitation of the legitimacy of human rights. His statement was recently quoted by the Daily Mail: 'human rights have become, like health and safety, a byword for foolish decisions by courts and administrators'. J. Groves, '"Europe's Human Rights Court Is Out of Control ... We Must Pull Out": Call by Top British Judge after Ruling That Prisoners Should Get the Vote', *Mail Online*, available at www.dailymail.co.uk/news/article-1354362/Europes-human-rights-court–control–pull-Call-British-judge-ruling-prisoners-vote.html#ixzz1RnFsH61j, accessed on 11 July 2011.

[17] K. Dzehtsiarou, *Interview with Judge Lech Garlicki* (European Court of Human Rights, Strasbourg, 2009).

with human rights norms when adopting new laws.[18] Therefore, if there is a consensus on a particular issue, one can presume that Convention rights were considered when national law was adopted. This presumption is rebuttable. In addition, European consensus is deployed only when the exact meaning of abstract provisions of the ECHR is not clear.[19]

Another recurring theme of the 'anti-majoritarian argument' is that the Court cannot legitimately deploy the will of the majority since human rights are precisely designed to protect against the will of the majority. Letsas argues that

> [i]f it makes no sense to let the majorities decide what rights individuals have, then it makes no sense either to resolve legal disagreement in human rights cases by appealing to what the majorities now believe or have legislated.[20]

This argument suggests that the will of the majority is not determinative in human rights litigation, especially at the supra-national level.[21] This argument seems fair if the will of the majority of the Contracting Parties is the only factor determining the meaning of the rights. However, European consensus only establishes a presumption in favour of particular solutions that were adopted by the majority of democratic States in Europe. European consensus is not decisive although it can be highly persuasive.[22] Therefore, the claim that the ECtHR imposes the dictates of the majority through European consensus is far-fetched.[23] The following section further outlines how the Court's treatment of minority rights undermines the

---

[18] In the United Kingdom, under the Human Rights Act, the Joint Human Rights Committee conducts legislative scrutiny of some laws to be adopted by Parliament.

[19] Dzehtsiarou, *Interview with Judge Egbert Myjer*.

[20] Letsas, 'The Truth in Autonomous Concepts', 304.

[21] Benvenisti argues that the Court 'stops short of fulfilling the crucial task of becoming the external guardian against the tyranny by majorities'. Benvenisti, 'Margin of Appreciation, Consensus, and Universal Standards', 852.

[22] K. Dzehtsiarou, *Interview with Michael O'Boyle* (European Court of Human Rights, Strasbourg, 2009).

[23] However, it should be noted that some commentators consider it to be paradoxical for an international judicial body to depend on national laws and rules in assessing the legality of certain measures adopted by the Respondent State. Y. Arai-Takahashi, *The Margin of Appreciation Doctrine and the Principle of Proportionality in the Jurisprudence of the ECHR* (2002), p. 192; W.J.G. van der Meersch, 'Reliance, in the Case-Law of the European Court of Human Rights, on the Domestic Law of the States', *Human Rights Law Journal*, 1 (1980), 13, 25. Common rules and principles were anticipated by the drafters of the Convention to be guiding principles for the development of human rights in Europe. Therefore, European consensus is neither an excessively innovative nor paradoxical tool of interpretation of the Convention.

'anti-majoritarian argument'. This is because in a number of cases consensus justified enhancing the protection of minority rights by the ECtHR.

Letsas concludes his argument by stating that the very essence of European consensus contradicts the purposes of the ECtHR as an institution designed to protect individuals against the State.[24] This argument does not take into account the nature of the Court and the Convention. The Convention was signed and the Court was created not to confront the Contracting Parties but to intensify cooperation and collective protection of human rights.

The themes of unity and commonality among the Contracting Parties are mentioned three times in the preamble to the Convention:

> [T]he aim of the Council of Europe is *the achievement of greater unity between its members* and that one of the methods by which that aim is to be pursued is the maintenance and further realisation of human rights and fundamental freedoms;
>
> fundamental freedoms are the foundation of justice and peace in the world and are best maintained on the one hand by an effective political democracy and on the other by a *common understanding and observance of the human rights* upon which they depend;
>
> the governments of European countries ... are *likeminded and have a common heritage* of political traditions, ideals, freedom and the rule of law.[25]

Commentators such as Brems argue that the origin of European consensus is the 'common heritage of political traditions' identified in the preamble; 'the ECHR is considered to be derived from the national systems of the European states'.[26] Van der Meersch adds that the Convention was inspired by the 'common law' of the European countries, and judgments which are based on European consensus reflect this inspiration.[27]

The drafters of the Convention conceived of legal unification as a safeguard against dictatorship in Europe and hence against new military conflicts. As Teitgen states:

---

[24] Letsas, 'The Truth in Autonomous Concepts', 293.
[25] Preamble to the Convention. Emphasis added.
[26] E. Brems, *Human Rights: Universality and Diversity* (Springer, 2001), p. 420. See also, P.G. Carozza, 'Uses and Misuses of Comparative Law in International Human Rights: Some Reflections on the Jurisprudence of the European Court of Human Rights', *Notre Dame Law Review*, 73 (1997–1998), 1217, 1227; A. Moravcsik, 'The Origins of Human Rights Regimes: Democratic Delegation in Post-War Europe', *International Organization*, 54 (2000), 217, 219.
[27] Van der Meersch, 'Reliance, in the Case-Law of the European Court of Human Rights, on the Domestic Law of the States', 15.

5.3 THE MINORITY RIGHTS CHALLENGE

[t]he adjudicating organ must either adopt a moral standard or defer to a relativistic approach based on a comparative analysis. The ECtHR has opted for the latter approach by developing the doctrine of consensus. This doctrine, coupled with the margins doctrine, poses another serious obstacle to the international protection of minority values.[36]

Benvenisti further points out that, 'most evident when minority rights and interests are involved, no margin and no consensus should be tolerated ... [a]nything less than the assumption of full responsibility would amount to a breach of duty by the international human rights organs'.[37]

This approach has not remained unchallenged in legal scholarship. Shany, for instance, states that the democratic deficit of international institutions would not necessarily favour acceptance of minority rights.[38] This section offers two additional arguments that can justify the application of European consensus to minority rights. First, the ECtHR has used European consensus in minority rights cases, and, arguably, this has not been to their detriment. Moreover, minority rights are quite well protected by the ECtHR; often, European consensus helps to further this protection by justifying the evolutive interpretation of the Convention. Second, it is argued that the application of consensus is appropriate in the European context but might be less so in other regional tribunals or worldwide. These two arguments are now discussed in turn.

The Court has deployed European consensus in considering gender,[39] linguistic,[40] religious,[41] ethnic and national rights of various minorities.[42] In these cases, European consensus was not applied *automatically*. As outlined in Chapter 2, the Court reserves some flexibility in the application of consensus. The Court can disregard European consensus if

---

[36] Benvenisti, 'Margin of Appreciation, Consensus, and Universal Standards', 851.
[37] Ibid., 854.
[38] Y. Shany, 'Toward a General Margin of Appreciation Doctrine in International Law?', *European Journal of International Law*, 16 (2005), 907, 921.
[39] See, for example, *Dudgeon v. the United Kingdom; E.B. v. France*, Application No 43546/02, Judgment of 22 January 2008; *Christine Goodwin v. the United Kingdom*, Application No 28957/95, Judgment of 11 July 2002.
[40] See, *Case 'Relating to Certain Aspects of the Laws on the Use of Languages in Education in Belgium' (Preliminary Objections)*, Application No 1474/62, 1677/62, 1691/62, 1769/63, 1994/63 and 2126/64, Judgment of 9 February 1967.
[41] *Kimlya and others v. Russia*, Application No 76836/01 and 32782/03, Judgment of 1 October 2010.
[42] *D.H. and others v. the Czech Republic*, Application No 57325/00, Judgment of 13 November 2007.

justification is provided, and the fact that the case concerns minority rights can be seen as such a justification.

The Court uses different types of consensus in the cases where minority rights are at stake. The ECtHR is capable of identifying consensus enshrined in international treaties and applies this type of consensus to a particular case rather than focusing on the individual laws of the Contracting Parties.[43] Furthermore, the Court can be satisfied with the existence of consensus at the level of principles, without requiring the existence of consensus at the level of rules.[44]

As the vast majority of the Council of Europe Member States has ratified the Framework Convention for the Protection of National Minorities, the ECtHR perceives this development in international law as an emerging consensus towards the recognition of national minority rights.[45] However, in *Chapman v. the United Kingdom*, the Court did not consider this consensus as concrete enough to decisively affect the outcome of the case. In this case, the government requested Roma settlers to remove their caravan which had been installed without the necessary planning permission. In relation to European consensus, the Court stated that

> the Court is not persuaded that the consensus is sufficiently concrete for it to derive any guidance as to the conduct or standards which Contracting States consider desirable in any particular situation. The Framework Convention, for example, sets out general principles and goals but the signatory States were unable to agree on means of implementation. This reinforces the Court's view that the complexity and sensitivity of the issues involved in policies balancing the interests of the general population, in particular with regard to environmental protection, and the interests of a minority with possibly conflicting requirements renders the Court's role a strictly supervisory one.[46]

The Court did not find a violation of the applicant's rights in this case because further convergence of rules in this area across Europe was required. In *D.H. and others v. the Czech Republic*,[47] *Oršuš and others v. Croatia*[48] and later *Horváth and Kiss v. Hungary*,[49] the ECtHR reconsidered this approach:

> In *Chapman* the Court ... observed that there could be said to be an emerging international consensus amongst the Contracting States of

---

[43] Chapter 3 provides a more detailed account of types of consensus deployed by the ECtHR.
[44] See, Chapter 2 for more details.   [45] *Chapman v. the United Kingdom*, para. 93.
[46] Ibid., para. 93–4.   [47] *D.H. and others v. the Czech Republic*.
[48] *Oršuš and others v. Croatia*, Application No 15766/03, Judgment of 16 March 2010.
[49] *Horváth and Kiss v. Hungary*, Application No 11146/11, Judgment of 29 January 2013.

in some areas, they are much more homogeneous in terms of human rights protection than States worldwide. Moreover, the members of the Council of Europe have achieved (at least in theory) a certain level of human rights protection; they are all (at least nominally) democracies, and it is unlikely that all these States will reduce the level of human rights protection within a short period of time.

Second, European consensus is a well-established argument in the case law of the ECtHR.[68] It has been deployed by the Parties,[69] then by the Commission[70] and by the Court,[71] starting from the very early cases adjudicated by the Strasbourg institutions. The ECtHR does not apply consensus automatically and it treats it as a rebuttable presumption. One can only guess what approach would be adopted by the tribunals which did not have a long tradition of application of such an argument. In circumstances where the overall level of protection is low and a human rights tribunal has not developed a well-established technique of interpretation, implementation of consensual decision-making may be troublesome. However, this does not apply to the deployment of consensus by the ECtHR.

5.4 Criticism of European consensus as a determinant of evolutive interpretation and the margin of appreciation

European consensus operates on the edge of the margin of appreciation and evolutive interpretation; both of these are necessary to maintain the stability of the Strasbourg system, with the former preventing the ECtHR from going too far in developing human rights standards and the latter ensuring that the ECHR does not turn into a meaningless instrument preserving views from 60 years ago when the Convention was drafted, signed and ratified by the original Contracting Parties. Having said that, both the margin of appreciation and evolutive interpretation have been criticised for the lack of clear and objective criteria determining their scope. This section argues that European consensus can be considered as one such criterion.

---

[68] *Greece v. the United Kingdom*, Application No 176/56, Judgment of 26 September 1958, para. 174.
[69] Ibid. See also, *Neumeister v. Austria*, Application No 1936/63, Judgment of 27 June 1968, para. 46.
[70] *Golder v. the United Kingdom*, Application No 4451/70, Judgment of 21 February 1975, para. 39.
[71] *Tyrer v. the United Kingdom*, Application No 5856/72, Judgment of 25 April 1978, para. 41.

5.4.1 *Criticism of evolutive interpretation and the margin of appreciation*

The margin of appreciation is criticised on the opposite basis upon which evolutive interpretation is criticised. However, they share commentators' concerns about the clarity of their scope and application. Commentators have identified key legitimacy concerns of evolutive interpretation. First, case law built on evolutive interpretation can amount to the exercise of a legislative role and bypass the sovereign consent of the Contracting Parties.[72] Evolutive interpretation is therefore considered as an inadequate tool of judicial activism.[73] Second, a 'counter-majoritarian difficulty'[74] may arise in determining the correct time for evolution since evolutive interpretation is determined by 'non-elected' judges.[75] Third, it has been argued that evolutive interpretation contradicts principles such as consistency in case law, legal certainty and predictability.[76] Hence, the process legitimacy of the case law may be undermined.[77] Fourth, even those commentators who accept evolutive interpretation in principle have

---

[72] The legitimacy of evolutive interpretation was challenged in *Golder* v. *the United Kingdom* by the dissenting judge. In this case, the ECtHR interpreted the Convention dynamically and stated that right to access a court is to be protected under Article 6 of the Convention. Judge Fitzmaurice in his separate opinion stated that the Contracting Parties cannot be expected to comply with an obligation which is not articulated or defined. *Golder* v. *the United Kingdom*, Separate Opinion of Judge Fitzmaurice, para. 30.

[73] L. Hoffmann, 'The Universality of Human Rights', *Law Quarterly Review*, 125 (2009), 416, 428–9. It should be noted here that there is no agreement in legal scholarship on what the definition of judicial activism is. For a more profound discussion of this issue, see K.D. Kmiec, 'The Origin and Current Meanings of "Judicial Activism"', *California Law Review*, 92 (2004), 1441, 1463–75; M. Cohn and M. Kremnitzer, 'Judicial Activism: A Multidimensional Model', *Canadian Journal of Law and Jurisprudence*, 18 (2005), 333, 334.

[74] The legitimacy of constitutional judicial review of legislation is often challenged from the point of view of the 'counter-majoritarian difficulty'. L.B. Tremblya, 'General Legitimacy of Judicial Review and the Fundamental Basis of Constitutional Law', *Oxford Journal of Legal Studies*, 23 (2003), 525. This difficulty relates to the fact that, in systems with judicial review of legislation, non-elected judges are able to scrutinise the decisions made by a democratically elected representative organ.

[75] In fact, the ECtHR judges are elected by the Parliamentary Assembly of the Council of Europe. They are elected from the list of three candidates submitted by the Contracting Party. Having said that, the judges cannot claim the same level of democratic legitimacy as national parliaments. See, K. Dzehtsiarou and D.K. Coffey, 'Legitimacy and Independence of International Tribunals: An Analysis of the European Court of Human Rights', *Hastings International and Comparative Law Review*, 37 (2014), 271.

[76] J.L.M. Gribnau, 'Legitimacy of the Judiciary', *Electronic Journal of Comparative Law*, 6 (2002), available at www.ejcl.org/64/art64-3.txt, accessed on 29 July 2014.

[77] For more details about process legitimacy, see, Chapter 6.

5.4 CRITICISM OF EVOLUTIVE INTERPRETATION

maintained that its application has been poorly supported by empirical data in the Court's reasoning.[78]

At the same time, the legitimacy of the margin of appreciation is challenged on grounds that are predominantly different to those of evolutive interpretation. First, it is argued that the margin of appreciation undermines the aspirational role of the ECHR and the universality of human rights.[79] Second, it is criticised for being a tool of excessive judicial self-restraint.[80] Third, the margin of appreciation is challenged on the basis that its scope is unclear, thereby creating uncertainties in the case law. Hence, the margin of appreciation undermines the process legitimacy of the ECtHR judgments.[81]

---

[78] A. Mowbray, 'The Creativity of the European Court of Human Rights', *Human Rights Law Review*, 5 (2005), 57, 61.

[79] Benvenisti argues that 'the judicial output of the ECHR and the other international bodies carries the promise of setting universal standards for the protection and promotion of human rights. These universal aspirations are, to a large extent, compromised by the doctrine of margin of appreciation.' Benvenisti, 'Margin of Appreciation, Consensus, and Universal Standards', 843. Judge De Meyer in his dissenting opinion stated that 'where human rights are concerned, there is no room for a margin of appreciation which would enable the States to decide what is acceptable and what is not. On that subject, the boundary not to be overstepped must be as clear and precise as possible. It is for the Court, not each State individually, to decide that issue, and the Court's views must apply to everyone within the jurisdiction of each State.' *Z. v. Finland*, Application No 22009/93, Judgment of 25 February 1997. Dissenting Opinion of Judge De Meyer.

[80] Morrisson categorised the margin of appreciation as a sign of judicial self-restraint. C.C. Morrisson, *The Dynamics of Development in the European Human Rights Convention System* (Martinus Nijhoff Publishers, 1981), pp. 6–7. Some commentators argue that 'the deferential attitude assumed by the Court and reflected in the margin of appreciation doctrine has resulted in an abdication by the Court of its responsibility to adjudicate complex and sensitive cases, leading it to accept without sufficient independent reflection the respondent government's claims'. O. Gross and F. Ní Aoláin, 'From Discretion to Scrutiny: Revisiting the Application of the Margin of Appreciation Doctrine in the Context of Article 15 of the European Convention on Human Rights', *Human Rights Quarterly*, 23 (2001), 625, 628. Burke points out that '[t]he practice of the Court and the Commission demonstrates the pernicious use of the doctrine to avoid conducting an independent examination of the evidence and the tendency to succumb to the position of the relevant national government'. K.C. Burke, 'Secret Surveillance and the European Convention on Human Rights', *Stanford Law Review*, 33 (1980), 1113, 1134.

[81] See, H.C. Yourow, *The Margin of Appreciation Doctrine in the Dynamics of European Human Rights Jurisprudence* (Martinus Nijhoff Publishers, 1995), p. 152; A. Lester, 'Universality versus Subsidiarity: A Reply', *European Human Rights Law Review* (1998), 73, 75–6; Gross and Ní Aoláin, 'From Discretion to Scrutiny', 629. Judge De Meyer pointed out that '[t]he empty phrases concerning the State's margin of appreciation – repeated in the Court's judgments for too long already – are unnecessary circumlocutions, serving only to indicate abstrusely that the States may do anything the Court does

It can be concluded from this outline that commentators have called for more consistency and coherence in the application of these doctrines.

5.4.2 European consensus: Between margin of appreciation and evolutive interpretation

It has been argued that European consensus 'injects European context and predictability' into the Court's deployment of the margin of appreciation and evolutive interpretation.[82] This argument is not endorsed by everyone in the academic community. Johnson, for example, argues that consensus is 'a construct through which the Court legitimizes its moral interpretation and because of this, as its case law shows, its use is unpredictable and variable'.[83] He further points out that '[a]s an epistemological construction, consensus analysis produces knowledge of reality in ways that are relational to, and dependent upon, the social position of those who apply the method'.[84] This is a fair observation, and the lack of a clear and consistent application of consensus by the Court has been criticised on a number of occasions.[85] These challenges, however, are not the result of certain inherent drawbacks of European consensus as an argument but exist due to some inconsistencies in its application which can be fixed. Moreover, this section argues that European consensus is much more objective than other possible criteria of margin of appreciation available to the Court. If the ECtHR applies European consensus clearly and consistently, then it will indeed inject European context and predictability into its reasoning.

5.4.2.1 European consensus and the margin of appreciation

The margin of appreciation is a useful tool of interpretation of the ECHR which gives States some ownership of the Convention rights and

---

not consider incompatible with human rights'. *Z. v. Finland*, Dissenting Opinion of Judge De Meyer. Carozza, 'Uses and Misuses of Comparative Law', 70.

[82] K. Dzehtsiarou, 'European Consensus and the Evolutive Interpretation of the European Convention on Human Rights', *German Law Journal*, 12 (2011), 1730, 1730.

[83] P. Johnson, *Homosexuality and the European Court of Human Rights* (Routledge, 2013), p. 77.

[84] Ibid., 78.

[85] L.R. Helfer, 'Consensus, Coherence and the European Convention on Human Rights', *Cornell International Law Journal*, 23 (1993), 133; M. Delmas-Marty, *The European Convention for the Protection of Human Rights. International Protection versus National Restrictions* (Kluwer Academic Publishers, 1992), p. 305; C. McCrudden, 'A Common Law of Human Rights? Transnational Judicial Conversations on Constitutional Rights', *Oxford Journal of Legal Studies*, 20 (2000), 499.

5.4 CRITICISM OF EVOLUTIVE INTERPRETATION

empowers them to solve complex dilemmas of human rights law. However, the vague and often imprecise scope of the margin of appreciation seems to permit overly broad judicial discretion in the assessment of the margin of appreciation[86] and makes the case law unpredictable.[87] Moreover, it allows States to argue that a matter at issue falls into the margin in nearly every case. Once Protocol 15 comes into force, the margin of appreciation will be mentioned in the preamble to the Convention.[88] Therefore, some commentators have urged the Court to clarify its approach in relation to the application of the margin of appreciation.[89] It is argued here that a properly identified and coherently applied European consensus is a criterion that determines the breadth of the margin of appreciation in a more objective, transparent and predictable manner than achieved through the application of other criteria: the nature of the Convention right, its importance, the nature of the interference or the object of interference.

The lack of clarity in application of the margin of appreciation is accepted by nearly all Convention commentators. Bakircioglu argues

---

[86] See, Z. v. Finland, Dissenting Opinion of Judge De Meyer; O. Bakircioglu, 'The Application of the Margin of Appreciation Doctrine in Freedom of Expression and Public Morality Cases', *German Law Journal*, 8 (2007), 711, 712; Gross and Ní Aoláin, 'From Discretion to Scrutiny', 627; Lester, 'Universality versus Subsidiarity: A Reply', 75–6; R.S. Macdonald, 'The Margin of Appreciation' in R. Macdonald, F. Matscher and H. Petzold (eds.), *The European System for the Protection of Human Rights* (Kluwer Law International, 1993), p. 85.

[87] Greer, for instance, argues that 'no simple formula can describe how it [the margin of appreciation] works ... [I]n spite of mountain of jurisprudence, its most striking characteristic remains its casuistic, uneven, and largely unpredictable nature.' S. Greer, *The Margin of Appreciation: Interpretation and Discretion under the European Convention on Human Rights* (Council of Europe Publishing, 2000), p. 5. See also Brauch, 'The Margin of Appreciation', 121; M.W. Janis, R.S. Kay and A.W. Bradley, *European Human Rights Law: Text and Materials* (Oxford University Press, 2008), p. 255.

[88] Article 1 of Protocol 15 provides that at the end of the preamble to the Convention, a new recital shall be added, which shall read as follows: 'Affirming that the High Contracting Parties, in accordance with the principle of subsidiarity, have the primary responsibility to secure the rights and freedoms defined in this Convention and the Protocols thereto, and that in doing so they enjoy a margin of appreciation, subject to the supervisory jurisdiction of the European Court of Human Rights established by this Convention.'

[89] Sottiaux and van der Schyff point out that '[t]here clearly is a need for greater predictability in applying the doctrine of the margin of appreciation'. S. Sottiaux and G. van der Schyff, 'Methods of International Human Rights Adjudication: Towards a More Structured Decision-Making Process for the European Court of Human Rights', *Hastings International and Comparative Law Review*, 31 (2008), 115, 135–6. See also, Bakircioglu, 'The Application of the Margin of Appreciation Doctrine', 712. Greer, *The Margin of Appreciation: Interpretation and Discretion under the European Convention on Human Rights*, p. 5.

that '[a]n over-subjective and unprincipled application of discretion might not only dilute the concept of legal certainty, but also undermine the delicate structure of the European Convention system, the existence of which is dependent upon the wilful cooperation of Member States'.[90] The principal objection to the margin of appreciation is that it introduces an unwarranted subjective element into the interpretation of various provisions of the ECHR.[91] Higgins argues that the margin of appreciation is 'increasingly difficult to control and objectionable as a viable legal concept'.[92] Macdonald maintains that it is not clear how the Court uses the doctrine: 'Being concerned with the appropriate scope of review, the margin is not susceptible to definition in the abstract, as it is, by its very nature, context dependent.'[93]

The need for clear standards and criteria is also emphasised by Gross and Ní Aoláin along the following lines:

> In resorting to the margin of appreciation doctrine the Court has frequently been satisfied with making a laconic mention of the doctrine without further explanation of the way it was applied to the particular circumstances of the case at hand. In yet other cases the doctrine has not even been mentioned or discussed explicitly, but is rather implicit in the Court's analysis and judicial reasoning.[94]

The Convention does not include a definition for margin of appreciation. O'Donnell argues that '[w]hile difficult to define, the margin of appreciation refers to the latitude allowed to the Member States in their observance of the Convention'.[95] Ostrovsky is of the view that the margin of appreciation is a way to distinguish matters that can be decided at the local level from matters that are so fundamental that they should be decided regardless of cultural variations. In other words, the doctrine allows human rights norms 'to take on a local flavour'.[96] Yourow defines the margin of appreciation in the following terms:

---

[90] Bakircioglu, 'The Application of the Margin of Appreciation', 712.
[91] N. Lavender, 'The Problem of the Margin of Appreciation', *European Human Rights Law Review* (1997), 380, 380.
[92] R. Higgins, 'Derogations under Human Rights Treaties', *British Yearbook of International Law*, 48 (1978), 281, 315.
[93] Macdonald, *The Margin of Appreciation*, p. 85.
[94] Gross and Ní Aoláin, 'From Discretion to Scrutiny', 635.
[95] T.A. O'Donnell, 'The Margin of Appreciation Doctrine: Standards in the Jurisprudence of the European Court of Human Rights', *Human Rights Quarterly*, 4 (1982), 474, 475.
[96] A.A. Ostrovsky, 'What's So Funny about Peace, Love, and Understanding? How the Margin of Appreciation Doctrine Preserves Core Human Rights within Cultural

5.4 CRITICISM OF EVOLUTIVE INTERPRETATION

> The national margin of appreciation or discretion can be defined in the European Human Rights Convention context as the freedom to act; manoeuvring, breathing or elbow room; or the latitude of deference or error which the Strasbourg organs will allow national legislation, executive, administrative and judicial bodies before it is prepared a national derogation from the Convention, or restriction, or limitation upon a right guaranteed by the Convention, to constitute a violation of one of the Convention's substantive guarantees.[97]

While the scope of the margin of appreciation is not always clearly articulated,[98] the Court has pointed out that European consensus is one of the factors which can help in determining it. In a number of cases, the Court reiterated that if there were no European consensus, then the margin of appreciation would be wider.[99]

The fact that the margin of appreciation is criticised for a lack of precise rules of application does not mean that the Court has not tried to explain how the margin of appreciation operates in its reasoning. In *S. and Marper* v. *the United Kingdom*, the Court has listed those criteria which it takes into account in assessing the width of the margin:

> The breadth of this margin [of appreciation] varies and depends on a number of factors including the nature of the Convention right in issue, its importance for the individual, the nature of the interference and the object pursued by the interference. The margin will tend to be narrower where the right at stake is crucial to the individual's effective enjoyment of intimate or key rights. Where a particularly important facet of an individual's existence or identity is at stake, the margin allowed to the State will be restricted. Where, however, there is no consensus within the Member States of the Council of Europe, either as to the relative importance of the interest at stake or as to how best to protect it, the margin will be wider.[100]

According to *S. and Marper* v. *the United Kingdom*, the breadth of the margin of appreciation depends on (i) the nature of the Convention right, (ii) its importance, (iii) the nature of the interference, (iv) the object of interference and (v) European consensus. One can argue that the first

---

Diversity and Legitimises International Human Rights Tribunals', *Hanse Law Review* (2005), 47, 47–8.

[97] Yourow, *The Margin of Appreciation Doctrine*, p. 13.
[98] See, for example, Gross and Ní Aoláin, 'From Discretion to Scrutiny', 629.
[99] *Dickson* v. *the United Kingdom*, Application No 44362/04, Judgment of 4 December 2007, para. 78. See *Evans* v. *the United Kingdom*, Application No 6339/05, Judgment of 10 April 2007, para. 59; *Lautsi and others* v. *Italy*, Application No 30814/06, Judgment of 18 March 2011, para. 70.
[100] *S. and Marper* v. *the United Kingdom*, Application No 30562/04 and 30566/04, Judgment of 4 December 2008, para. 102.

four criteria are subjective in nature and provide a broad scope for judicial discretion.[101] The meaning of each of these criteria is not entirely clear. They are hard to measure, and different stakeholders can rationally disagree as to their meaning.

Moreover, the importance and nature of the Convention right at stake and the nature of interference can be determined by reference to European consensus. For example, in *Dickson v. the United Kingdom*, the Court pointed out that

> [w]here ... there is no consensus within the Member States of the Council of Europe, either as to the relative importance of the interest at stake or as to how best to protect it, the margin will be wider. This is particularly so where the case raises complex issues and choices of social strategy: the authorities' direct knowledge of their society and its needs means that they are in principle better placed than the international judge to appreciate what is in the public interest.[102]

It seems that those criteria which are mentioned in *S. and Marper* can themselves at least partially depend on European consensus.

Paczolay explains how European consensus determines the scope of the margin of appreciation:

> The margin of appreciation is complementary to consensus; this is demonstrated by the fact that their boundaries move together: the extent of the margin of appreciation fluctuates from 'slight' and 'certain' to 'wide'. Complementarily, the range of consensus might shift to the extent of being 'broad'.[103]

This means that the extent of the margin is dependent on how well established consensus is. This rule does not eliminate a subjective element from the determination of the scope of the margin of appreciation; this section merely argues that other criteria are either linked to European consensus, such as the importance and the nature of the interference, or they allow the Court to use almost unlimited discretion, such as the importance and the sensitivity of the object of interference. Arguably, every case (unless it is a repetitive application) poses important and sensitive moral questions. If a sensitive issue is at stake and

---

[101] Delmas-Marty, *The European Convention for the Protection of Human Rights. International Protection versus National Restrictions*, p. 333.
[102] *Dickson v. the United Kingdom*, para. 78.
[103] P. Paczolay, 'Consensus and Discretion: Evolution or Erosion of Human Rights Protection' in *Dialogues between Judges* (European Court of Human Rights, 2008), p. 109.

5.4 CRITICISM OF EVOLUTIVE INTERPRETATION

there is no European consensus on the matter, the Court can conclude that the law is in a transitional stage and allow a wide margin of appreciation.

The case of *Fretté v. France* illustrates this point. The Court was asked to consider whether the prohibition of adoption by homosexuals complied with the Convention. The Court pointed out that, since the delicate issues raised within the case touched on areas where there was little common ground amongst the Member States of the Council of Europe and, generally speaking, the law appeared to be in a transitional stage, a wide margin of appreciation must be left to the authorities of each State.[104] The issue of adoption is important. However, the importance of this issue could not reduce the area of margin of appreciation established by assessing European consensus.

The same issue occurred in *Evans v. the United Kingdom*, where the Court stated that

> [w]here a particularly important facet of an individual's existence or identity is at stake, the margin allowed to the State will be restricted. Where, however, there is no consensus within the Member States of the Council of Europe, either as to the relative importance of the interest at stake or as to the best means of protecting it, particularly where the case raises sensitive moral or ethical issues, the margin will be wider.[105]

The case of *A., B. and C. v. Ireland* is probably the only one where the sensitivity of the issue and national consensus trumped European-wide consensus. This case is discussed in more detail in Chapter 3.

European consensus is not an ideal and totally objective criterion for the margin of appreciation. It leaves some space for discretion of the judges and it should not be applied automatically. Having said that, European consensus is a more precise and externally verifiable determinant of the margin, or, as O'Donnell points out, 'it would seem that an examination of the laws and practices of the Member States in search for consensus or its lack is one of the surest methods for determining the latitude the Court will grant the government when the margin of appreciation is a consideration'.[106]

---

[104] *Fretté v. France*, Application No 36515/97, Judgment of 26 February 2002, para. 41.
[105] *Evans v. the United Kingdom*, para. 77.
[106] O'Donnell, 'The Margin of Appreciation Doctrine', 483; Delmas-Marty, *The European Convention for the Protection of Human Rights. International Protection versus National Restrictions*, p. 333. See also, I. Moral, 'The Increasingly Marginal Appreciation of the Margin of Appreciation Doctrine', *German Law Journal*, 7 (2006), 611, 617.

5.4.2.2 European consensus and evolutive interpretation

European consensus can be conceptualised as a way of mediating between the margin of appreciation and evolutive interpretation. If there is no European consensus, the issue will fall in the area of the margin of appreciation, and as soon as consensus is established, the ECtHR can apply evolutive interpretation and wrest this issue from State discretion. This section argues that evolutive interpretation is necessary for the ECHR to remain a meaningful and effective mechanism of human rights protection. This section also assumes that evolutive interpretation can be seen as an assault on legal certainty and predictability. It is central to the argument of this section that European consensus can act as an objective determinant of evolutive interpretation.

Interpretation of the Convention requires fluidity, flexibility and a dynamic approach.[107] In *Scoppola v. Italy (No 2)*, the ECtHR stated that

> [i]t is of crucial importance that the Convention is interpreted and applied in a manner which renders its rights practical and effective, not theoretical and illusory. A failure by the Court to maintain a dynamic and evolutive approach would risk rendering it a bar to reform or improvement.[108]

A former president of the Court, Judge Wildhaber, writing extrajudicially, has emphasised that evolutive interpretation is fundamental to the effectiveness of the Convention system and the ECtHR's authority.[109] Judge Rozakis points out that a 'failure by the Court to maintain a dynamic and evolutive approach would indeed risk rendering it a bar to reform or improvement'.[110] A dynamic reading of the Convention ensures that the Convention's rights are made practical and effective.[111] Evolutive interpretation provides the necessary degree of flexibility to ECHR law in a rapidly changing environment.[112]

---

[107] M. Fitzmaurice, 'Dynamic (Evolutive) Interpretation of Treaties (Part II)' in J.G. Lammers (ed.) *Hague Yearbook of International Law* (Martinus Nijhoff Publishers, 2009), p. 29; M. Varju, 'Transition as a Concept of European Human Rights Law', *European Human Rights Law Review* (2009), 170, 172.

[108] *Scoppola v. Italy (No 2)*, Application No 10249/03, Judgment of 17 September 2009, para. 104.

[109] L. Wildhaber, 'European Court of Human Rights' in D.M. McRae (ed.) *Canadian Yearbook of International Law* (UBC Press, 2002), p. 310.

[110] A. Mowbray, 'An Examination of the European Court of Human Rights' Approach to Overruling Its Previous Case Law', *Human Rights Law Review*, 9 (2009), 179, 183.

[111] Letsas, *A Theory of Interpretation*, p. 79.

[112] Varju, 'Transition as a Concept of European Human Rights Law', 172.

5.4 CRITICISM OF EVOLUTIVE INTERPRETATION

The correlation between consensus and evolutive interpretation is often explained by the Court in the following terms:

> The existence of a consensus has long played a role in the development and evolution of Convention protections ... the Convention being considered a 'living instrument' to be interpreted in the light of present-day conditions. Consensus has therefore been invoked to justify a dynamic interpretation of the Convention.[113]

Starting with *Tyrer v. the United Kingdom*, the Court has continued to deploy consensus as evidence for evolutive interpretation.[114]

The correlation is significant since, on occasion, a lack of consensus has prevented the Court from a dynamic reading of the Convention. If the Court is not in a position to establish European consensus, which is necessary for evolutive interpretation, it then usually regards the matter at issue as falling within the State's margin of appreciation.

Despite being very useful in human rights adjudication, to some extent, the doctrine of effectiveness of rights and its corollary of evolutive interpretation undermines the process legitimacy of the Court's judgments.[115] In order to make rights effective, the Court sometimes has to change its stance, and this reduces the predictability of the outcomes.[116] If the Court is satisfied that evolutive interpretation should be deployed, a previous judgment or judgments may be overruled.[117]

The Contracting Parties may invest certain financial and organisational resources into complying with rules interpreted in a certain way at a given time. These rules can then change subsequently as a consequence of dynamic interpretation. To counter this challenge, Letsas argues that the Court cannot enter into a cost-benefit calculation in deciding its approach to interpretation; the problems created by a lack of predictability must be trumped by the moral value of human rights.[118] Letsas correctly focuses on the moral value of human rights. However, it cannot

---

[113] *A., B. and C. v. Ireland*, Application No 25579/05, Judgment of 16 December 2010, para. 234.
[114] *Tyrer v. the United Kingdom*, para. 183. *Tyrer* was the first case where the Court deployed evolutive interpretation.
[115] By process legitimacy, I mean legitimacy based on the Court's adherence to such principles as predictability, legal certainty and foreseeability. See Chapter 6 for details.
[116] See, for example, T.W. Merrill, 'Originalism, *Stare Decisis* and the Promotion of Judicial Restraint', *Constitutional Commentary*, 22 (2005), 271, 285–6.
[117] See, *Christine Goodwin v. the United Kingdom*; *Vilho Eskelinen and others v. Finland*, Application No 63235/00, Judgment of 19 April 2007; *Société Colas Est and others v. France*, Application No 37971/97, Judgment of 16 July 2002.
[118] Letsas, *A Theory of Interpretation*, p. 74.

be the only justification for otherwise seemingly arbitrary decisions to deploy evolutive interpretation.

On a number of occasions, the Court has reiterated its adherence to such principles as consistency, legal certainty and predictability of the case law.[119] For example, although previous case law is not binding, the Court does not depart from precedents without good reason.[120] The reasons for a departure from preceding case law are rooted in phenomena such as developments in law,[121] societal changes[122] and technical progress.[123] These developments should be of such significance that they should affect the interpretation of a pre-existing text.[124] Therefore, the Court should elaborate reasonably clear measurements for weighing these developments.

Mowbray points out that the ECtHR deploys evolutive interpretation but sometimes does so without providing adequate justification for its use of the living instrument doctrine.[125] Mowbray maintains that the Court has not overstepped its legitimate interpretative role by being involved in dynamic interpretation. However, the lack of clear determining factors creates a fear that dynamic interpretation is simply a cover for subjective 'ad-hockery'.[126] This section argues that properly identified European consensus can reduce the subjectivity and arbitrariness of evolutive interpretation.

European consensus provides evidence confirming that dynamic interpretation of the Convention is in line with the contemporary understanding of human rights. From the mid-1970s, the Court has deployed consensus as evidence of changing conditions in Europe.[127] The ECtHR treats European consensus as a justification of evolutive interpretation, an argument that allows the Court to depart from its previous case law:

> The existence of a consensus has long played a role in the development and evolution of Convention protections ... the Convention being

---

[119] Gribnau, 'Legitimacy of the Judiciary'.
[120] *Mamatkulov and Askarov* v. *Turkey*, Application No 46827/99 and 46951/99, Judgment of 4 February 2005, para. 121; *Vilho Eskelinen and others* v. *Finland*, para. 56.
[121] *Micallef* v. *Malta*, Application No 17056/06, Judgment of 15 October 2009.
[122] *Cossey* v. *the United Kingdom*, Application No 10843/84, Judgment of 27 September 1990, para. 35.
[123] *S.H. and others* v. *Austria*, Application No 57813/00, Judgment of 3 November 2011, para. 81.
[124] D. French, 'Treaty Interpretation and the Incorporation of Extraneous Legal Rules', *International and Comparative Law Quarterly*, 55 (2006), 281, 285.
[125] Mowbray, 'The Creativity of the European Court of Human Rights', 61.
[126] Ibid., 69–71. [127] *Tyrer* v. *the United Kingdom*, para. 183.

5.4 CRITICISM OF EVOLUTIVE INTERPRETATION

considered a 'living instrument' to be interpreted in the light of present-day conditions. Consensus has therefore been invoked to justify a dynamic interpretation of the Convention.[128]

The Court has confirmed on a number of occasions that European consensus can justify evolutive interpretation. The case of *Bayatyan v. Armenia* is an example of this. The Court was called to determine whether the conviction of a conscientious objector – a Jehovah's Witness – for his refusal to perform military service was compatible with Article 9 of the ECHR. In the past, the European Commission of Human Rights[129] decided that mandatory military service in similar circumstances did not violate Article 9 of the ECHR.[130] At that time, this issue was considered to fall within the margin of appreciation of the States. In *Bayatyan*, the Court concluded that there was a clear indication of European consensus and therefore evolutive interpretation could be applied.[131] In this case, it was relatively easy to foresee that the Court would shift its position in relation to conscientious objections due to the overwhelming support from the Contracting Parties. The Court emphasised that

> since the Commission's decision in *Grandrath v. the Federal Republic of Germany* and its follow-up decisions the domestic law of the overwhelming majority of Council of Europe member States, along with the relevant international instruments, has evolved to the effect that at the material time there was already a virtually general consensus on the question in Europe and beyond. In the light of these developments, it cannot be said that a shift in the interpretation of Article 9 ... was not foreseeable.[132]

Properly identified European consensus can mitigate the adverse effects of evolutive interpretation on the process legitimacy of certain judgments since it increases the predictability of such decisions. Koch and Vedsted-Hansen observe that

> the dynamic or evolutive interpretation of human rights treaties is in no way unrelated to sources of law which are under the current influence by democratically legitimised bodies such as domestic legislatures ... As a

---

[128] *A., B. and C. v. Ireland*, para. 234.
[129] The commission was a decision-making body of the Strasbourg system of human rights protection until 1998.
[130] *Grandrath v. the Federal Republic of Germany*, Application No 2299/64, Commission report of 12 December 1966; *X. v. Austria*, Application No 5591/72, Commission decision of 2 April 1973, p. 161.
[131] *Bayatyan v. Armenia*, Application No 23459/03, Judgment of 7 July 2011, para. 109.
[132] Ibid., para. 108.

primary source of reference, the Court usually examines whether a common standard or even consensus has evolved among the European States parties to the Convention.[133]

5.5 Conclusion

This chapter argues that the drawbacks of European consensus identified by commentators are often exaggerated and the alternatives suggested to replace consensus are insufficient. The European consensus argument does not pose much of a threat to human rights in the European context as on a number of occasions it has been used to expand the scope of rights. The alternative to European consensus is adjudication based on the moral standpoint of the judges, but this is open to criticism as an arbitrary decision-making approach. Such decision-making can hardly add clarity to the scope of the margin of appreciation and evolutive interpretation. In contrast, European consensus is one of the most objective criteria available to the ECtHR in determining the scope of the margin of appreciation or the 'tipping point' for evolutive interpretation.

---

[133] I.E. Koch and J. Vedsted-Hansen, 'International Human Rights and National Legislatures – Conflict or Balance?', *Nordic Journal of International Law*, 7 (2006), 53, 12.

6

Legitimacy of the Court and legitimacy of its judgments

6.1 Introduction

Human rights tribunals cannot function effectively if they are perceived to be illegitimate. The fact that the term legitimacy is currently so widely used and discussed does not add much clarity to understanding which factors can enhance it.[1] To argue that a particular aspect of a judgment is likely to increase its legitimacy might seem an exercise in futility. In the case of the European Court of Human Rights (ECtHR or Court), such a legitimising factor could be the high moral value of human rights. Having said that, this chapter aims to argue that moral superiority of human rights is not enough to legitimise each and every decision delivered by the ECtHR. Both the moral value of human rights and the fact that the Contracting Parties have agreed to be supervised by the ECtHR contribute to the initial legitimacy of the Court. However, over time, its initial legitimacy may fade. This chapter focuses on the challenges to the legitimacy of the ECtHR, and the potential reasons for its fading legitimacy. It continues by testing European consensus against these challenges and aims to conclude that European consensus is capable of reducing the tensions associated with these challenges. In general terms, legitimacy can be understood as the respect and support for the Court that emanates from stakeholders' conviction that the Court will decide cases consistently and in a manner that respects the nature of both the European Convention on Human Rights (ECHR or Convention) (as a human rights instrument) and its jurisdiction (as subsidiary and limited), as well as by reference to clear and transparent evidence.[2]

---

[1] See, T.M. Franck, 'Why a Quest for Legitimacy', *UC Davis Law Review*, 21 (1987), 535; J. Brunnee and S.J. Toope, *Legitimacy and Legality in International Law* (Cambridge University Press, 2010).

[2] F. de Londras and K. Dzehtsiarou, 'Managing Judicial Innovation in the European Court of Human Rights' (on file with the author).

This chapter will first argue that the legitimacy of the ECtHR is questionable from at least two perspectives. First, its legitimacy deficit stems from the fact that the ECtHR is an international court. This difficulty is closely linked to a State's fierce protection of its sovereignty. This challenge will be termed the international constitutional challenge. Second, the Court's legitimacy is problematic because it is a court which is entitled to call into question the decisions of democratically elected governments based on vaguely defined human rights norms. This challenge is similar to the so-called counter-majoritarian difficulty that national constitutional (supreme) courts face. This will be termed the national constitutional challenge.

After establishing these two rather uncontroversial legitimacy challenges of the ECtHR, this chapter offers some thoughts on how the effects of these challenges can be minimised. It examines various aspects of international constitutional challenges and considers how consensus can mitigate these challenges.

In the final section of the chapter, the claim will be made that the ECtHR faces national constitutional challenges. The key challenge is the counter-majoritarian difficulty which claims that courts endowed with the competence to carry out constitutional review do not have the democratic mandate to review decisions of democratically legitimate authorities. This section argues that consensus integrates democratic decisions into the decision-making of courts of constitutional review, thus improving their legitimacy.

6.2 Lost legitimacy?

The ECtHR has preconditions to being considered as a legitimate institution in international law because it is based on the ECHR, which was signed and ratified by the Contracting Parties. The ECHR entrusts the ECtHR with the authority to ensure 'the observance of the engagements undertaken by the High Contracting Parties in the Convention and the Protocols'.[3] However, this initial legitimacy does not apply to all judgments that come from the Court, and legitimacy of the ECHR can fade over time.[4] The Contracting Parties can, for example, challenge certain

---

[3] ECHR, Article 19.

[4] This is also the case with legitimacy of constitutions. Raz points out that 'even if new constitutions may derive their authorities from the authority of their makers, old constitutions, if morally valid at all, must derive their authority from other sources'. J. Raz, 'On the Authority and Interpretation of Constitutions: Some Preliminaries' in L. Alexander

6.2 LOST LEGITIMACY?

activist decision-making by the Court, which is often labelled as a 'living instrument' doctrine[5] or evolutive interpretation. It provides that the Convention can evolve over time following the evolution of European society. When the Convention was drafted, its provisions may have meant something significantly different to what these provisions now mean. Therefore, such meaning is unlikely to be covered by the original consent of the Contracting Parties which ratified the Convention. Original consent cannot legitimise a new meaning of the Convention. The Court has to ensure some other sources of legitimacy of its judgments, especially once the ECtHR resorts to judicial innovation, such as evolutive interpretation.

Are there any signs of lost legitimacy? Is the process of fading legitimacy real? One can argue that the legitimacy of an international tribunal mainly depends on how the Contracting Parties react to its decisions. This reaction not only is limited to compliance rates[6] but also focuses on whether State officials, media or other stakeholders openly criticise the Court in the public domain.[7] The Contracting Parties can comply with the judgments of the Court while criticising them; this would damage the legitimacy of the ECtHR and prepare the foundation for future failures to comply. It is important not only to be legitimate but also to be perceived as being legitimate.[8] This section predominantly discusses the Court's relation with the Contracting Parties. This does not necessarily mean that other stakeholders, such as applicants, non-governmental organisations (NGOs) or the academic community, have no impact on the legitimacy of the ECtHR. De Londras and Dzehtsiarou argue that

---

(ed.), *Constitutionalism Philosophical Foundation* (Cambridge University Press, 1998), p. 169.

[5] See, *Tyrer v. the United Kingdom*, Application No 5856/72, Judgment of 25 April 1978, para. 31.

[6] Carrubba and Gabel argue that compliance is a significant aspect of a court's legitimacy. They observe the vicious circle of legitimacy when 'legitimacy enhances compliance and compliance enhances legitimacy'. C.J. Carrubba and M.J. Gabel, 'Courts, Compliance, and the Quest for Legitimacy in International Law', *Theoretical Inquires in Law*, 14 (2013), 505, 509. Although compliance is important, it is not the only factor of legitimacy. See also, Y. Shany, 'Assessing the Effectiveness of International Courts – A Goal-Based Approach', *American Journal of International Law*, 106 (2012), 225, 244–7.

[7] Dothan links legitimacy and criticism of the Court by pointing out that 'States can damage a court's legitimacy by criticizing its judgments ... criticism can expose the weaknesses in a court's judgment and make the international community perceive it as wrong, unjust or biased and thereby damage the court's legitimacy'. S. Dothan, 'How International Tribunals Enhance Their Legitimacy', *Theoretical Inquires in Law*, 14 (2013), 455, 460.

[8] A. Buchanan and R.O. Keohane, 'The Legitimacy of Global Governance Institutions', *Ethics and International Affairs*, 20 (2006), 405, 407.

the Court has a particular need to maintain functioning relationships with contracting parties, i.e. states. This is because states are prominent actors in on-going reform efforts, central to the resourcing of the Court's structure and institutional architecture, and critical actors in the processes of enforcement and execution of judgments. In this respect, individual states are both responsible for the execution of adverse judgments against them and play a more general role as members of the Committee of Ministers, which has a supervisory role in the execution of judgments. Taking this into account it is clear that the Court may have rather a lot to lose if states (and particularly high-compliance states) begin to withdraw diffuse support and/or seriously question its legitimacy.[9]

The ECtHR has been criticised over the full 50 years of its existence. Governments started threatening to leave the Convention system nearly as soon as they joined. Up until 1998 when Protocol 11 came into force, the Contracting Parties were in possession of two 'useful' tools – optional clauses to the ECHR that could have been accepted only temporarily: jurisdiction of the Court and right of individual petition. On a number of occasions, the governments considered not renewing acceptance of these clauses.[10] Over the last few decades, the Court has grown in its importance and influence. Optional clauses have been removed from the Convention; thousands of people submit their applications to the Court. It is often said that the Court has become the victim of its own success, meaning that it cannot cope with the increasing numbers of applications.[11] However, the keyword here is success: the ECtHR is the most influential regional human rights court in the world. Success also means responsibility, and the Court's role is crucial for human rights protection in Europe. The collapse of the Strasbourg system now could be detrimental, especially in certain Eastern European States. Therefore, the Court must maintain its legitimacy now even more than ever. Even if lost

---

[9] De Londras and Dzehtsiarou, 'Managing Judicial Innovation in the European Court of Human Rights'.

[10] In reaction to the *Iversen* case, the Norwegian authorities renewed their declaration of acceptance of optional clauses for one year only. E. Bates, *The Evolution of the European Convention on Human Rights* (Oxford University Press, 2010), p. 220. Bates quotes a memorandum of the British Home Secretary from 1972 which among other issues points out that '[u]nless there is a marked change of heart by the Commission, or unless the tendency of the Commission towards developing a new jurisprudence by extending the meaning of the Convention is corrected by a decision of the European Court, continued acceptance of these optional articles by the United Kingdom is likely to bring us neither benefit nor credit'. Ibid., p. 288. These threats, however, have never been followed.

[11] See, K. Dzehtsiarou and A. Greene, 'Legitimacy and the Future of the European Court of Human Rights: Critical Perspectives from Academia and Practitioners', *German Law Journal*, 12 (2011), 1707, 1707.

legitimacy does not lead to a complete collapse of the system, it will effectively prevent the Court from being able to set standards in the area of human rights protection.[12]

In recent years, the Court has been widely criticised by nearly all stakeholders – national governments,[13] local judges,[14] the media,[15] Convention commentators[16] and even the Pope.[17] While some of these challenges are linked to profound disagreement with the

[12] See, T.S. Clark, 'The Separation of Powers, Court Curbing, and Judicial Legitimacy', *American Journal of Political Science*, 53 (2009), 971, 974.

[13] British Prime Minister David Cameron in his speech on the European Court of Human Rights stated that '[a]ll states agreed that the Court was, in some cases, too ready to substitute its judgment for that of reasonable national processes and all agreed that that was not its role'. He also expressed the view that 'we need to work together to ensure that ... the Court remains true to its original intention: to uphold the Convention and prevent the abuse of human rights'. D. Cameron, 'Speech on the European Court of Human Rights', *New Statesman*, available at http://www.newstatesman.com/politics/2012/01/human-rights-court-national, accessed on 31 July 2014. See also, 'The Backbench Parliamentary Debates, "Prisoners' Right to Vote"', available at http://www.publications.parliament.uk/pa/cm201011/cmhansrd/cm110210/debtext/110210-0002.htm, accessed on 3 July 2011. A former ambassador of Malta to the Council of Europe has also fiercely criticised the ECtHR. J. Licari, 'Government by Foreign Courts', *Times of Malta*, available at http://www.timesofmalta.com/articles/view/20130915/opinion/Government-by-foreign-courts.486215#.UpTOMD9uqSo, accessed on 31 July 2014.

[14] See, for example, critical statements of the head of the Russian constitutional court, B. Bejlin, 'Russia May Stop Listening to the European Court' (Россия Может Перестать Слушать Европейский Суд), *Vesti*, available at http://www.vesti.ru/doc.html?id=403698, accessed on 21 November 2011; the President of the Belgian Constitutional Court has also criticised a few judgments delivered by the ECtHR: see, S. Smet, 'President of Belgian Constitutional Court Criticizes European Court of Human Rights', *Strasbourg Observers*, available at http://strasbourgobservers.com/2010/05/17/president-of-belgian-constitutional-court-criticizes-european-court-of-human-rights, accessed on 21 November 2011. See also, L. Hoffmann, 'The Universality of Human Rights', *Law Quarterly Review*, 125 (2009), 416, 428–9.

[15] See, for example, J. Slack, 'Named and Shamed: The European Human Rights Judges Wrecking British Law', *Daily Mail*, available at http://www.dailymail.co.uk/news/article-1353860/Named-shamed-The-European-human-rights-judges-wrecking-British-law.html#ixzz1QNTg8Uz2, accessed on 3 August 2011; J. Groves, '"Europe's Human Rights Court Is Out of Control ... We Must Pull Out": Call by Top British Judge after Ruling That Prisoners Should Get the Vote', *Mail Online*, available at http://www.dailymail.co.uk/news/article-1354362/Europes-human-rights-court-control–pull-Call-British-judge-ruling-prisoners-vote.html#ixzz1RnFsH61j, accessed on 11 July 2011.

[16] Weiler, for instance, characterised the judgment of the Chamber in Lautsi as 'an embarrassment'. J. Weiler, 'Lautsi: Crucifix in the Classroom Redux', *European Journal of International Law*, 21 (2010), available at http://www.ejiltalk.org/lautsi-crucifix-in-the-classroom-redux, accessed on 31 July 2014.

[17] Pope Benedict XVI criticised the Chamber judgment in *Lautsi* v. *Italy*; see, D. McGoldrick, 'Religion in the European Public Square and in European Public Life – Crucifixes in the Classroom?', *Human Rights Law Review*, 11 (2011), 451, 452.

European project[18] and cannot be changed by any means, some critics share the commitment to cooperation in Europe in the area of human rights but are rather unhappy with how the Court adjudicates human rights cases.

In his extrajudicial writing, former judge of the ECtHR Egbert Myjer observes that

> [e]very now and then the first reaction to a new judgment of the Court by national politicians was to announce that they would investigate whether it was worthwhile to remain a Party to the ECHR. Needless to say, such threats were never followed up. In many cases, the reaction on the national level is either one of shame or one of indignation: how dare this international Court criticise something that has been approved by national parliamentarians or assessed (and approved) by national judges?[19]

This quotation captures well the two challenges that the Court's constitutional legitimacy is facing. First, the Court is an international tribunal and it suffers from legitimacy deficit for being a 'foreign court'; most of these challenges are shared by other international institutions and international law in general. Second, it is called to review decisions often adopted by the democratically elected governments, and therefore the counter-majoritarian difficulty which is faced by national constitutional courts is also attributable to the ECtHR. These challenges overlap, and the Court is usually accused of being foreign and insensitive to local needs when it reviews a decision of a democratically legitimate institution. However, for the purposes of this chapter, these challenges will be considered separately as they might attract different enhancement techniques.

---

[18] It includes both the Council of Europe and the European Union. These two are often intertwined in public opinion. See, among many others, M. Hall, 'Britain in the EU: This Must Be the End', *Daily Express*, available at http://www.express.co.uk/news/uk/228428/Britain-in-the-EU-This-must-be-the-end, accessed on 4 March 2014. In this article, the journalist discusses the reaction of the British Members of Parliament to the prisoners' voting judgment by the ECtHR. A more recent example is M. Champion, 'No Time Off for a Terrorist's Good Behavior', *Bloomberg View*, available at http://www.bloomberg-view.com/articles/2014-02-26/no-time-off-for-a-terrorist-s-good-behavior, accessed on 4 March 2014. The author claims that '[t]he UK abolished the death penalty in 1969 for all crimes but treason, and for treason in 1998; it can't restore executions so long as it is a member of the European Union. Last July, the Grand Chamber of the European Court of Human Rights in Strasbourg ruled that life without the prospect of release upon rehabilitation is torture.' Ibid.

[19] E. Myjer, 'Why Much of the Criticism of the European Court of Human Rights Is Unfounded' in S. Flogaitis, T. Zwart and J. Fraser (eds.), *The European Court of Human Rights and Its Discontents Turning Criticism into Strength* (Edward Elgar, 2013), p. 40.

6.3 International constitutional challenges

The first legitimacy challenge relates to the question of how the ECtHR can accommodate State consent in its reasoning. This is necessary mainly due to the voluntary nature of international law. This section argues that European consensus can be conceptualised as an updated consent of the Contracting Parties to a particular regulation or principle. By integrating consent into its reasoning, the Court can limit the negative effect of not engaging in originalist interpretation of the Convention. The second challenge to legitimacy is that it would quickly fade if the Court found itself in conflict with the Contracting Parties. Hence, the Court should not establish relations of superiority-inferiority with the Contracting Parties but rather maintain synergistic relations; European consensus can be a channel for such relations. Third, the legitimacy of the ECtHR would perhaps vanish if it were perceived as an institution that made arbitrary judgments without due respect to legal norms. This section argues that European consensus can be traced back to customary international law, and this improves the legality of the ECtHR rulings. Finally, the Court is sometimes accused of not honouring the principle of subsidiarity. This means that the Court should only be an addition to national systems of human rights protection, not a substitution thereof. In this respect, consensus can be conceptualised as an argument that reminds the stakeholders that the Court takes subsidiarity seriously.

6.3.1 State consent

The most traditional source of legitimacy in international law is, of course, State consent.[20] International law was created by States in order to regulate relations between those States which agreed to participate. It was only in the twentieth century that international law began to occupy new territories. With the emergence of *jus cogens* and widespread binding human rights treaties, the agreement of a State to participate ceased to be the only precondition for international law to exist and operate. Benvenisti suggests that the consent-based model of international law is an old-fashioned nineteenth-century concept which should not be taken into account when fundamental rights and freedoms are at stake.[21] It seems that Benvenisti captures the need to depart from the model of

---

[20] Buchanan and Keohane, 'The Legitimacy of Global Governance Institutions', pp. 412–3.
[21] E. Benvenisti, 'Margin of Appreciation, Consensus, and Universal Standards', *Journal of International Law and Politics*, 31 (1999), 843, 851.

international law solely based on State consent, but it cannot be totally abandoned because State consent is still a key factor in State-centred international law.

The Court references to the original consent of the Contracting Parties and the original meaning of the Convention are rare and problematic.[22] The ECHR was drafted in the late 1940s, and Europe has changed considerably since then. The ECtHR must reflect these changes by means of evolutive interpretation. However, the ECtHR cannot deploy evolutive interpretation arbitrarily; rather, it should reflect a real change in human rights protection – not a perceived or desired one. European consensus gives the Court an opportunity to prove the reality of the change and for the States to consent to it. It is submitted that incorporation of such consent positively impacts the legitimacy of the ECtHR as it prevents the Court from going beyond those developments that the Contracting Parties are able to accept.

The ECtHR has developed the meaning of the ECHR through the deployment of evolutive interpretation. In the 1950s, when the 'founding States' ratified the Convention, they could not anticipate with precision how the Court would interpret the Convention.[23] Original consent to the ECHR is not as old as in the case of, for example, the US constitution. This means that the original meaning of the ECtHR is not as outdated as the meaning of the US constitution. Moreover, it is important to remember that the Convention was not ratified by all Contracting Parties in the 1950s. A significant number of former communist European States acceded to the Convention in the 1990s, and their consent is arguably still 'fresh'.[24] When the 'new States' joined, the main doctrines of interpretation had already been established, and these States cannot argue that evolutive interpretation of the Convention took them by surprise. Does this mean that the Court has to apply different standards depending on when a State Party ratified the Convention? The answer is perhaps 'no'. It is not in the spirit of the Convention to divide the Contracting Parties

---

[22] Letsas claims that 'the Court's interpretative ethics has been both anti-textualist and anti-originalist'. G. Letsas, 'The ECHR as a Living Instrument: Its Meaning and Legitimacy' in A. Føllesdal, B. Peters and G. Ulfstein (eds.), *Constituting Europe: The European Court of Human Rights in a National, European and Global Context* (Cambridge University Press, 2013), p. 123.

[23] Bates, *The Evolution of the European Convention*, pp. 297–301.

[24] Albania in 1995, Bulgaria in 1992, Croatia in 1996, the Czech Republic in 1991, Bosnia and Herzegovina in 2002, Estonia in 1993, Azerbaijan in 2001, Georgia in 1999, Hungary in 1990 and others.

6.3   INTERNATIONAL CONSTITUTIONAL CHALLENGES   151

into groups and apply different rules to different Parties.[25] Moreover, even founding States have had their chance to 'officially' oppose the way that the Court interprets the Convention, for example by not signing and ratifying new protocols to the Convention.[26] All Contracting Parties have renewed their support by ratifying Protocol 11 in 1998, which fundamentally restructured the Strasbourg system, and Protocol 14 in 2010, which introduced further procedural reforms.[27]

This does not mean that continuing formal support of the Contracting Parties through ratification of the Protocols removes all limits for the Court in interpreting the Convention. Buchanan argues that

> [e]ven though ... [international] institutions are created by State consent and cannot function without State support, they engage in ongoing governance activities, including the generation of laws and/or law like rules that are not controlled by the 'specific consent' of States. Hence, the problem of bureaucratic distance looms large, even if the States that create these institutions are democratic; the links between the popular will in democratic States that consent to the creation of global governance institutions and the governing functions these institutions perform seem too anaemic to confer legitimacy.[28]

The voluntarism of international law determines the fact that the Contracting Parties to the Convention should express continuing agreement to being supervised by the ECtHR.[29] Helfer and Slaughter argue that acknowledging the sovereignty of the Contracting States by the Court helps legitimise the jurisprudence of the ECtHR, even when the

---

[25] A different attitude to different Contracting Parties can also damage the Court's legitimacy. Dothan points out that '[g]reater restraint towards [certain] states ... may indicate that a court is biased ... This can cause significant damage to a court's legitimacy which relies partly on the image of the court as impartial.' Dothan, 'How International Tribunals Enhance Their Legitimacy', 461.

[26] Russia, for example, has significantly delayed the ratification of Protocol 14.

[27] Protocol 11 has changed the Court from being a part-time institution to a permanent tribunal as well as a number of key provisions of the Convention including election of judges and institutional composition of the Strasbourg system. See, Bates, *The Evolution of the European Convention*, pp. 460–5. Protocol 14 slightly simplified the procedure of disposal of inadmissible complaints.

[28] A. Buchanan, 'The Legitimacy of International Law' in S. Besson and J. Tasioulas (eds.), *The Philosophy of International Law* (Oxford University Press, 2010), p. 91.

[29] Christiano argues that consent still plays an important role in international law because it derives its legitimacy from the voluntary association of States. T. Christiano, 'Democratic Legitimacy and International Institutions' in S. Besson and J. Tasioulas (eds.), *The Philosophy of International Law* (Oxford University Press, 2010), pp. 122–3.

decision in question cuts against the States.[30] Macdonald, a former judge of the ECtHR, has pointed out that the whole system of European human rights protection 'rests on the fragile foundations of the consent of the Contracting Parties'.[31] While more than 50 years of the Strasbourg Court might suggest that original consent is of limited relevance to a consideration of the Court's legitimacy,[32] States continue to return to it (expressly or impliedly) in their critique of the Court.[33]

The Court has to have the Contracting Parties on board while engaging in judicial innovation, such as evolutive interpretation. Given that original consent is hardly applicable to this situation because judicial innovation arguably cuts specifically against original consent, the Court should thus seek updated consent. It is impractical and barely possible to request formal consent[34] in relation to a particular case in the form of a protocol, and, therefore, the Court has to rely on implicit and up-to-date consent: European consensus.

European consensus can be conceptualised as an updated consent because it reflects the current state of law and practice in the Contracting Parties. It means that the majority of them agreed to and accepted a certain legal regulation. It is true that European consensus is not normally deployed in cases where the law in question falls within the commonly accepted standards. Much more often, European consensus is deployed if the law or practice under consideration by the Court deviates from consensus.[35] The Contracting Party against which the European consensus argument is deployed might object on the ground that a democratic decision taken by this Contracting Party is overridden by

---

[30] L.R. Helfer and A.-M. Slaughter, 'Toward a Theory of Effective Supranational Adjudication', *Yale Law Journal*, 107 (1997), 273, 317.

[31] R.S. Macdonald, 'The Margin of Appreciation' in R.S. Macdonald, F. Matscher and H. Petzold (eds.), *The European System for the Protection of Human Rights* (Martinus Nijhoff Publishers, 1993), p. 123.

[32] G. Letsas, 'The Truth in Autonomous Concepts: How to Interpret the ECHR', *European Journal of International Law*, 15 (2004), 304.

[33] In 2009, Lord Hoffmann pointed out that 'it would be valuable for the Council of Europe to continue to perform the functions originally envisaged in 1950, that is, drawing attention to violations of human rights in Member States and providing a forum in which they can be discussed'. Hoffmann, 'The Universality of Human Rights', 431. It would appear that this is primarily so when politicians speak about the legitimacy of the Court; see, B. Çalı, A. Koch and N. Bruch, 'The Legitimacy of the European Court of Human Rights: The View from the Ground' (2011), available at http://ecthrproject.files.wordpress.com/2011/04/ecthrlegitimacyreport.pdf, accessed on 31 July 2014.

[34] Ratification of Protocols or any other forms of consent.

[35] *Bayatyan v. Armenia*, Application No 23459/03, Judgment of 7 July 2011.

6.3 INTERNATIONAL CONSTITUTIONAL CHALLENGES   153

the democratic decisions made in other Contracting Parties.[36] However, this argument appears to misinterpret the rationale behind European consensus. The Court does not hold that there is a violation of European consensus, but that there is a violation of the Convention. European consensus supports the Court in finding the meaning of the Convention rights. Through consensus, the Contracting Parties implicitly consent to a particular meaning of the right in question.

It is not unanimously accepted by commentators that consent should play any role in the interpretation of the Convention. Letsas has developed an argument that can potentially undermine the value of reliance on State consent by the ECtHR. As outlined in Chapter 5, Letsas argues that the ECtHR judges have to engage in a moral reading of the Convention and that moral values of human rights legitimise judgments and judicial innovations from the ECtHR.[37] Moreover, the fear of losing legitimacy is grossly overrated due to the fact that the 'Court has earned respect and recognition at both national and international levels'.[38] It seems that the Court earned this respect because it kept a low profile in the early years of its existence, and preferred incremental and gradual changes to revolutionary human rights protection.[39] This respect is the result of taking State consent seriously. State consent is not understood here as the expectations of States in each and every case of individual application where they act as respondents. Their expectations are fairly clear – they wish to be condemned for human rights violations as rarely as possible (preferably never).[40] However, giving the Contracting Parties *carte*

[36] Murray argues that '[i]f a State through the democratic process makes difficult ethical and moral choices reflecting issues deeply rooted in the social fabric of its society is it for an international judicial body (or indeed a national one) to negate those difficult choices under the cloak of consensus?' L. Murray, 'Consensus: Concordance, or Hegemony of Majority' in *Dialogues between Judges* (Council of Europe, 2008), p. 66. Legg argues that current State practice or in other words European consensus is legitimate because of the 'nature of international agreements as emanations of state consent'. A. Legg, *The Margin of Appreciation in International Human Rights Law* (Oxford University Press, 2012), p. 106.
[37] G. Letsas, *A Theory of Interpretation of the European Convention on Human Rights* (Oxford University Press, 2009), p. 3. This is the crux of the anti-majoritarian argument discussed in Chapter 5.
[38] Ibid., p. 125.
[39] See, Bates, *The Evolution of the European Convention*; N. Krisch, *Beyond Constitutionalism, The Pluralist Structure of Postnational Law* (Oxford University Press, 2010), pp. 144–5.
[40] In exceptional cases, a third State might intervene in the case and support finding a violation. The case of *Kononov* v. *Latvia* is a good example of such a scenario. The applicant was a Russian partisan who was prosecuted in Latvia for war crimes committed during the Second World War. In its third-party intervention, Russia opposed the

blanche would probably undermine the whole idea behind the ECtHR as an effective international human rights arbiter. Consent is understood as a collective acceptance of a particular rule or a particular approach – a common European attitude or commonly accepted rules that build up European public order as reflected by European consensus.

This is not to say that the moral value of human rights is not important for the legitimacy of the Court and its judgment. It is one of the key legitimising factors. However, international human rights adjudication cannot rest solely on the moral superiority of human rights, because, as Waldron has rightly argued, people can disagree about rights.[41] Moreover, application of broad and sparse human rights definitions can lead to different, often mutually exclusive, results.[42] In those cases, some more objective and palpable grounds other than a moral reading are desirable; otherwise, such decision-making can be perceived as arbitrary and political, reflecting subjective beliefs of the majority of seven or seventeen judges of the Court,[43] and therefore illegitimate. The moral value of the judgments of the ECtHR is an important but insufficient element of the legitimacy of the ECtHR judgments.

State consent is important in understanding the legitimacy of the Court. States agree to be bound by the Convention and the Court's judgments up to a certain point. If this point is reached, the States might stop executing the Court's judgments[44] and they can even threaten to denounce the Convention. This usually happens when States are of the opinion that the Court has gone too far,[45] or acted *ultra vires*.[46] It seems that, in order to

---

conviction and argued that Latvia had violated Article 7 of the Convention. *Kononov* v. *Latvia*, Application No 36376/04, Judgment of 17 May 2010, para. 170–7. However, this is an exceptional situation and happens fairly rarely.

[41] J. Waldron, *Law and Disagreement* (Oxford University Press, 1999).

[42] Very few judgments of the Grand Chamber of the ECtHR are free of dissenting opinions of judges.

[43] Meritorious cases are decided by the committees of three judges, chambers of seven and grand chambers of seventeen. The Committee can decide meritorious cases on the basis of well-established case law and they do not normally deal with hard cases.

[44] See, prisoners' voting saga and the UK's reluctance to execute the judgments in *Hirst* v. *the United Kingdom (No 2)*, Application No 74025/01, Judgment of 6 October 2005, and *Greens and M.T.* v. *the United Kingdom*, Application No 60041/08 and 60054/08, Judgment of 23 November 2010, discussed in Chapter 3.

[45] J. Doyle, '"Human Right Judges Go Too Far", Says Grayling as He Ratchets Up Hostilities with Strasbourg Court', *Daily Mail*, available at http://www.dailymail.co.uk/news/article-2249723/Human-right-judges-far-says-Grayling-ratchets-hostilities-Strasbourg-court.html, accessed on 24 December 2013.

[46] A. Føllesdal, B. Peters and G. Ulfstein, 'Conclusions' in A. Føllesdal, B. Peters and G. Ulfstein (eds.), *Constituting Europe* (Cambridge University Press, 2013), pp. 394–5.

ensure cooperation from States, the Court should not overstep a certain point. This point will be called a legitimacy wall[47] – a point beyond which the Court should not go in order to maintain its legitimacy.[48] The key question here is how to establish where this legitimacy wall stands.

Some commentators suggest that in order to avoid reaching or overreaching the legitimacy wall, the Court should maintain a low profile and adhere to the concept of due deference.[49] Krisch argues that the Court has not yet overstepped its legitimacy wall in the majority of cases because it has kept the cost of compliance fairly low.[50] Having said that, a low profile usually means maintaining the status quo in human rights protection. However, it is crucial for the effectiveness of the Strasbourg system to change and develop in order to reflect changes in society and to be an engine behind the improvement of human rights protection in Europe. The Court cannot be an institution of human rights mummification but rather it should develop the standards. European consensus can marry these two competing interests by staying within the framework acceptable to States yet reflecting evolving ideas in Europe.

European consensus can be conceptualised as an implicit consent which can act as a substitute to formal consent within the Strasbourg system. The latter is a classical legitimising factor in international law which arguably lost its hegemony in the twentieth century. However, it did not lose its importance completely.

6.3.2 Dialogue between the ECtHR and the Contracting Parties

This section argues that European consensus can enhance the legitimacy of the Court not only as a signpost of a legitimacy wall or as an updated consent to a particular solution but also as a means of a dialogue between the Court and the Contracting Parties. The conceptualisation of

---

[47] This term was suggested by de Londras while drafting the article: de Londras and Dzehtsiarou, 'Managing Judicial Innovation in the European Court of Human Rights'. This term did not end up in the final version of that paper but it appears to capture this challenge well.

[48] Carrubba and Gabel argue that international courts 'cannot successfully push interpretations of international law that are inconsistent with underlying government preferences. To put it differently, the court can only help facilitate compliance that the member state governments are ultimately willing to enforce'. Carrubba and Gabel, 'Courts, Compliance, and the Quest for Legitimacy', 533.

[49] Legg suggests that one of the reasons for deference exercised by the ECtHR is respect for the democratic legitimacy of the States' actions. Legg, *The Margin of Appreciation*, p. 25.

[50] Krisch, *Beyond Constitutionalism*, pp. 144–5.

consensus as an implicit consent of the Contracting Parties cannot fully explain why there are cases in which consensus is disregarded by the Court. If consensus is conceptualised as a form of consent, then the ECtHR has to rigorously follow it.[51] However, this book does not advocate the automatic application of consensus and argues that European consensus is the medium through which the ECtHR can establish a dialogical node with the Contracting Parties. This understanding of consensus demonstrates that the Court can have some impact on emerging consensus by providing feedback through its judgments.

Krisch explains that the classical dichotomy between international and national law is no longer useful.[52] International and national laws 'do not form an integrated whole, neatly organised according to rules of hierarchy and a clear distribution of tasks'.[53] Both national and international laws go through a transformation because more and more functions appear to be delegated to the international level.[54] The ECtHR is increasingly seen, not as an international or regional Court, but as a constitutional actor[55] that participates in the formation of European public order. At the same time, 'the Convention's constitutional landscape is also undeniably pluralistic, polyvalent, and heterarchical, rather than unitary, monistic, and rigidly hierarchical'.[56] In these circumstances, the Court has to be open to communication from the States and be mindful of the signals that have been sent to the Court from national authorities. In such a case, the Court can expect reciprocity, meaning that the signals sent by the Court will be taken seriously at the national level. Walker points out that 'the only acceptable ethic of political responsibility for the new Europe is one that is premised upon mutual recognition and respect between national and supranational authorities'.[57] Such mutual recognition is usually conceptualised as

---

[51] T. Zwart, 'More Human Rights Than Court: Why the Legitimacy of the European Court of Human Rights Is in Need of Repair and How It Can Be Done' in S. Flogaitis, T. Zwart and J. Fraser (eds.), *The European Court of Human Rights and Its Discontents* (Edward Elgar, 2013), pp. 90–2.

[52] N. Krisch, 'The Open Architecture of European Human Rights Law', *Modern Law Review*, 71 (2008), 183, 184.

[53] Krisch, *Beyond Constitutionalism*.   [54] Ibid., p. 13.

[55] S. Greer and L. Wildhaber, 'Revisiting the Debate about "Constitutionalising" the European Court of Human Rights', *Human Rights Law Review*, 12 (2012), 655.

[56] Ibid., p. 685.

[57] N. Walker, 'The Idea of Constitutional Pluralism', *Modern Law Review*, 65 (2002), 317, 337. Perhaps Walker meant communication between the EU and the Member States, but it seems that it is also relevant to the ECtHR-Contracting Parties relations.

6.3 INTERNATIONAL CONSTITUTIONAL CHALLENGES 157

a dialogue or interaction between the ECtHR and the Contracting Parties.

The need for interaction and close communication between the ECtHR and the Contracting Parties was acknowledged in the Brighton Declaration, which enshrines section B, entitled 'Interaction between the Court and national authorities'.[58] The declaration urges the Court to take national decisions into account by means of increasing deployment of the margin of appreciation. However, as has been argued elsewhere, the doctrine of margin of appreciation cannot enhance dialogue as the Court merely defers from assessing the actions of the respondent State which fall within certain boundaries.[59] Having said that, the need for interaction is clearly emphasised by the Contracting Parties, and it is safe to suggest that engagement in dialogue enhances the legitimacy of the Court and the judgments it produces.

Unlike margin of appreciation, European consensus is clearly a tool used by the Court to engage in dialogue with the Contracting Parties.[60] The ECtHR takes into account the common voice of the Contracting Parties through European consensus. The ECHR not only is an agreement between the Contracting Parties[61] but it also creates a new notion – the notion of a European law of human rights. This does not mean that the Court has the ultimate power in determining the standards of this new law because the Court is not a legislator. All Contracting Parties to the Convention should have a say in this dialogue (polylogue). Rather than the Court,[62] it should be the Contracting Parties at the forefront of human rights protection as the Court's role is simply to

---

[58] Brighton Declaration adopted on 20 April 2012. Section B.
[59] K. Dzehtsiarou, 'Interaction between the European Court of Human Rights and Member States: European Consensus, Advisory Opinions and the Question of Legitimacy' in S. Flogaitis, T. Zwart and J. Fraser (eds.), *The European Court of Human Rights and Its Discontents* (Edward Elgar, 2013), p. 118.
[60] Petkova argues that 'consensus analysis demonstrates knowledge of majoritarian trends in, and creates a dialogical node with, the courts' constituents, in particular by addressing non-legal considerations'. B. Petkova, 'The Notion of Consensus as a Route to Democratic Adjudication?', *Cambridge Yearbook of European Legal Studies*, 14 (2012), 663, 675.
[61] Drzemczewski points out that '[t]he Convention has ... created a new form of law. It is a treaty in form rather than a treaty in substance. This instrument is not a simple contract based on reciprocity; it is a treaty of a normative character, developing an evolving notion of "Convention law" which interpenetrates and transcends both the international and domestic legal structures. Its organs have the rather delicate and difficult task of interpreting this "common law".' A. Drzemczewski, 'The *Sui Generis* Nature of the European Convention on Human Rights', *International and Comparative Law Quarterly*, 29 (1980), 54, 61.
[62] It is so due to its limited character and subsidiary nature. See, J. Christoffersen, 'Individual and Constitutional Justice: Can the Power Balance of Adjudication Be Reversed?' in

encourage such developments. This dialogical node helps to legitimise the Court's decisions.[63]

Such dialogue is possible because both national and ECHR laws use the same language; the language of commitment to the common values of human rights. De Londras suggests that the relationship between international and domestic human rights protection should be reflective and synergistic.[64] If a synergistic relationship is established, then domestic standards should develop in parallel with international ones without immediate superiority or subordination. In the view of de Londras:

> Domestic constitutional and other rights-protecting standards can be invigorated by international human rights law, and international human rights law can evolve by reference to domestic standards in general with international adjudicatory bodies attempting to recognise 'tipping points' based on State practice as well as on principle and clearly articulated treaty-based standards.[65]

It seems that international law is more than merely the law that regulates relations between sovereign States; it has grown in importance and assumed responsibilities that were traditionally seen as purely domestic. It seems that the ECtHR is an element of the constitutional pluralist regime which lacks traditional legal relations of hierarchy and subordination. With that in mind, legitimacy of human rights courts should be grounded on instruments that are capable of accommodating the input of the Contracting Parties; European consensus is just such an instrument.

6.3.3 Consensus as a source of international law

Arbitrary decision-making is a significant challenge to the Court's legitimacy. European consensus can be linked to recognised sources of international law, and, therefore, if consensus is applied properly, it can hardly be argued that the Court simply selected the option that the judges liked the most. In this case, the judges select an option that is supported by international law. It is central to this argument to point out that

---

J. Christoffersen and M.R. Madsen (eds.), *The European Court of Human Rights between Law and Politics* (Oxford University Press, 2011), pp. 200–2.

[63] Dothan points out that 'international Courts can gain legitimacy by interacting with legitimate national courts'. Dothan, 'How International Tribunals Enhance Their Legitimacy', 458.

[64] F. de Londras, 'International Human Rights Law and Constitutional Rights: In Favour of Synergy', *International Review of Constitutionalism*, 9 (2009), 307, 311.

[65] Ibid., 312.

European consensus is capable of enhancing the process legitimacy of the ECtHR if applied consistently and coherently and if it is based on verified data. One can distinguish between two partially overlapping schools in relation to the legitimacy of legal norms or institutions: process or procedural legitimacy and substantive legitimacy. Process theorists, such as Weber,[66] Kelsen[67] and Dahl,[68] define legitimacy as an attribute which a norm, decision or institution possesses only if it was adopted or created in accordance with accepted procedures. Weber argues that readiness to conform to a rule follows from the fact that it is 'formally correct and imposed by accepted procedures'.[69] In contrast to process theory, substantive legitimacy takes into account the content of a rule. For example, Habermas proposes that legitimacy is conferred by scientific empiricist reasoning which produces a rational result.[70] Dworkin argues that fair procedure is not enough for a legal provision to be legitimate.[71]

Process legitimacy can ensure that a court enjoys diffuse support[72] from the stakeholders, meaning that judgments that are procedurally correct and unbiased can be supported even if the stakeholders do not agree with the outcome.[73] In contrast, a member of the public who agrees with the substance of the decision would express specific support.[74]

Legal commentators argue that the legitimacy of the courts' rulings depends on whether they honour principles like consistency, coherence,

---

[66] M. Weber, *Wirtschaft und Gesellschaft* (Verlag von J.C.B. Mohr, 1972, first published in 1922), p. 19.

[67] H. Kelsen, *Pure Theory of Law* (1989, first published in 1938), p. 198.

[68] Dahl argues that 'even the best-designed judicial system can guarantee only procedural justice; it cannot guarantee substantive justice. A constitution can ensure a right to a fair trial; it cannot absolutely guarantee that a fair trial will always lead to the right verdict. But it is precisely because no such guarantee is possible that we place such a high value on a fair trial'. R.A. Dahl, *Democracy and Its Critics* (Yale University Press, 1989), p. 169.

[69] Weber, *Wirtschaft und Gesellschaft*, p. 19. See also, J.L.M. Gribnau, 'Legitimacy of the Judiciary', *Electronic Journal of Comparative Law*, 6 (2002), available at http://www.ejcl.org/64/art64-3.txt, accessed on 31 July 2014.

[70] J. Habermas, *Communication and the Evolution of Society* (Beacon Press, 1979), p. 183.

[71] R. Dworkin, *Law's Empire* (Harvard University Press, 1986), pp. 178–86.

[72] See, J.L. Gibson, G.A. Caldeira and L.K. Spence, 'Why Do People Accept Public Policies They Oppose? Testing Legitimacy Theory with a Survey-Based Experiment', *Political Research Quarterly*, 58 (2005), 187, 188.

[73] Dothan, 'How International Tribunals Enhance Their Legitimacy', 456.

[74] See, Y. Lupu, 'International Judicial Legitimacy: Lessons from National Courts', *Theoretical Inquiries in Law*, 14 (2013), 437, 440–1.

legal certainty and predictability.[75] An enforcement mechanism can be legitimate if the rules are reasonably clear and legal consequences are predictable.[76] Clarity and foreseeability of the Court's reasoning are considered to be key concepts in ensuring process legitimacy of the ECtHR judgments.[77] In other words, process legitimacy is tightly linked to principles of rule of law.[78] The ECtHR has declared its adherence to such principles.[79]

An opposite logical alternative to the rule of law is arbitrariness; if the decisions of the Court are seen as arbitrary, its legitimacy may suffer as a result. A decision of a court is much less likely to be challenged as arbitrary if it is grounded on the recognised sources of law. All judgments of the ECtHR are based on the Convention, and one can argue that this is enough to support the process legitimacy of the Court. However, as it has already been pointed out on a number of occasions, the ECHR does not provide answers to all interpretive puzzles that can occur in the Court's practice. In this situation, the Court has to resort to other sources. In international law, customs and general principles of civilised nations are the recognised sources of law.[80] This section argues that the Court's adherence to customs and general principles of civilised nations may enhance its process legitimacy, and European consensus can be seen as a tool akin to these sources of international law.

---

[75] See, Gribnau, 'Legitimacy of the Judiciary'; J. Gerards, 'Judicial Deliberations in the ECtHR' in N. Huls, M. Adams and J. Bomhoff (eds.), *The Legitimacy of Highest Courts' Rulings. Judicial Deliberations and Beyond* (T.M.C. Asser Institute, 2008), available at http://papers.ssrn.com/sol3/papers.cfm?abstract_id=1114906, accessed on 31 July 2014.

[76] A. Buchanan, 'Human Rights and the Legitimacy of the International Order', *Legal Theory*, 14 (2008), 39, 41.

[77] Lady Justice Arden lists the qualities that the ECtHR should demonstrate to improve the implementation of the Convention system. 'Quality of reasoning and ability to communicate clearly with their constituents' was one of these qualities. M. Arden, 'Address at the Seminar "The Convention Is Yours" Organised by the ECtHR', *Dialogues between Judges* (Council of Europe, 2010), p. 23.

[78] '[T]he commitment to the rule of law is the commitment to resolving or managing conflicts by effectively institutionalizing the impartial application of publicly known general rules that are based on the assumption that there is to be an accommodation of interests.' Buchanan, 'The Legitimacy of International Law', 89.

[79] In *Demir and Baykara* v. *Turkey*, the Court stated that 'it is in the interests of legal certainty, foreseeability and equality before the law that the Court should not depart, without good reason, from precedents established in previous cases'. *Demir and Baykara* v. *Turkey*, Application No 34503/97, Judgment of 12 November 2008, para. 153.

[80] Article 38(1) of the Statute of the International Court of Justice lists customs as the source of law alongside treaties, general principles of law and 'teachings of the most highly qualified publicists'.

Article 38 of the International Court of Justice (ICJ) Statute lists legitimate and widely recognised sources of international law. International courts can increase their legitimacy if they are seen to apply these generally accepted rules of international law.[81] As a result, they will be perceived as impartial and unbiased. Moreover, reliance on these sources can create an impression of predictability and foreseeability of the judgments.

The Court has ruled that customary norms are important for the interpretation of the Convention. In *Hirsi Jamaa and others v. Italy*, the Court stated that it was basing its interpretation of Article 1 of the Convention related to the notion of jurisdiction on 'customary international law and treaty provisions'.[82] The ECtHR judge, Inete Ziemele, writing extrajudicially, points out that the Court uses customary international law in at least two instances: first, when the Court deals with an issue which is governed by international law;[83] and second, when the Court seeks to establish European consensus.[84]

Custom is not an uncontroversial source of international law. For an international court to acknowledge a custom, it should be consistent, applied and generally accepted as law.[85] The practice that the Court identifies as reflecting European consensus is not necessarily reflective of a traditionally understood regional custom; for consensus, the practice of the Contracting Parties should not be long established and often the Court is satisfied with trends which show an ongoing legal transformation.[86] While it is justifiable for the Court to push certain trends forward

---

[81] Lupu, 'International Judicial Legitimacy', 444.

[82] *Hirsi Jamaa and others v. Italy*, Application No 27765/09, Judgment of 23 February 2012, para. 75.

[83] I. Ziemele, 'Customary International Law in the Case Law of the European Court of Human Rights – The Method', *Law and Practice of International Courts and Tribunals*, 12 (2013), 243, 246.

[84] Ibid., 248.

[85] J. Crawford, *Brownlie's Principles of Public International Law*, 8th edn (Oxford University Press, 2012), pp. 24–5.

[86] In the case of *Stanev v. Bulgaria*, the Court had to decide whether the Contracting Party could limit access to court to mentally handicapped individuals. The Court established that 'eighteen of the twenty national legal systems studied in this context provide for direct access to the courts for any partially incapacitated persons wishing to have their status reviewed. In seventeen States such access is open even to those declared fully incapable. This indicates that there is now a trend at European level towards granting legally incapacitated persons direct access to the courts to seek restoration of their capacity' (para. 243). After that, the Court stated that 'in the light of the foregoing, in particular the trends emerging in national legislation and the relevant international instruments, the Court considers that Article 6 § 1 of the Convention must be interpreted

and develop human rights, it makes European consensus more remote from the classical definition of custom.

It is clearly beyond the scope of this study to analyse the notion of custom in international law, but certain key features of international customs and European consensus match. The Court bases its conclusion about the presence or absence of consensus on the rules and current practice that exist in the Contracting Parties and are accepted as binding in their national legal systems. The same is true in relation to custom. As Tzevelekos concludes, '[i]f this [consensus] is not custom, then it is extremely close to it'.[87]

Cassese links European consensus to another source of international law mentioned in Article 38 of the ICJ Statute: the 'general principles of law recognised by the civilized nations'.[88] These principles, while being a subject of legal debate in terms of their definition, scope and function,[89] are often seen as the most fundamental governing postulates of national law that can be deployed in international law.[90] International courts use comparative data to establish general principles, and for that reason they are akin to European consensus.[91] Having said that, general principles can only partially explain European consensus.

The ECtHR sometimes deploys consensus at the level of principles as Chapter 2 suggested, and, in this case, European consensus can be conceptualised as a general principle of law. Principles can be understood as fundamental standards that require more precise rules to regulate a particular situation; principles can only point in a particular direction

as guaranteeing in principle that anyone who has been declared partially incapable, as is the applicant's case, has direct access to a court to seek restoration of his or her legal capacity' (para. 245). *Stanev* v. *Bulgaria*, Application No 36760/06, Judgment of 17 January 2012.

[87] V. Tzevelekos, 'The Making of International Human Rights Law' in C.-M. Brölmann and Y. Radi (eds.), *International Law-Making in a Post-National Setting* (forthcoming, 2015). The former president of the International Court of Justice Rosalyn Higgins, writing extrajudicially, points out that 'present-day conditions ... are to be found largely by reference to the developing practice of the member States themselves, in an approach that is now *well established*. This is not identical to the interpretation of obligations by reference to contemporary customary international law, but the underlying approach is very similar.' R. Higgins, 'Time and the Law: International Perspectives on an Old Problem', *International and Comparative Law Quarterly*, 46 (1997), 501, 517 (emphasis added).

[88] S. Cassese, 'The constellation of global and national courts: Jurisdictional redundancy and interchange' (on file with the author).

[89] See, for example, M.C. Bassiouni, 'A Functional Approach to "General Principles of International Law"', *Michigan Journal of International Law*, 11 (1989–1990), 768.

[90] Ibid., 771. [91] Ibid., 773.

6.3 INTERNATIONAL CONSTITUTIONAL CHALLENGES

and need an intermediary norm to be effective. For example, in the case of *D.H. v. the Czech Republic*, the Court established that there was consensus on the level of principles to confirm that national minorities should be effectively protected.[92] However, this general recognition must be translated into more precise rules. Such European consensus is similar to general principles of international law. However, if the Court looks for exact rules of how certain issues are regulated, then it is engaged in an exercise which is more akin to the establishment of a regional custom. In *A., B. and C. v. Ireland*, for example, the Court was looking for similarities in concrete rules regulating abortion.[93] In this case, the Court was not looking to establish the principle that the foetus' life or the mother's choice should be protected, but precise rules of how these principles were accommodated in the Contracting Parties.

It is not the purpose of this section to label European consensus as a custom or general principle of law. In terms of the legitimacy of international law, it is more important that European consensus can be logically connected to the sources of international law. The exact nature of these sources can depend on the type of consensus at stake, but, in any case, the Court's approach to consensus can be located within the structure of the sources of international law. This seems to enhance the process legitimacy of the ECtHR judgments as these judgments would not appear to be arbitrary because they are based on the sources of international law.

It is arguably not enough to link a particular argument to established sources of law; European consensus should also be seen as part of reasoning that is solidly grounded in law. Formalists argue that judges can legitimately demand to be obeyed only when 'their decisions stem from fair interpretation of commands laid down in the texts'.[94] While the judges have rather broad discretion in the application of constitutional norms,[95] judicial decision-making should nevertheless be conducted on a non-arbitrary basis.

---

[92] *D.H. and others v. the Czech Republic*, Application No 57325/00, Judgment of 13 November 2007, para. 181.

[93] *A., B. and C. v. Ireland*, Application No 25579/05, Judgment of 16 December 2010; *Tyrer v. the United Kingdom*, Application No 5856/72, Judgment of 25 April 1978, para. 112.

[94] F.H. Easterbrook, 'Method, Result, and Authority: A Reply', *Harvard Law Review*, 98 (1985), 622, 629.

[95] See, B.Z. Tamanaha, *Beyond the Formalist-Realist Divide* (Princeton University Press, 2010), pp. 79–84. King points out that judicial discretion will remain in any model. J.A. King, 'Institutional Approaches to Judicial Restraint', *Oxford Journal of Legal Studies*, 28 (2008), 409, 412; P. Pettit, 'Legitimate International Institutions: A Neo-Republican

In order to ensure that the judgments are not arbitrary, the Court has to provide clear reasons and explain why a particular State action does or does not violate the Convention. Çalı, Koch and Brunch argue that '[t]he only tool that the Court has to offset the risk of legitimacy erosion in advanced democracies is the reasoning structure of its judgments – and in this reasoning structure it should try not to upset domestic institutions'.[96] Process legitimacy theorists argue that the ECtHR can enhance its legitimacy through clear and consistent reasoning based on legal rules.[97] The legality of a decision does not fully explain legitimacy of decision-making. Legitimacy is a broader term than legality,[98] especially in circumstances where the legal basis is particularly thin.[99] Therefore, since consensus is based on legitimate norms, it can transfer legitimacy to the judgment of the Court.

European consensus is a solid reason for a particular decision due to at least two factors. First, by using European consensus, the Court creates an impression that it is constrained by a legal argument and instead of making political decisions just follows in the footsteps of what has been decided by the majority of the Contracting Parties. An international court enhances its legitimacy if it is seen to be constrained by objectively verified legal arguments.[100] Second, European consensus and the comparative law that it is based upon play an important informational role.[101] National judges are much better placed to predict the expectations of

---

Perspective' in S. Besson and J. Tasioulas (eds.), *The Philosophy of International Law* (Oxford University Press, 2010), p. 143.

[96] B. Çalı, A. Koch and N. Bruch, 'The Legitimacy of Human Rights Courts: A Grounded Interpretivist Analysis of the European Court of Human Rights', *Human Rights Quarterly*, 35 (2013), 955, 982.

[97] Dothan argues that '[t]he reasoning is a tool judges can use to serve their strategic goals to improve legitimacy'. Dothan, 'How International Tribunals Enhance Their Legitimacy', 468. Judge Corstens has pointed out that 'the Court must steer the protection of human rights by delivering clear and well-reasoned judgments that enable the domestic authorities and courts to ascertain how the Convention should be interpreted in specific cases'. G. Corstens, 'Address at the Seminar "The Convention Is Yours" Organised by the ECtHR' in *Dialogues between Judges* (Council of Europe, 2010), p. 11.

[98] See, D.M. Bodansky, 'The Concept of Legitimacy in International Law', *University of Georgia Research Paper Series*, 07–013 (2007), 1, 3.

[99] The norms of the Convention are imprecise and can sometimes lead to conflicting results.

[100] See, Dothan, 'How International Tribunals Enhance Their Legitimacy', 469.

[101] For a more detailed account of the informational role of comparative law, see, K. Dzehtsiarou and V. Lukashevich, 'Informed Decision-Making: The Comparative Endeavours of the Strasbourg Court', *Netherlands Quarterly of Human Rights*, 30 (2012), 272, 278–85.

their audiences;[102] European consensus can inform the ECtHR about these expectations, and this should prevent the Court from going beyond the legitimacy wall in its reasoning.

6.3.4 Subsidiarity

The Contracting Parties have urged the Court to take subsidiarity seriously.[103] The President of the ECtHR, Dean Spielmann, speaking extrajudicially, has pointed out that subsidiarity is a key structural principle for the Convention system.[104] Moreover, once Protocol 15 comes into force, a reference to subsidiarity will be included in the preamble to the Convention.[105] The link between the legitimacy of an international tribunal and its subsidiarity has been clearly made.[106] Subsidiarity can be understood in two senses: procedural and substantive. From the procedural point of view, subsidiarity means that the ECtHR can only come into play after the Contracting Parties have had a chance to remedy a human rights violation. This form of subsidiarity is covered by admissibility requirements enshrined in Article 35 of the Convention. While this understanding of subsidiarity can enhance the legitimacy of the ECtHR

---

[102] Lupu, 'International Judicial Legitimacy', 438.
[103] This point was made in all three declarations on the future of the ECtHR: Interlaken, Izmir and Brighton.
[104] D. Spielmann, 'Judgments of the European Court of Human Rights Effects and Implementation. Keynote Speech', available at http://www.echr.coe.int/Documents/Speech_20130920_Spielmann_Gottingen_ENG.pdf, accessed on 11 December 2013, 5.
[105] Pursuant to Article 1 of Protocol 15 at the end of the preamble to the Convention, a new recital will be added, which will read as follows: 'Affirming that the High Contracting Parties, in accordance with the principle of subsidiarity, have the primary responsibility to secure the rights and freedoms defined in this Convention and the Protocols thereto, and that in doing so they enjoy a margin of appreciation, subject to the supervisory jurisdiction of the European Court of Human Rights established by this Convention.'
[106] Helfer states that 'normatively, subsidiarity helps to legitimize ECtHR review by providing a measure of deference to national actors in situations where such deference is appropriate'. L.R. Helfer, 'Redesigning the European Court of Human Rights: Embeddedness as a Deep Structural Principle of the European Human Rights Regime', *European Journal of International Law*, 19 (2008), 125, 159. See also, P.G. Carozza, 'Subsidiarity as a Structural Principle of International Human Rights Law', *American Journal of International Law*, 97 (2003), 38; P. Mahoney, 'Universality versus Subsidiarity in the Strasbourg Case Law on Free Speech: Explaining Some Recent Judgments', *European Human Rights Law Review* (1997), 634; R. Ryssdal, 'The Coming of Age of the European Convention on Human Rights', *European Human Rights Law Review*, 1 (1996), 18, 24; M. Kumm, 'The Legitimacy of International Law: A Constitutionalist Framework of Analysis', *European Journal of International Law*, 15 (2004), 907, 920–1.

since procedural subsidiarity prevents the Court from replacing the national system of human rights protection, this understanding does not exhaust the meaning of subsidiarity.

Subsidiarity can be understood in a more substantive fashion. This means that the Court should not only follow the national system in procedural terms but also take into account the substance of the decision taken at a national level. The court is not there to substitute the decisions made on the national level but only to check if these decisions have violated human rights. This type of subsidiarity is much more complex and controversial and requires closer attention. Subsidiarity seems to imply a degree of judicial deference, and this is capable of underpinning the stability of the Strasbourg system. This section argues that European consensus is a tool of substantive subsidiarity which helps the Court to see when it can fine-tune the direction in which a particular State is developing in terms of human rights protection and bring it into line with common European developments.

European consensus is a tool of substantive subsidiarity which ensures that the Court takes the collective views of the Contracting Parties seriously.[107] In this context, European consensus can be conceptualised as a collectively accepted solution that gives the Court a green light to impose this solution on the diverging States once the majority has made up its mind. If such agreement has not been reached, the Court should not impose its own view on this human rights issue; in this sense, the ECHR is a subsidiary system to the decisions that are reached separately by the majority of the Contracting Parties.

This section has analysed the challenges to legitimacy posed by the fact that the ECtHR is an international tribunal. It has offered four different but interlinked justifications of how consensus can contribute to minimising the negative effect of these challenges: European consensus reflects the updated consent of the Contracting Parties, it facilitates dialogue between the Court and the Contracting Parties, it is linked to the sources of international law and it is a tool of substantive subsidiarity. In order to prove that European consensus does not provide an answer to some legitimacy challenges that the ECtHR is facing, opponents of

---

[107] Lübbe-Wolff argues that '[t]he doctrines developed in the case-law of the Court concerning national margins of appreciation and the role of consensus (not to be confused with unanimity) are abstract expressions of substantive subsidiarity'. G. Lübbe-Wolff, 'How Can the European Court of Human Rights Reinforce the Role of National Courts in the Convention System?' in *Dialogues between Judges* (Council of Europe, 2008), p. 15.

consensus must argue that none of these justifications is applicable to the ECtHR case law.

6.4 National constitutional challenges

This section deals with the challenges of legitimacy of the ECtHR which are similar to the ones that national constitutional courts face or may face. Some of these issues may resemble concerns discussed in the previous section. For instance, the issue of consent is not unknown to national constitutional courts.[108] However, it is clear that consent in the case of the ECtHR has a significant international law component – namely consent of the States, not consent of the individuals or the executives.

The ECHR provides that it is the Court that has the ultimate interpretive authority with regard to its provisions and their meanings.[109] Such an interpretive power places the Court at the heart of the process of developing the Convention and elucidating on the precise nature of State obligations under it. As a result, some argue that the Court itself has become a constitutional court.[110] For Wildhaber, this can be substantiated by three points: the Court's development from a bulwark against totalitarianism to something more akin to a domestic constitutional court adjudicating on daily issues of rights enforcement;[111] its promotion of core constitutional values of democracy and human rights; and its use of constitutionalism as an analytical tool to distinguish between adjudicatory decisions and more serious constitutional questions.[112] Constitutionalisation does not come without costs. The legitimacy of constitutional courts, including the ECtHR, can be challenged since they

---

[108] Petkova, 'The Notion of Consensus', 675. [109] ECHR, Article 32(1).
[110] See, Greer and Wildhaber, 'Revisiting the Debate'; S. Greer, *The European Convention on Human Rights. Achievements, Problems and Prospects*.
[111] L. Wildhaber, 'Rethinking the European Court of Human Rights' in J. Christoffersen and M.R. Madsen (eds.), *The European Court of Human Rights between Law and Politics* (Oxford University Press, 2011), pp. 226–7. See also, Bates, *The Evolution of the European Convention*.
[112] Wildhaber argues that this understanding of the constitutional nature of the Court is a reaction to the overwhelming backlog of mostly inadmissible and repetitive applications. Wildhaber, 'Rethinking the European Court'. See also, Greer, *The European Convention on Human Rights. Achievements, Problems and Prospects*; F. de Londras, 'Dual Functionality and the Persistent Frailty of the European Court of Human Rights', *European Human Rights Law Review*, 1 (2013), 38; Greer and Wildhaber, 'Revisiting the Debate'.

review decisions adopted by democratically elected national legislators[113] or even national constitutions.[114] This means that a body of judges that has never been tested against the majoritarian support can overrule something that was decided by a democratically legitimate government. This challenge is called the counter-majoritarian difficulty.[115] In legal scholarship, this difficulty is usually attributed to national constitutional judicial review; judicial review conducted by the ECtHR is somewhat similar.[116] Therefore, some analogies seem appropriate here.[117]

It should be noted that a counter-majoritarian difficulty usually emerges in cases where an unelected judiciary reviews laws adopted by a national parliament. The ECtHR does not only scrutinise laws adopted by the parliaments or people through referendums. In many cases, the ECtHR has found administrative or judicial practice to be in violation of the Convention.[118] However, this does not resolve the

---

[113] *Odièvre v. France*, Application No 42326/98, Judgment of 13 February 2003; *S.H. and others v. Austria*, Application No 57813/00, Judgment of 3 November 2011.

[114] *Sejdić and Finci v. Bosnia and Herzegovina*, Application No 27996/06 and 34836/06, Judgment of 22 December 2009; *A., B. and C. v. Ireland*.

[115] A. Stone, 'Judicial Review without Rights: Some Problems for the Democratic Legitimacy of Structural Judicial Review', *Oxford Journal of Legal Studies*, 28 (2008), 1, 1–2. See also, J. Waldron, 'Deliberation, Disagreement and Voting' in H.H. Koh and R.C. Slye (eds.), *Deliberative Democracy and Human Right* (Yale University Press, 1999); S.P. Croley, 'The Majoritarian Difficulty: Elective Judiciaries and the Rule of Law', *University of Chicago Law Review*, 65 (1995), 689; R. Bork, 'Neutral Principles and Some First Amendment Problems', *Indiana Law Journal*, 74 (1971), 10.

[116] It has been argued that constitutionalisation is an ongoing process within the Court and the ECtHR is more and more akin to a constitutional court of Europe. Greer, for instance, argues that 'the primary purpose of the judicial process is not to benefit individual applicants at all, but remains, as it always has been, to enable the Court to address the most serious defects with Convention compliance in Member States "constitutional justice"'. Greer, *The European Convention on Human Rights. Achievements, Problems and Prospects*, p. 59. See also, S. Gardbaum, 'Human Rights and International Constitutionalism' in J. Dunoff and J. Trachtman (eds.), *Ruling the World? Constitutionalism, International Law and Global Governance* (Cambridge University Press, 2009), p. 233; F. de Londras, 'The European Court of Human Rights, Dual Functionality, and the Future of the Court after Interlaken', *UCD Working Papers in Law, Criminology and Socio-Legal Studies Research Paper*, 45 (2011), available at http://ssrn.com/abstract=1773430, accessed on 7 July 2011. See also, Wildhaber, 'Rethinking the European Court'; Greer and Wildhaber, 'Revisiting the Debate'.

[117] Krisch, 'The Open Architecture', 184; Helfer, 'Redesigning the European Court', 127.

[118] For example, in *McCann and others v. the United Kingdom*, the Court considered whether the operation of the UK special forces was compliant with the Convention. *McCann and others v. the United Kingdom*, Application No 18984/91, Judgment of 27 September 1995. In *M.C. v. Bulgaria*, the Court considered the practice of the Bulgarian police to press charges against rapists only in cases where the victim physically resisted. *M.C. v. Bulgaria*, Application No 39272/98, Judgment of 4 December 2003.

6.4 NATIONAL CONSTITUTIONAL CHALLENGES

counter-majoritarian difficulty, as the mere ability of a tribunal to overrule a decision supported (at least in theory) by the majority might negatively affect support for the Court's rulings.

An academic debate on the role of judicial review in human rights protection is usually centred on the views of Waldron. This debate is particularly heated over the systems that have a strong judicial review of the American type.[119] In this type of review, the judges are able to strike down a piece of legislation they deem to be unconstitutional. However, this challenge is also discussed in the context of constitutional tribunals of European States, some of which have in place weak judicial review. This means that an act of parliament can be declared incompatible with the constitution or the ECHR but it does not automatically stop its application – an additional decision by the parliament is necessary.[120] The ECtHR also exercises weak judicial review because ultimately the judgments are implemented by the Contracting Parties through their legislative process, and they often retain wide discretion over how to implement these judgments. The counter-majoritarian difficulty cannot be fully applied to the ECtHR precisely due to the fact that it does not have the power to strike down any piece of legislation. This is so even despite the fact that the debate surrounding the legitimacy of the ECtHR questions whether it can interfere in 'internal matters' where national parliaments are the ultimate decision-makers.

---

[119] B. Friedman, 'The Counter-Majoritarian Problem and the Pathology of Constitutional Scholarship', *Northwestern University Law Review*, 95 (2001), 933, 932–45. 'Constitutional scholarship by law professors has been so intensely fixated on the counter-majoritarian difficulty, that the paradigm has been alternately referred to as an "obsession", a "preoccupation", and even a "platitude", by others within the academy.' A.M. Martens, 'Reconsidering Judicial Supremacy: From the Counter-Majoritarian Difficulty to Constitutional Transformations', *Perspectives on Politics*, 5 (2007), 447, 448. See also, R. Masterman, *The Separation of Powers in the Contemporary Constitution* (Cambridge University Press, 2011), p. 39.

[120] 'Counter-majoritarian difficulty' is discussed in relation to a few European constitutional courts: the German Constitutional Court in D.E. Finck, 'The United States Supreme Court versus the German Constitutional Court', *Boston College International and Comparative Law Review*, 20 (1997), 123, 130–1; the French Constitutional Council in M. Tushnet, 'Policy Distortion and Democratic Debilitation: Comparative Illumination of the Counter-Majoritarian Difficulty', *Michigan Law Review*, 94 (1995), 245, 250–75; 'counter-majoritarian difficulty' of judicial review under the Human Rights Act in the United Kingdom – see M.J. Perry, 'Protecting Human Rights in a Democracy: What Role for the Courts', *Wake Forest Law Review*, 38 (2003), 635, 667–70; for a comparison between some European constitutional courts and the US Supreme Court, see M. Rosenfeld, 'Constitutional Adjudication in Europe and the United States: Paradoxes and Contrasts', *International Journal of Constitutional Law*, 2 (2004), 633.

This section will first briefly discuss the debate of legitimacy of constitutional judicial review which mainly deals with the US Supreme Court. It will then consider whether certain challenges should be taken seriously by the ECtHR. Finally, this section will outline the role of consensus (or counting) in trumping counter-majoritarian difficulty. It is argued that European consensus and comparative law can inform the ECtHR about the democratic preferences of the Contracting Parties. This, in turn, helps the Court to show that it is mindful of these preferences by following European consensus.

In a nutshell, opponents of the judicial review of legislation argue that judicial review is undemocratic and therefore illegitimate. Waldron maintains that judges who are unelected and unaccountable cannot review the decisions of democratically elected bodies. Even if judges are appointed by elected officials, they are still less legitimate than the directly elected legislators.[121] According to Waldron, since rational disagreements are possible in relation to the content of rights, judges are called to make political decisions in the framework of judicial review. However, judges do not possess a democratic mandate to make such decisions. Waldron further suggests that the quality of the decisions produced by constitutional courts is no better than that of the decisions of parliaments; therefore, judicial decision-making is not preferable on grounds of quality.[122]

Those commentators who do not share Waldron's conviction tend to defend judicial review on the following grounds. First, judicial review offers a more objective and unbiased view than democratically elected governments, which have to be populist, at least to some extent. Kavanagh points out that

> [s]ince the court upholding an entrenched Bill of Rights has no interests of its own to further, and is relatively unaccountable to the various political interests in society, it can provide an impartial forum in which the issues can be decided in light of constitutional principles. This procedure is preferable precisely because judges are not directly affected by their own

---

[121] J. Waldron, 'The Core of the Case against Judicial Review', *Yale Law Journal*, 115 (2006), 1346, 1353.

[122] Waldron points out that '[t]he right answer as some sort of guiding star or objectively existing Holy Grail of inquiry does not distinguish the judge from the popular representative. I guess it is possible that someone might want to defend judicial review along the following line. At least judges often purport to seek the right answer about rights, whereas legislators seldom do; the legislative "inquiry" is almost always a cover for self-interest.' J. Waldron, 'Moral Truth and Judicial Review', *American Journal of Jurisprudence*, 43 (1998), 75, 82.

6.4 NATIONAL CONSTITUTIONAL CHALLENGES

decision. As unelected officials, they can provide a corrective to some of the energies which animate normal politics, such as those of political interest and power.[123]

Second, critics observe that Waldron expresses an overly simplistic and technical view of democracy.[124] Kavanagh argues that legitimacy does not suggest that all decision-making procedures should be designed in a purely majoritarian fashion.[125] Constitutional judicial review provides an 'additional layer of governmental accountability which allows individuals and groups to challenge executive (and possibly legislative) action'.[126] Lever suggests that democratic representation can be achieved through other means rather than only through universal suffrage.[127]

Third, Fallon uses a utilitarian argument, pointing out that judicial review helps to protect human rights and having courts with a veto power does enhance the legitimacy of the political system as the whole.[128] Finally, judicial review based on human rights is often unpopular because it allows the most 'unpopular' persons in society to be heard. It would be hard to do so through a normal political process.[129] For that reason, constitutional courts should use interpretation that is capable of

---

[123] A. Kavanagh, 'Participation and Judicial Review: A Reply to Jeremy Waldron', *Law and Philosophy*, 22 (2003), 451, 472.

[124] Kavanagh points out that 'procedural egalitarianism is different from equal consideration of people's interests. The latter is result-orientated, because it requires institutions that are most likely to respect people's interests equally. It refers to the output of political decisions, rather than the input and Waldron's focus is on the latter.' Kavanagh, 'Participation and Judicial Review', 453. Posner argues that 'Waldron is not sufficiently realistic about the legislative process. He has a too starry-eyed view of it.' R.A. Posner, 'Review of Jeremy Waldron, "Law and Disagreement"', *Columbia Law Review*, 100 (2000), 582, 590. Freeman maintains that democracy should not be simply understood in the sense of majoritarian procedures. Democracy also includes such principles as rule of law, civil liberties, and equalities of opportunities. S. Freeman, 'Constitutional Democracy and the Legitimacy of Judicial Review', *Law and Philosophy*, 9 (1990), 327, 367. Kyritsis points out that 'Waldron's challenge trades on an ambiguity regarding the relationship between legislators and their constituents and the concept of representation that this relationship is based on. More specifically, it underestimates the distance between them.' D. Kyritsis, 'Representation and Waldron's Objection to Judicial Review', *Oxford Journal of Legal Studies*, 26 (2006), 733, 740.

[125] Kavanagh, 'Participation and Judicial Review', 457.

[126] Masterman, *The Separation of Powers*, p. 41.

[127] A. Lever, 'Is Judicial Review Undemocratic?', *Public Law* (2007), 280, 286–7.

[128] R. Fallon, 'The Core of an Uneasy Case for Judicial Review', *Harvard Law Review*, 121 (2008), 1693, 1699.

[129] A. Kavanagh, *Constitutional Review under the UK Human Rights Act* (Cambridge University Press, 2009), p. 341.

improving their legitimacy – this will help to ensure diffuse support for even unpopular decisions.

One of the ways to counter the arguments of illegitimacy of the decisions of the courts of constitutional review is to ground them solidly in the law that these courts are designed to enforce. It has been argued on a number of occasions that diffuse support for courts increases if they are seen as rules-bound and not political actors.[130] The counter-majoritarian difficulty is complicated by the fact that the discretion of the judges in constitutional adjudication is not sufficiently limited by rules.[131] The counter-majoritarian difficulty can be confronted by including European consensus in the decision-making, which is not only an (at least in theory) objectively verified argument but also one linked to democracy and majoritarian decision-making. While this feature of European consensus has become the main reason for its criticism, it is capable of bringing some democratic credentials to the decisions of constitutional courts. Even though the deployment of European consensus is not a suitable response to all constitutional challenges, it reduces some pressure on the ECtHR. The US Supreme Court often uses the same tactic to reduce the pressure on its legitimacy.

It would perhaps be more justifiable if the ECtHR is compared with a constitutional court from one of the Contracting Parties to the Convention. However, this is hardly possible due to the fact that either most European federal States are formed of too few regions and so counting would not bring any meaningful results,[132] or competences of the regions are so limited that key rules are adopted on the federal level and can only be slightly amended by the regions.[133] For this reason, this section will first outline counting as it is conducted by the US Supreme Court and then briefly analyse the debate surrounding it.

The US Supreme Court is comparable to the ECtHR for the following reasons.[134] First, the US is a federal State with diverse state legislation and a clear divide between federal and state powers. This makes the decision-making of the ECtHR in terms of European consensus/counting

---

[130] See, Gibson, Caldeira and Spence, 'Why Do People Accept Public Policies They Oppose?', 188; and Lupu, 'International Judicial Legitimacy', 444.

[131] R. Dworkin, *Taking Rights Seriously* (Harvard University Press, 1977), p. 84.

[132] For example, Bosnia and Herzegovina or Belgium.

[133] For example, Germany or Russia.

[134] On a more general issue of fruitfulness of comparison between international and national courts, see, J.K. Staton and W.H. Moore, 'Judicial Power in Domestic and International Politics', *International Organization*, 65 (2011), 553, 556-7.

6.4 NATIONAL CONSTITUTIONAL CHALLENGES

somewhat similar to the US Supreme Court. Both can rely on analysis of differences or similarities between the States (either Contracting Parties in the case of the ECtHR or US states in the case of the US Supreme Court). Second, the ECtHR and the US Supreme Court have to decide real and hard cases on the basis of outdated definitions of vague Bills of Rights, and both have been criticised for being counter-majoritarian.[135] Third, both courts are involved in dynamic interpretation, under the banner of either evolutive interpretation or living constitutionalism.[136] Both courts feel the need to rely on something more stable than simply the judges' conviction that society has changed in order to be able to confront counter-majoritarian difficulty. Therefore, they resort to counting.

The US Supreme Court has used counting on a number of occasions. In *Lawrence*, the US Supreme Court struck down a Texas statute criminalising homosexual intercourse, overturning its own previous decision in *Bowers* v. *Hardwick*.[137] This judgment does not take into account the fact that such laws had been part of the history and tradition of the United States,[138] emphasising instead an 'emerging awareness' over the past 50 years that 'liberty gives substantial protection to adult persons in deciding how to conduct their private lives in matters pertaining to sex'.[139] The US Supreme Court used counting to justify this finding. Since *Bowers*, the number of states with laws of this nature has reduced from 24 to 13, and even in the remaining states there is a pattern of non-enforcement against consenting adults acting in private.[140] Thus, the court in *Lawrence* was influenced both by consensus and by developments across states of the union in a remarkably similar way to *Dudgeon*.[141] It is worth pointing out that the ECtHR deployed

---

[135] The US Constitution is more outdated but this does not change the argument.
[136] K. Dzehtsiarou and C. O'Mahony, 'Evolutive Interpretation of Rights Provisions: A Comparison of the European Court of Human Rights and the US Supreme Court', *Columbia Human Rights Law Review*, 44 (2013), 309, 316.
[137] *Bowers* v. *Hardwick*, 478 US 186 (1986).
[138] Justice Scalia dissented in *Lawrence* partly on the basis that 'an "emerging awareness" is by definition "not deeply rooted in this Nation's history and tradition[s]", as we have said "fundamental right" status requires'. *Lawrence* v. *Texas*, 539 US 558 (2003), 598.
[139] Ibid., 572.
[140] Ibid., 573. It should be noted that consensus, while cited by the Court to support its decision, was not the decisive factor. For a variety of reasons relating to the analysis in the judgment concerning the relationship between law and morality, the Court concluded that *Bowers* 'was not correct when it was decided, and it is not correct today'. Ibid., 578.
[141] Ibid., 573.

European consensus in *Dudgeon*.[142] *Lawrence* is not the only case in which the US Supreme Court has deployed counting, and the US Supreme Court's counting practice is well documented.[143]

The fact that the interpretation settled on by the court enjoyed widespread support in other states across the United States makes ultimate acceptance of the court's evolutive interpretation significantly more likely.[144] It can be seen that where interpretation of a provision is based on consensus, the court handing down the decision is following rather than leading public opinion. Sunstein argues that

> the Supreme Court sometimes entrenches a new constitutional principle or a novel understanding of an old principle. But even when it does so, it is never acting in a social vacuum. Often it is endorsing, fairly late, a judgment that has long attracted widespread social support from many minds.[145]

The practice of consensus identification is generally accepted by the judges. They are mostly concerned not with counting itself but rather with how counting is done. Justice Scalia of the US Supreme Court has famously pointed out that the US Supreme Court is selective in its counting. He said that 'all the Court has done today ... is to look over the heads of the crowd and pick out its friends'.[146] Concerns about the sub-optimal methodology of consensus identification have been voiced by judges[147] and academics[148] in relation to the ECtHR practice of

---

[142] *Dudgeon v. the United Kingdom*, Application No 7525/76, Judgment of 23 September 1981, para. 60.

[143] 'State Law as "Other Law": Our Fifty Sovereigns in the Federal Constitutional Canon', *Harvard Law Review*, 120 (2007), 1670, 1674–9; Petkova, 'The Notion of Consensus', 676–9.

[144] See, K. Dzehtsiarou, 'European Consensus and the Evolutive Interpretation of the European Convention on Human Rights', *German Law Journal*, 12 (2011), 1730.

[145] C.R. Sunstein, *A Constitution of Many Minds* (Princeton University Press, 2009), p. 4. Sunstein argues that *Brown* v. *Board of Education* is an example of this pattern: 'By 1954, the American public was no longer committed to racial segregation, and there can be little doubt that most of the nation and its leaders rejected it ... We can see *Brown* as a case in which national experience, including moral growth over time, led to an understanding of the Constitution's equality principle that would not have been possible a few decades earlier.' Ibid., p. 41. Similar arguments have been made by J.M. Balkin, *Living Originalism* (Harvard University Press, 2011).

[146] *Roper v. Simmons* (2005) 543 US 551, 617 (Scalia J., dissenting).

[147] Dissenting Opinion of Judges Tulkens, Cabral Barreto, Fura-Sandström, Spielmann and Jebens. *D.H. and others v. the Czech Republic*; Dissenting Opinion of Judge Jungwiert, *D. H. and others v. the Czech Republic*.

[148] Y. Arai-Takahashi, *The Margin of Appreciation Doctrine and the Principle of Proportionality in the Jurisprudence of the ECHR* (Intersentia, 2002), pp. 196–7; L.R.

counting. However, this does not undermine the value of properly identified consensus as an instrument that enhances the legitimacy of a constitutional tribunal.

It seems that the practice of counting reduces the pressure of counter-majoritarian difficulty. This means that if the court grounds its decision-making on consensus, it ensures that there is popular support for its decision. It also means that the courts have to overcome certain difficulties. For example, Jacoby argues that the practice of counting states is a violation of the separation of powers between the federal government and the states because, with counting, the court actually removes certain powers from the states simply because this practice does not conform to the majority.[149] It was also argued that the fact that a particular rule is widely accepted by the states does not mean that this rule is indeed supported by the majority of US citizens.[150] Despite these limitations, counting does create an impression, if not of a real acceptance, at least of a perceived acceptance of a particular rule.[151] This, in turn, improves the legitimacy of the rulings, or, in other words, it allows diffuse support for the decisions of the court.

6.5 Conclusion

The ECtHR is a foreign court which can find a legal norm or practice adopted by the democratically elected national representatives to be incompatible with the ECHR. This creates two tiers of legitimacy challenges: international and national. The ECtHR has to respond to these challenges to continue to be an effective decision-maker in human rights adjudication.

The original legitimacy of the ECtHR cannot justify every judgment, especially if the Court deploys evolutive interpretation. In these circumstances, the ECtHR has to look for other sources of legitimisation. This chapter argues that European consensus is such a source because it can be conceptualised as an updated implied consent of the States, it

---

Helfer, 'Consensus, Coherence and the European Convention on Human Rights', *Cornell International Law Journal*, 23 (1993), 133, 164.

[149] T. Jacoby, 'The Subtle Unraveling of Federalism: The Illogic of Using State Legislation as Evidence of an Evolving National Consensus', *North Carolina Law Review*, 84 (2006), 1089, 1092.

[150] 'State Law as "Other Law"', 1685.

[151] Petkova argues that the US Supreme Court started using counting as a response to accusations 'of ignoring public opinion'. Petkova, 'The Notion of Consensus', 678.

facilitates the dialogue between the Court and the Contracting Parties and it ensures that the States participate in a decision-making process and that the Court honours its subsidiary role. European consensus can also be linked to the sources of international law, and this increases the legality of the judgments where consensus was deployed. Finally, European consensus adds a democratic mandate to the 'counter-majoritarian' judgments of the ECtHR.

7

European consensus

Perceptions of the ECtHR judges

7.1 Introduction

This chapter summarises the interviews conducted with the 33 former and currently sitting judges of the European Court of Human Rights (ECtHR or Court) who agreed to talk to the author about European consensus and who explained their perceptions and ideas about the comparative law method deployed by the ECtHR.

Section 7.2 of this chapter explains the methodology of the research and what it was aiming to achieve. All interviews were semi-structured; there was not a strict set of questions but rather a number of topics that were discussed with the judges.

The research design employed was set up to test a set of three hypotheses. The first hypothesis was that the judges of the ECtHR consider European consensus to be a legitimate tool of interpretation. Since legitimacy is a multifaceted concept, the judges were not asked about legitimacy directly. Instead, all judges were asked why the ECtHR deployed European consensus in its reasoning. Even though legitimacy was not mentioned in the questions, some judges acknowledged that enhancing legitimacy was a key function of consensus. Section 7.3 of the chapter therefore explores the reasons why the Court deploys consensus.

The second hypothesis was that European consensus is a persuasive argument affecting the judgments of the ECtHR. To verify this hypothesis, the judges were asked questions about their personal perception of European consensus and whether they thought that the deployment of European consensus could persuade the Contracting Parties to execute the judgment of the ECtHR. Section 7.4 explores two levels of persuasive effect of European consensus: on the judges of the ECtHR and on the Contracting Parties.

The third and final hypothesis was that the judges of the Court do not accept European consensus unconditionally. Two types of challenges related to consensus were considered in this part. The first are the challenges that the judges face at the stage of identification of consensus. Questions about the appropriateness of comparative analyses conducted by the ECtHR were asked in order to determine whether the judges were satisfied with the materials they received from the Research Division of the Court. Moreover, judges were asked if these materials could or should be complemented by third-party interventions. The second are the challenges associated with the application of European consensus. Questions about the appropriateness of European consensus in human rights adjudication were posed in order to reveal the judges' perceptions of this matter. Sections 7.5 and 7.6 deal with these two challenges, respectively.

7.2 Research design and methodology

The judges of the ECtHR have not been asked about their views on the European consensus argument before, nor have their answers been incorporated into a published academic article or monograph.[1] Some judges have expressed general views in their extrajudicial writings,[2] but an in-depth qualitative survey of the judges' approach to European consensus had not been conducted prior to this research. Such a survey might shed light on what the judges of the Court consider to be the rationale behind the European consensus argument. The survey was conducted by means of interviews with the judges of the Court and the lawyers of the Court's Registry. The aim of the interviews was to find out whether the judges and lawyers considered European consensus to be a legitimising tool. In this aspect of the research, the choice was made not to focus on the attitude of national stakeholders, such as national lawyers, judges and governments, but instead to concentrate on those 'within' the ECtHR, namely the judges of the Court and the lawyers of the Registry. While national stakeholders' perceptions of European consensus are important in order to assess the perceived legitimacy of European

---

[1] Only English-language sources were taken into account for this statement.
[2] See, R. Ryssdal, 'The Coming of Age of the European Convention on Human Rights', *European Human Rights Law Review*, 1 (1996), 18; C. Rozakis, 'The European Judge as Comparatist', *Tulane Law Review*, 80 (2005), 257; L. Wildhaber, 'The European Convention on Human Rights and International Law', *International and Comparative Law Quarterly*, 56 (2007), 217; L. Wildhaber, A. Hjartarson and S. Donnelly, 'No Consensus on Consensus? The Practice of the European Court of Human Rights', *Human Rights Law Journal*, 33 (2013), 248.

7.2 RESEARCH DESIGN AND METHODOLOGY

consensus within the Member States,[3] they cannot directly influence the application of European consensus by the Court itself. In contrast, the judges of the ECtHR can avoid using European consensus if they perceive it to be illegitimate. Moreover, the judges are usually well placed to assess how certain arguments are perceived by the stakeholders in their respective countries. This perception can to some degree predetermine their own attitude to European consensus.

While the focus is on the judges' perceptions of European consensus, the present research does not underestimate the role of the Court's Registry in drafting the judgments.[4] The decision in a case is made by the judges of the Court; however, the draft of the judgment is normally prepared by the Court's Registry.[5] Therefore, the Deputy Registrar of the Court, Michael O'Boyle, was interviewed for this research project. Approaching other lawyers of the Registry was complicated, and those who agreed to be interviewed specifically asked not to be recorded and/or mentioned by name in relation to this research. Besides Michael O'Boyle, fifteen other lawyers of the Registry were interviewed.[6]

The author approached 50 judges of the ECtHR and requested an interview. The interviews were conducted between 2008 and 2014, mainly in Strasbourg. The selection process was made on the basis of the broad geographical representation of the States the judges were elected from, their gender and their lengths of experience as judges of the Court. The initial research plan did not aim to interview all of the 47 sitting judges of the Court due to the complicated process of setting up an interview. Nonetheless, it can be asserted that the 33 judges[7] of the Court who were subsequently interviewed represented a substantive sample of the Court's judiciary, which was big enough to draw conclusions about the judges' perceptions of European consensus. It cannot be said that the

---

[3] B. Çalı, A. Koch and N. Bruch, 'The Legitimacy of the European Court of Human Rights: The View from the Ground' (2011), available at http://ecthrproject.files.wordpress.com/2011/04/ecthrlegitimacyreport.pdf, accessed on 23 July 2014, p. 6.

[4] The role of the Registry is officially acknowledged by Protocol 14, which established the role of non-judicial rapporteur. According to Article 26 of the Convention, when sitting in a single-judge formation, the Court will be assisted by rapporteurs, who will function under the authority of the President of the Court. They will form part of the Court's Registry.

[5] The author's experience as a trainee lawyer at the ECtHR.

[6] Among the lawyers interviewed, there were filtering lawyers dealing mainly with inadmissible applications, as well as more experienced lawyers dealing with the Chamber and Grand Chamber cases.

[7] See the list of judges interviewed with the dates and lengths of interviews attached in Appendix 1.

author interviewed 33 judges out of 47 sitting judges of the Court as some of the judges had retired from the bench. On a few occasions, two judges elected from the same country were interviewed.[8]

The interview as a tool of research was deliberately chosen for this project. Questionnaires submitted to the judges could have been an alternative to interviews in revealing their perceptions of European consensus. However, interviews are generally seen as a more satisfactory tool of research despite the fact that they are more time and resource demanding.[9] Interviews were chosen since it could not be guaranteed that the judges would fill out the questionnaires themselves. These questionnaires could easily have been ignored or filled out by interns or assistants. In the case of an interview, this potential drawback is excluded since the judges were interviewed personally by the author.[10]

However, a difficulty that interviews as an empirical research tool face is that it cannot be guaranteed that the informants are revealing their genuine motives for the application of European consensus. Epstein and King point out that

> asking someone to identify his or her motive is one of the worst methods of measuring motive. People often do not know, or cannot articulate, why they act as they do. In other situations, they refuse to tell, and in still others, they are strategic both in acting and in answering the scholar's question. This is obvious from the example of asking justices about how they reach decisions.[11]

---

[8] For example, two judges elected from the Netherlands were interviewed: Judge Myjer and Judge Silvis.

[9] For a comparison of the advantages and disadvantages of interviews and other empirical methods of research, see, D.C. Miller and N.J. Salkind, *Handbook of Research Design and Social Measurement*, 6th edn (Sage Publications, 2002), p. 301–12; J.D. Brewer, *The A–Z of Social Research: A Dictionary of Key Social Science Research Concepts* (Sage Publications, 2003), pp. 253–5. For instance, among the advantages of the personal interview method, Miller and Salkind mention the possibility of explaining questions if they are unclear, and the more spontaneous answers of the respondents. Higher costs and lower response rates are mentioned among the disadvantages of interviews. Moreover, the personal interview usually takes more time than other empirical methods. Miller and Sankind, *Handbook of Research Design*, pp. 310–1.

[10] Brewer points out that, at the interview, '[o]ne can ensure that the correct (sampled) person gives the responses. A respondent can easily hand a questionnaire to someone else and ask them to fill it in for them.' Brewer, *The A–Z of Social Research*, p. 254.

[11] L. Epstein and G. King, 'The Rules of Inference', *University of Chicago Law Review*, 69 (2002), 1, 93. See also B. Flanagan and S. Ahern, 'Judicial Decision-Making and Transnational Law: A Survey of Common Law Supreme Court Judges', *International and Comparative Law Quarterly*, 60 (2011) 1, 7; J. Segal and H. Spaeth, 'The Authors Respond', *Law and Courts*, 4 (1994), 3, 16.

To minimise this problem, some empirical researchers guarantee that their informants will not be identified.[12] The approach taken in the present research was quite different. The informants were warned that their names might be revealed upon their consent and some parts of their interviews would be quoted with a view to increasing the transparency of the research. It was decided to request specific consent from each judge who was quoted in the book and who was still acting as a judge of the ECtHR in 2014. The author received mixed responses from the judges. A significant number of the judges agreed for their names to be revealed. Having said that, some judges preferred to remain unnamed while they were still on the bench. In the interests of consistency, it was decided to encode the names of all sitting judges of the ECtHR who were interviewed for this project.

Nevertheless, it can be argued that the motives of the judges are quite objectively outlined in this research. First, the interview format increased the chances that the judges would provide an objective account of their motives and perceptions. Bailey points out that unpreparedness of the informant is one of the advantages of interviews: 'The respondent does not have the chance to retract his or her first answer and write another.'[13] Moreover, the judges were not informed about the list of questions to be asked at the interview, and therefore they answered spontaneously, which arguably increased the fairness of their responses. Before their interviews, most of the judges were merely informed about a general topic of discussion, namely European consensus, and were not provided with any further details of the interview. Second, the interviews were conducted in a semi-structured format.[14] The judges were asked to speak

---

[12] Flanagan and Ahern, 'Judicial Decision-Making', 7–8.

[13] K.D. Bailey, *Methods of Social Research* (Free Press, 1994), p. 174.

[14] For a description of semi-structured interviews, see T. Wengraf, *Qualitative Research Interviewing: Biographic Narrative and Semi-Structured Methods* (Sage Publications, 2001), p. 5; S. Kvale, *Interviews: An Introduction to Qualitative Research Interviewing* (Sage Publications, 1996); I. Dobinson and F. Johns, 'Qualitative Legal Research' in M. McConville and W.H. Chui (eds.), *Research Methods for Law* (Edinburgh University Press, 2007). Wengraf points out that '[s]emi-structured interviews are designed to have a number of interviewer questions prepared in advance but such prepared questions are designed to be sufficiently open that the subsequent questions of the interviewer cannot be planned in advance but must be improvised in a careful and theorized way. As regards such semi-structured interviews, they are ones where research and planning produce a session in which most of the informant's responses cannot be predicted in advance and where you as interviewer therefore have to improvise probably half and maybe 80% or more of your responses to what they say in response to your initial prepared question or questions.' Wengraf, *Qualitative Research Interviewing*, p. 5.

freely about their perceptions of European consensus. In this format, the judges sometimes expressed unexpected opinions about European consensus.[15] Of course, it is hardly possible to negate all bias that can impact the motives of the judges. Some responses were perhaps influenced by the judges' loyalty to their colleagues, their position within the Court's structure and other reasons. The fact that 33 interviews were conducted and the judges expressed a variety of views about European consensus significantly reduced the effect of any individual bias on the research project overall.

The majority of the interviews was digitally recorded. These interviews were subsequently transcribed, and then the scripts were sent to the judges for comments and editing. The scripts were then analysed, and the most representative quotes were included in the text below. At the final stage of preparation, all sitting judges were asked to confirm that these quotes properly reflected their views about consensus.

7.3 Why does the Court use European consensus?

All judges interviewed for this project were asked questions about the reasons why the Court deployed European consensus. The answers can be divided into two groups. These answers are not mutually exclusive but highlight a particular aspect of European consensus. Some judges pointed out that European consensus was simply an inherent and natural argument for the Court as a regional human rights court. Other judges argued that consensus was deployed to fulfil a particular function in the Court's reasoning. This section will first present the former argument and then turn to the discussion of the functions of European consensus as seen by the judges of the ECtHR.

Many judges pointed out that European consensus was an instrument which was inherent in the character of both the ECtHR as a regional court, and the European Convention on Human Rights (ECHR or Convention) as a regional human rights treaty. Judge Jaeger observed that

> [w]e use it [European consensus] because we are the European court. That is a simple answer. If you are a national court – you are looking into

---

[15] For instance, Judge Jaeger mentioned the possibility of a respondent State implementing solutions adopted by other European States outlined by the Court in its comparative research. K. Dzehtsiarou, *Interview with Judge Renate Jaeger* (European Court of Human Rights, Strasbourg, 2010). The author did not consider this possibility when this project was initially planned.

national law, you also look into national policy or politics... But if you are a European court we are looking into different countries.[16]

According to some judges, it was the nature of the Convention to discover and maintain high standards of human rights protection, and therefore the Court deployed European consensus. Judge 4 observed that

> there is some serious reason for seeking such guidance [from the Contracting Parties through European consensus] and that would be the setting of generally applicable standards for the entire continent. The very idea of the Convention and countries acceding to it is to maintain at the general level an equally high standard of respect to human rights in all the different countries ... The necessity ... should be seen in the attempt of the Court and the goal of the Court to maintain the same standard of application of the Convention throughout all Member States.[17]

Judge Kovler shared the same opinion as Judge 4 and added that European consensus allowed the Court to use common approaches in interpreting the Convention.[18] For Judge 9, 'the Convention is itself a product of a comparative study'.[19] Judge 12 also emphasised that

> [y]ou are in an international court; the jurisprudence 20–30 years ago was practically non-existent. From what source did you plug information to inform your values, to inform your interpretation? If you are a judge, if you are a curious lawyer, when dealing with a matter you would want to know things such as – what is the French position, for instance? You will get this information from your fellow judges; they will be speaking about their own systems. That is not a haphazard. The first answer for me is that it is a natural process for a lawyer to want to know the law in other countries.[20]

This suggests that the nature of the ECtHR and the ECHR is a precondition of deployment of the European consensus argument.

Some judges attempted to justify deployment of European consensus not merely through references to the natural fit of European consensus to the ECtHR but also through analysis of the functions of consensus. These judges mentioned the following functions in their interviews:

---

[16] Ibid.
[17] K. Dzehtsiarou, *Interview with Judge 4* (European Court of Human Rights, Strasbourg).
[18] K. Dzehtsiarou, *Interview with Judge Kovler* (European Court of Human Rights, Strasbourg, 2009).
[19] K. Dzehtsiarou, *Interview with Judge 9* (European Court of Human Rights, Strasbourg).
[20] K. Dzehtsiarou, *Interview with Judge 12* (European Court of Human Rights, Strasbourg).

1. enhancing the legitimacy of the ECtHR especially in cases in which the ECtHR deployed evolutive interpretation;
2. persuading the Contracting Parties and making the judgments more acceptable;
3. avoiding arbitrary decision-making (i.e. when the judges imposed their personal moral views on the Contracting Parties);
4. determining the scope of the margin of appreciation; and
5. assisting the Court in dealing with novel issues of interpretation (of the Convention) or issues of particular importance or controversy.

Some of these functions can overlap; some judges listed more than one function that consensus strived to fulfil. This classification only shows that different judges placed emphasis on different aspects of consensus. These functions are now discussed in turn.

First, some of the judges emphasised enhancement of legitimacy as the key function of the European consensus argument. Judge 14 pointed out that

> [t]he idea of European consensus somehow emerged in the Court's case law. The first idea that comes to one's mind is the idea of legitimacy. If there is consensus then the decision or the verdict is legitimate because everyone agrees.[21]

For Judge 17, 'European consensus assessment is a method which is important in finding justice and obtaining legitimacy for a certain outcome of the case'.[22] Judge 11 linked legitimacy, evolutive interpretation and European consensus, emphasising that European consensus made the Court's conclusions more persuasive for the stakeholders. She pointed out that

> [t]he reason why [the Court deploys European consensus] is that the European Convention is a living instrument. If interpreted in that way as it would have been interpreted in the [19]50s it would be a dead instrument. So, there is a Convention that has to be adapted but the question is how it should be adapted. We cannot take decisions from the air – and here we have a question about legitimacy. The Court has to find convincing arguments of how the values changed.[23]

One of the functions of legitimacy is to persuade the losing party to execute and abide by the judgment of the Court.[24] Judge 12 stated that

---

[21] K. Dzehtsiarou, Interview with Judge 14 (European Court of Human Rights, Strasbourg).
[22] K. Dzehtsiarou, Interview with Judge 17 (European Court of Human Rights, Strasbourg).
[23] K. Dzehtsiarou, Interview with Judge 11 (European Court of Human Rights, Strasbourg).
[24] See, for example, L.R. Helfer and A.-M. Slaughter, 'Toward a Theory of Effective Supranational Adjudication', Yale Law Journal, 107 (1997), 273, 317.

7.3 WHY DOES THE COURT USE EUROPEAN CONSENSUS?

European consensus helped to 'legitimise judgments of the international court'.[25] Some of the judges did not discuss the legitimacy of the judgments but rather mentioned the persuasiveness of the judgments in which European consensus had been deployed. The second function of European consensus is to persuade the Contracting Parties to accept the judgment of the Court.

Judge 18 emphasised that acceptance of the ECtHR judgments was the key reason for deployment of European consensus:

> The Court is very careful and it is very much concerned with the acceptance of its judgments. So, if it embarks on uncharted waters it is very important to have a look at the evolution of society and how Member States deal with similar issues in order to make a decision acceptable, not only for the State concerned but also for other Member States who have similar problems.[26]

Judge 6 also expressed a similar idea, stating that 'when a national court[27] attempts to reach a decision on an issue involving "an essentially contested concept", that decision is thought to be more persuasive whenever the court is able to demonstrate that most of the world, or at least Europe, adheres to that perception which is supported by that court'.[28] According to Judge Tulkens:

> The rationale behind it [deployment of European consensus] seems to be that for the judgment to be accepted by the States they should be in the mainstream. And that is a practical rationale because our case law should be accepted by the States. So, we have to progress gradually, pedagogically. So, we have to accompany the movement unless it is obvious. We do not want to create some resistance.[29]

The third function that was mentioned by the judges was that European consensus either created an impression of non-arbitrary decision-making from the Court or reduced the overly broad discretion of the judges. Judges Rozakis, Myjer and Judge 8 claimed that the judges should not merely impose their personal moral beliefs on the Contracting Parties

---

[25] Dzehtsiarou, *Interview with Judge 12*.
[26] K. Dzehtsiarou, *Interview with Judge 18* (European Court of Human Rights, Strasbourg).
[27] Judge 6 was mainly talking about national courts in this particular quote but it seems that the same principle is applicable to the ECtHR. K. Dzehtsiarou, *Interview with Judge 6* (European Court of Human Rights, Strasbourg).
[28] Ibid.
[29] K. Dzehtsiarou, *Interview with Judge Françoise Tulkens* (European Court of Human Rights, Strasbourg, 2010).

but also back up their findings with evidence. Judge Rozakis observed that

> knowing that European States should abide by our judgments, respect them and execute what we impose on them; what we really do not want to do is legislate – we do not want to impose on the States what is totally unknown to them. These matters make us to look out and see, in the particular circumstances of a specific case, what are the answers given on this matter by European States. For instance, let us take bioethics which is a relatively novel issue in Europe – artificial insemination. To decide simply and purely on the basis of our own consciousness, saying that we feel that within this practice or procedure there has been a violation on the part of the State – by not allowing people to enter into artificial insemination would be enslaving in a way. In order to avoid that, knowing that we harmonise rules on the European level, we have to look around and ask – do they accept that?[30]

Judge Myjer also condemned arbitrary and groundless decision-making in the following terms:

> I am one of those who believe that the biggest danger for the Court is that it turns into a purely academic church of human rights believers who say that we preach the new Gospel of human rights. What we consider from our purest internal conviction as the biggest failures in Europe should not be pronounced and followed in all of Europe.[31]

Judge 8 observed that

> [we use consensus] in order not to give an impression that we are dealing with things in a very abstract way – in an ivory tower. I think that it is very important to send a message to an outside world that we know, or at least tend to know, what is going on in the various Member States of the Council of Europe. It is very important to know in what sense an international court should decide to stay in touch with what is going on in Europe.[32]

It seems that some judges saw European consensus as a tool that could persuade the stakeholders that the decision was not made arbitrarily and that it was not merely the personal point of view of seven[33] or seventeen[34] judges.

---

[30] K. Dzehtsiarou, *Interview with Judge Christos Rozakis* (European Court of Human Rights, Strasbourg, 2010).
[31] K. Dzehtsiarou, *Interview with Judge Egbert Myjer* (European Court of Human Rights, Strasbourg, 2009).
[32] K. Dzehtsiarou, *Interview with Judge 8* (European Court of Human Rights, Strasbourg).
[33] Pursuant to Article 26, the Chamber of the Court should consist of seven judges.
[34] There are 17 judges sitting in every Grand Chamber case.

7.3 WHY DOES THE COURT USE EUROPEAN CONSENSUS? 187

Fourth, some judges perceived European consensus only as a tool of interpretation that predominantly determined the scope of the margin of appreciation. Judges Garlicki and Malinverni and Judges 10, 15 and 17 expressed the opinion that the key purpose of European consensus was to shape the scope of the margin of appreciation. Judge Garlicki pointed out that

> [s]ometimes we use it [European consensus] to say that there is no violation because what the State did was within the margin of appreciation, or sometimes we involve the margin of appreciation in the reasoning but say that unfortunately this particular action or situation is not covered by what margin of appreciation leaves to the States. There are, of course, different criteria by which to determine whether this margin of appreciation should be wider or narrower in a particular situation, but the existence of European consensus or common ground/trend can determine the width of the margin of appreciation.[35]

Judge 17 commented that the presence of European consensus narrowed the margin of appreciation, but that there might still be some discretionary room left. He maintained that 'the Court's view is that whenever there is a consensus the margin of appreciation of the State will be limited. However, the State not being in line with such consensus does not automatically imply that there is a violation to be found. The Court has to take into account all relevant aspects of the case.'[36]

Judge Malinverni observed that 'the question of European consensus is mainly related to the limits of the margin of appreciation of the States'.[37] For Judge 10, the key interpretative value of European consensus was as a middle ground between evolutive interpretation and the margin of appreciation. He commented that

> [t]he concepts in the Convention are not crystal clear. Consequently, there is always an issue of interpretation involved, in particular, when we are facing new issues. There is this old discussion about, on the one hand, the need for the Convention to be a living instrument, and on the other hand, the need to take into account States' margin of appreciation and to be in a field where people would perceive the solution as clearly a human rights issue. And, in that balance there is a European consensus or an evolving European consensus which is a tool that offers some

---

[35] K. Dzehtsiarou, *Interview with Judge Lech Garlicki* (European Court of Human Rights, Strasbourg, 2009).
[36] Dzehtsiarou, *Interview with Judge 17*.
[37] K. Dzehtsiarou, *Interview with Judge Giorgio Malinverni* (European Court of Human Rights, Strasbourg, 2009).

guidance as to whether there is a violation at this stage or there is no violation.[38]

Judge 15 also emphasised the importance of European consensus as a criterion for the margin of appreciation. He mentioned that the value of European consensus depended on the nature of the issue that was at stake. Neither European consensus nor the margin of appreciation is deployed by the ECtHR in every case, and therefore, some judges, including Judge 15, argued that the function of European consensus was to assist the Court in dealing with complex or novel legal issues. This was the fifth function of consensus listed by the judges.

Judge 15 pointed out that 'the Court refers to European consensus at least in my perception in order to identify some solutions which are more or less advanced especially in fields which are linked with society's problems and when assessing the famous margin of appreciation'.[39] The fact that European consensus was more applicable in relation to certain legal issues was also emphasised by a number of other judges. They explained that the Court needed consensus to deal with 'existential social problems',[40] 'the most sensitive areas',[41] 'essentially contested concepts'[42] and those issues in relation to which there was no 'clearly established legal position'[43] of the Court.

Some judges saw the role of consensus as a tool that helped the Court to deal with novel issues in relation to which there was no case law of the ECtHR. Judge 19 pointed out that

> [w]hen we look upon some new elements, some of which were never before discussed in the Court – then we say they should be accepted by consensus. Judges of international courts as well as judges of constitutional courts should look at the wider picture, not only individual cases, because sometimes by making a decision on individual cases we know that our message has implications and is not only regarding a particular individual or a particular State.[44]

Judge 20 expressed a narrower understanding of consensus. She pointed out that 'the Court uses consensus if it has not developed a clear position

---

[38] K. Dzehtsiarou, *Interview with Judge 10* (European Court of Human Rights, Strasbourg).
[39] K. Dzehtsiarou, *Interview with Judge 15* (European Court of Human Rights, Strasbourg).
[40] K. Dzehtsiarou, *Interview with Judge Lucius Caflisch* (European Court of Human Rights, Strasbourg, 2008).
[41] Dzehtsiarou, *Interview with Judge Myjer*.
[42] Judge 6 with reference to Walter Bryce Gallie. K. Dzehtsiarou, *Interview with Judge 6*.
[43] K. Dzehtsiarou, *Interview with Judge 20* (European Court of Human Rights, Strasbourg).
[44] K. Dzehtsiarou, *Interview with Judge 19* (European Court of Human Rights, Strasbourg).

on the issue. If such position exists then European consensus is not needed that much.'[45] Judge Rozakis commented that 'we do not need European consensus if there is already established case law of the Court'.[46]

It seems that the great majority of the judges saw European consensus as a legitimate tool of interpretation of the ECHR. However, they came to this conclusion through different routes. Some judges mentioned that this was due to the special nature of the ECtHR as a regional court and therefore it was almost bound to use a comparative method and deploy its results in the Court's reasoning. Many others emphasised the nature of consensus as a tool that could fulfil various functions in the Court's jurisprudence.

This section has confirmed that European consensus is a useful tool, but it has not yet established that European consensus affects the decision of the Court, and not just through a *post factum* rationalisation of the decision. In order to do this, the following section will determine how persuasive European consensus is for the judges and for the Contracting Parties.

7.4 How persuasive is European consensus?

The key purpose of this section is to establish what the judges think about the persuasive effect of European consensus. In this sense, this section argues that consensus is useful on at least two 'levels'. First, European consensus can arguably persuade the judges to adopt a particular decision in the case under consideration. This role of consensus is hard to detect from the reasoning as the Court does not have a system by which one can 'weigh' different arguments. If European consensus can persuade the judges to follow the rule supported by consensus, then one can say that European consensus can amount to a legal argument that influences the decision-making of the Court. Second, European consensus can be understood as a tool that can enhance the acceptability of the judgments by the Contracting Parties. In other words, it is a tool that can persuade the Contracting Parties to execute the judgment. Some judges have pointed out that this is one of the functions of consensus, and this section explores to what extent it is so. If the judges shared this belief, it could mean that they saw European consensus as an argument that was capable of enhancing the legitimacy of the ECtHR judgments.

---

[45] Dzehtsiarou, *Interview with Judge 20*. [46] Dzehtsiarou, *Interview with Judge Rozakis*.

Some judges were asked whether they would follow European consensus even if it were at odds with their personal convictions. The majority of the judges thought that it was unlikely that they would disregard European consensus even in such an event. Judges Bîrsan and Tulkens were of the opinion that the situations where they would go against consensus would be extremely rare. Judge Bîrsan observed that 'it is difficult for me to accept that I can go against the consensus. It is difficult to imagine that situation – I do not exclude this though.'[47] Judge Tulkens said that 'I am not here to impose my personal views. That is impossible. I want to see that my views are confirmed by the views of others and European consensus can be very useful in that.'[48]

The majority of judges explained that they would follow European consensus unless there were convincing reasons against it. This approach is similar to the approach advocated in this book, namely that European consensus can be conceptualised as a rebuttable presumption. Judge 6 also described this approach:

> If a judge's opinion runs against the European consensus, what matters is whether that opinion is based on the provisions of the Convention or on the existing Court's case law, or at least (especially in the absence of the Court's case law) the case law of other national or supranational courts, or on the European legal tradition (true, not so easily discernible). If this is so, then that opinion is law based and shall be used as an argument in a case. But if it is just a 'private' opinion, the existence of European consensus would probably present a stronger argument. For instance, in cases involving religion even a non-believer judge, who has a very critical attitude towards religious beliefs and practices, must recognise a person's freedom of religion, and defend it if it is infringed upon.[49]

Some judges pointed out that whether they could be persuaded by European consensus or not depended on the subject matter of the case. Judge Garlicki concluded that the effect of European consensus depended on a number of factors:

> [Consensus] depends on the nature of the problem. In most cases, if there is a common ground then I think that the States should not depart too much from this. But I also can imagine that there are some important values for a judge, whether it be, for example, abortion, capital punishment, some elements of human dignity. If there is some kind of fundamental conflict between values and a position of even the majority of

---

[47] K. Dzehtsiarou, *Interview with Judge Corneliu Bîrsan* (European Court of Human Rights, Strasbourg, 2010).
[48] Dzehtsiarou, *Interview with Judge Tulkens*. [49] Dzehtsiarou, *Interview with Judge 6*.

7.4 HOW PERSUASIVE IS EUROPEAN CONSENSUS? 191

> European legislators, I would stick to the values. However, this is only in an extreme situation which is, by definition, very rare. We do not have too many examples of judges dissenting merely on the basis that it is too fundamental and too important to accept any other solutions. We do not have too many cases dealing with, let's say, super-fundamental values. If it is related to trade union rights, electoral rights, and the definition of missing persons – in this case we would follow European consensus. But it is my personal belief that there is a limit and as long as this limit is not reached, I think that most judges are ready to accept the collective wisdom of their colleagues from other countries.[50]

A conflict between values and European consensus was also mentioned by Judge 18. He was asked whether he could imagine a situation where his personal convictions could go against European consensus. Judge 18 offered the following answer:

> I could imagine such a scenario, although I have never been confronted by such a scenario. It is not far-fetched. Let's take the fight against terrorism. If at some point there is a consensus to use inhuman treatment in order to get results and that for instance, all the EU Member States agree that there would be a good idea to be tough in the fight against terrorism and to use methods that would be totally inconsistent with our Convention, there I see a real problem because the underlying values of the Convention should always prevail; notwithstanding that consensus among the States could run against these values. But this is highly hypothetical problem because on the EU level they are very much attached to human rights ... But I am very much attached to the values of the Convention; non-derogable rights can never be superseded by a hypothetical consensus.[51]

According to Judges Malinverni and Jaeger, the nature of the issue at hand would influence the persuasive value of European consensus. For Judge Malinverni, certain sensitive subjects should not be decided by following European consensus. He observed that

> as a rule I would follow the general European trend. If there is a majority of States who have the same or almost the same legislation in the field, I will tend to follow it. But there might be some issues related to morals, to religion in which I can imagine that I can disagree with the majority of the States ... So, if I am really convinced and if I have a very firm opinion on the topic, then I would tend to stick to this opinion even if there is a majority of States which adopted the new legislation.

Judge Jaeger also emphasised the conditional character of European consensus, but, for her, the nature of the provisions of the Convention

---

[50] Dzehtsiarou, *Interview with Judge Garlicki*.   [51] Dzehtsiarou, *Interview with Judge 6*.

predetermined the effect of European consensus. Judge Jaeger pointed out that

> the first question to be asked is whether the solution followed in the majority of countries is allowed or prescribed by the Convention. If it is only allowed – if it is one of the possible solutions ... then any other solutions may be also in conformity with the Convention. So, the first question is whether there is only one solution under the Convention or there are a few possibilities ... If you come to the conclusion that there are a few possible solutions then your own approach is just your own ethical approach but not a judicial one ... You have to see the difference between you as a person and you acting as a judge.[52]

For Judge 20, European consensus would only have persuasive value if she did not have any previous convictions in relation to the matter at hand. She acknowledged that

> if I have a very strong conviction then the fact that Europe thinks otherwise is not entirely persuasive for me. If I think that in the circumstances of this case my decision is based on correct interpretation of the Convention then European consensus would not convince me to act differently. Another issue would be if I am not sure and there are competing arguments supporting both positions. Here European consensus is a very strong argument, but everything would depend on the circumstances of the case.[53]

It seems that the judges saw consensus as a strong argument that pointed in a particular direction. Having said that, for some judges, this argument could be trumped by personal convictions, the nature of the Convention right or the particular circumstances of the case.

Even more important for the argument of this book is what the judges thought about whether European consensus could enhance acceptability and improve the execution of the judgments of the ECtHR. The vast majority of the judges was of the opinion that European consensus supported the execution of judgments, while only two of them[54] thought otherwise.

Judge 1 pointed out that 'it is true that if out of 47 States, let's say 40 States have this particular provision in their law then it should seem reasonable that the other 7 States should try to introduce a provision not exactly identical but similar'.[55] Judge 4 observed that European consensus 'encourages the national authorities to reach a better standard that is

---

[52] Dzehtsiarou, *Interview with Judge Jaeger*.   [53] Dzehtsiarou, *Interview with Judge 20*.
[54] Judges 8 and 22.
[55] K. Dzehtsiarou, *Interview with Judge 1* (European Court of Human Rights, Strasbourg).

7.4 HOW PERSUASIVE IS EUROPEAN CONSENSUS? 193

acceptable under the Convention and which is already implemented in other countries'.[56] Judge Tulkens pointed out that 'we have to have convincing judgments. If we have total rejection from the States – it is hopeless. We are not here to write nice articles. We have this responsibility to give guidelines to the countries.'[57]

Some judges thought that European consensus could help both the Contracting Parties and the applicant to understand the ECtHR judgments. Judge 10 commented that

> I think that consensus works both ways. It certainly – and I am sure that there is an agreement on this – shows that there is a variety of solutions. It can also explain to the applicant side, for example, that there is no agreement when it comes to defining human rights in present day society. This argument about consensus does not really support your position. This is about the applicant or the applicants who are not successful. But, on the other hand, when the conclusion goes another way it is something which could assist in explaining the situation to the Government when they are told that this was a violation of the Convention. So, I think that the consensus argument can be useful to both sides not only to one side.[58]

Judge 17 agreed with Judge 10's main point and added that

> I think that European consensus can positively influence the Contracting Parties and other stakeholders. Moreover, it might have a positive effect on the Committee of Ministers. If a particular solution is respected in many countries and the ECtHR accepts it this might add a bit of sympathy to the decision of the Court. The Committee of Ministers respect our judgments even without European consensus, of course. However, I am inclined to think that it would help if the decision falls within shared domestic conscience among a large majority of States.[59]

Those judges who were of the opinion that European consensus could enhance acceptance of the judgments by the Contracting Parties also acknowledged that it might not necessarily happen in all cases. Judge 1 explained that 'if a judgment is supported also by consensus that in theory should make it easier for the dissenting States to accept the case, to implement the decision. But this is not always been the case.'[60] Many judges pointed out that factors such as the subject matter of the case and which particular Contracting Party had been found in violation of the Convention were important in assessing the persuasive value of European consensus. Judge 5 concluded that

---

[56] Dzehtsiarou, *Interview with Judge 4*. [57] Dzehtsiarou, *Interview with Judge Tulkens*.
[58] Dzehtsiarou, *Interview with Judge 10*. [59] Dzehtsiarou, *Interview with Judge 17*.
[60] Dzehtsiarou, *Interview with Judge 1*.

> [the persuasive value of European consensus] depends on the subject ... Turkey [for example] is the last country to recognise conscientious objections ... These judgments [where Turkey was condemned for not recognising them] are also pending before the Committee of Ministers ... but Turkey still resists introducing new rules into the legal system.[61]

According to Judges 9 and 11, European consensus could help to execute the ECtHR judgments by means of its pedagogic function. Judge 9 concluded that

> the reason why there is more information on comparative law now given in judgments and greater recourse to the comparative-law method in the reasoning is presumably to make the judgments more convincing. Unlike the judgments of the Court of Justice of the European Union, the judgments of the Strasbourg Court do not, by virtue of the Convention, have direct, binding effect within the national legal orders – they do, by virtue of the national law, in some countries; and while national practice is coming more and more to this position, there is still a long way to go. The Strasbourg Court needs to have the support of the national judges if the Convention system is to be fully effective. If too much is expected of this Court, the Convention protection machinery will become top-heavy: too many cases will come here rather than being dealt with in the national legal systems and the Court will become asphyxiated. As a consequence, the Convention system really needs the national judges to be doing their work under Article 1 – that is to say, offering judicial protection capable, wherever possible, of ensuring that the Convention rights are properly implemented at the national level ... The Strasbourg Court therefore needs to establish an effective collaboration with the national courts. For national judges to collaborate with the Strasbourg Court, they have to have confidence in the quality of its judgments. Not just the judgments concerning their own country, but also the case-law in general. One way of achieving that is to convincingly explain why decisions have been arrived at: the supportive reasoning. This Court thus has a pedagogic function as a generator of a Europe-wide human rights case law as well as an adjudicatory function in individual cases. Part of that pedagogic function is to explain why Convention law ... is 'evolving' – in other words, changing in content over time or extending into new areas – in the way that it is. That is, I suspect, one reason why there is nowadays more extensive material on comparative law being set out in the preliminary part of the judgments and greater recourse to the comparative-law method in the reasoning.[62]

Judge 11 emphasised the informational function of consensus and pointed out that telling the respondent State that it was one of the last

---

[61] K. Dzehtsiarou, *Interview with Judge 5* (European Court of Human Rights, Strasbourg).
[62] Dzehtsiarou, *Interview with Judge 9*.

7.4 HOW PERSUASIVE IS EUROPEAN CONSENSUS? 195

remaining States in Europe with a certain legal regulation could encourage it to change such regulation. She explained that

> [European consensus] has an informational value ... It is good to understand that the others [Contracting Parties] find other solutions ... So, it [European consensus] helps some people to understand why they are criticised. Especially if they live in countries like say – Switzerland, the Netherlands, Norway, Sweden, Germany. They think that their own legal system is good – why do they [judges of the ECtHR] criticise us so often?[63]

Judges 15 and 21 pointed out that they were not in a position to assess whether certain arguments could enhance the acceptability of ECtHR judgments, and that this was a question for the Contracting Parties or the Committee of Ministers.[64] Judge 15 pointed out that

> [t]his is not a question for the Court I would say because, as you know, the execution of judgments is mainly within the responsibility of the Committee of Ministers. I would not say that it is a totally political exercise but it is, of course, not a judicial exercise. I do not know the dynamics of the Committee of Ministers on this ... Article 46 is mandatory, so there is normally no political consideration which should assist the execution of the judgment – the judgment should be executed.[65]

Judge 21 pointed out that she did not 'see the connection with execution. Maybe there is but that should be asked of the governments.'[66]

Two of the judges interviewed doubted whether European consensus could convince the Contracting Parties to execute judgments. Judge 22 pointed out that 'the role of the judgment of the Court is not to convince. It is nice if it is convincing but the role of the judgment is to put an end to the matter.'[67] Judge 8 was of the opinion that this argument could have an opposite effect on the Contracting Parties. He explained that

> [the deployment of European consensus is] more for the European Court to defend itself against all sorts of criticism ... But that does not mean that for those States to which the judgment is addressed this consensus idea is going to be very convincing. To the contrary, I can imagine that sometimes the country would say – you see we lose our case not because in principle our arguments were not right but because the rest of Europe thinks that we are wrong. If we have a State that is not very fond of Europe,

---

[63] Dzehtsiarou, *Interview with Judge 11*.
[64] According to Article 46 of the Convention, the Committee of Ministers supervises the execution of the Court's judgments.
[65] Dzehtsiarou, *Interview with Judge 15*.
[66] K. Dzehtsiarou, *Interview with Judge 21* (European Court of Human Rights, Strasbourg).
[67] K. Dzehtsiarou, *Interview with Judge 22* (European Court of Human Rights, Strasbourg).

I do not think that it is a very convincing argument. They would rather see a more thorough examination and analysis of their point of view, like their own courts do it, rather than comparing what is happening in other countries.[68]

Despite the fact that many judges saw value in European consensus as an argument that both influenced the decision-making process in the Court and affected the execution of the Court's judgments, it was not accepted by all judges unanimously. Having said that, there was a minority of sitting judges who doubted that European consensus had some persuasive value to the judges (as a whole) and to the Contracting Parties. Holding that European consensus could be a persuasive argument did not mean that the judges on the Court did not see any challenges in its identification and application. The next two sections explore the criticism of European consensus by the judges of the ECtHR.

7.5 How satisfactory is comparative research that leads to European consensus?

Critical remarks expressed by the judges can be divided into the procedural and the substantive. This section deals with procedural criticism, namely the criticism of comparative law and the way consensus identification is taking place. Due to professional courtesy, the judges interviewed did not offer much criticism of the comparative legal research conducted by the Court's Registry. Judge 5 mentioned that 'we have a very, very good Research Department. So, in many cases we ask them to prepare a report – comparative law reports',[69] which are 'of very high level'.[70] Judge 19 confirmed that 'we are very fortunate to have the Research Division. It is extremely important especially when we discuss some issues which the Court is facing for the first time.'[71]

The judges also confirmed that the comparative research reports prepared by the Research Division did not only contain summaries of the laws of the Contracting Parties but also covered 'other international approaches to the issue',[72] including materials from the United States, Canada, South Africa and other jurisdictions.[73] Some comparative reports 'deal not only with domestic laws but also international law materials. This gives us a perspective.'[74] Judge 10 said that 'I am

---

[68] Dzehtsiarou, *Interview with Judge 8*.   [69] Dzehtsiarou, *Interview with Judge 5*.
[70] K. Dzehtsiarou, *Interview with Judge 3* (European Court of Human Rights, Strasbourg).
[71] Dzehtsiarou, *Interview with Judge 19*.   [72] Dzehtsiarou, *Interview with Judge 3*.
[73] Dzehtsiarou, *Interview with Judge Bîrsan*.   [74] Dzehtsiarou, *Interview with Judge 5*.

7.5 HOW SATISFACTORY IS COMPARATIVE RESEARCH? 197

impressed by the quality of what we receive from our Research Division ... And it seems to me that there are methods here to ensure that what we get is up to quality.'[75] Judge 14 maintained that '[t]he quality of the reports is very high. I can assure you – they are very structured ... It is controlled by the Judges and there are no complaints about the reports made by the Court.'[76] Judge 11 emphasised the fact that there were lawyers from nearly all 47 Contracting Parties in the Court and that this made the comparative reports very authoritative. She pointed out that

> it is very valuable what we get here and it is wonderful that we have lawyers from all those countries. No university can do a comparative analysis on that scale. When I used to work at the university, we compared five or six countries but we would never have countries like San Marino. They might have no specific regulations in these small countries but still we have this wonderful possibility and ... it was very interesting to me to see the results of comparative reports. But, of course, we are not researchers – it is something that the lawyers have to do sideways. This is not their focus, and very often these questions [questions asked by the judge rapporteur] are quite tricky. Sometimes when I see the questions about ... [my national] law I think that these are questions that I have never thought about.[77]

Judge 21 identified another challenge of comparative law conducted by the ECtHR that might be less applicable in the cases at hand. She observed that 'I have been many times in that situation where I think the research report does not provide the full picture, but not because of the people doing the research but because of the request posed to them'.[78]

The judges disagreed over the extent to which the comparative law prepared by the Court should enquire into the reasons for a particular legal regulation. Some judges were in favour of more in-depth research, while others thought that it was unrealistic to enter into too much depth.

Judge Tulkens offered some comments on how comparative law was produced by the ECtHR:

> [Comparative analysis] is useful if it is properly done. It is not that easy to do. What we do – we ask the lawyer to see in the literature what the position of national law is. But legislation can be very different from the case law. It is very hard for the lawyer to be aware of all the recent developments ... It is very difficult to do an accurate comparative law analysis not only in the text but also in reality. When they ask to conduct

---

[75] Dzehtsiarou, *Interview with Judge 10*. [76] Dzehtsiarou, *Interview with Judge 14*.
[77] Dzehtsiarou, *Interview with Judge 11*. [78] Dzehtsiarou, *Interview with Judge 21*.

comparative research they ask all judges here to confirm it. And it is very sensible to have a report with a situation with the law today ... So, comparative analysis – yes, but you should rely on it very carefully.[79]

Judge 18 pointed out that the Court should try to reveal the reasons for a particular legal situation in Europe, especially if there was no consensus on the matter at issue. He observed that

> if you look at what is happening in domestic jurisdictions – the fact that there is no consensus does not mean that the states do not want this solution but there can be various reasons why they do not enact new legislation ... – because it is not politically interesting, because no one thinks that it is needed except some applicants who are always a minority; because the government is too busy with other things. Sometime the State needs the judgment of the Court to make them aware that the change is needed. The fact that there is no consensus does not need to mean that the State opposes this solution and we always bear it in mind when we say that there is no consensus. We have to look very carefully at what is at stake and then ask ourselves why there is no consensus. There might be a strong opposition among the Member States in some direction, but it might be very different that there is no awareness of the problem ... I think that the Rapporteur should ask sometimes the following question – if there is no consensus could the Research Division indicate why there is no consensus.[80]

Judge 6 convincingly argued that there were two aspects to comparative research: legal and sociological. The Court's ability to produce comprehensive reports depended on whether the issue at stake was of a sociological or a legal nature. Judge 6 stated that

> on legal issues, such as comparative criminal procedure or the administration of justice, lawyers are able to produce very informative reports. But in areas that require not only legal knowledge one cannot rely only on lawyers' insights, especially if one tries to determine whether there is European consensus on an issue, because any consensus is not only a legal but also a social and a cultural, and a psychological phenomenon. In my own practice as a constitutional judge, I was inclined to the view that experts in fields outside the realm of law had to be consulted, as *amicus curiae*, whenever the law in question dealt with matters beyond lawyers' professional competence.[81]

Some judges were mindful of the natural limitations of the comparative legal research prepared by the Court. Judge 8, for instance, observed that

---

[79] Dzehtsiarou, *Interview with Judge Tulkens*. [80] Dzehtsiarou, *Interview with Judge 18*.
[81] Dzehtsiarou, *Interview with Judge 6*.

7.5 HOW SATISFACTORY IS COMPARATIVE RESEARCH? 199

an ideal comparative report would have some sociological studies which revealed the rationale of certain regulations. However, then he pointed out that

> the courts do not do that and I do not think that the courts should do that. The courts should make a reasonable effort to find out what is happening in various countries. I must say that if, as you have seen in a number of cases, you get information from the countries – maybe not information of the same level; some information is more detailed than information from another country – simply because there is more available. But that does not exclude that you get a pretty good overview of what is going on. Maybe the Court does not know all that details and I am not sure that the comparative report put together by the Research Division is up to all academic standards, but for the Court it is probably enough to see in what direction the countries are going. The Court is not a research unit. We are working differently than academics would work. So, we are not looking for the results such as there were 35 countries out of 47 that accepted that ... It is more about the tendencies that we are interested in and that we have the information to establish these tendencies.[82]

Judge 17 expressed a similar point of view by stating that

> you have to be careful with the normative value of this [European consensus] argument. One of the issues might be the methodology of identification of consensus. This methodology is soft and sometimes not rigorous enough for the purposes of legal scholarship, for example. However, it is quite acceptable for the purpose of the decision-making at the Court to seek a general impression on a given subject. In order to see whether same sex marriage is accepted or not, a Polaroid snapshot of the legal state of affairs in Europe will do, you do not need rigorous analysis for that purpose. Such a snapshot does not contain any in-depth analysis or assessment of the various legal positions.[83]

For some judges, it was important that the comparative analysis prepared by the Court was supplemented by reports from the non-governmental organisations (NGOs) working in the area. For example, Judge 4 pointed out that, when conducting a comparative study, the Court uses its own sources but that

> our ... [backlog] does not really allow for a timely research or broad enough research ... On the other hand, the Court resorts to the third parties' interventions and I have always been in favour of this system not only as a person who comes from a civil society organisation, but also because I believe that the third-party interveners would be capable of offering an

[82] Dzehtsiarou, *Interview with Judge 8*.   [83] Dzehtsiarou, *Interview with Judge 17*.

objective analysis in comparison to the ones of the parties. In this regard, I do prefer to rely or to consult the positions of third-party interveners as long as they are not involved with some interests in this question.[84]

In contrast, Judge Jaeger did not think that the NGO submissions should have much impact on the decision-making of the Court. She observed that

> I think that the NGOs' reports are just a matter of politeness. We know that NGOs do a lot of very good work ... we need NGOs and their assistance in the implementation process, but not for the reasoning.[85]

Judge Malinverni maintained that NGOs 'play a minor role in the work of the Court contrary to what happens in the UN treaty bodies'.[86]

The majority of judges interviewed offered comments that can be placed between these two polar approaches, namely that NGOs reports were useful, but that the agenda of the NGOs in these human rights cases must also be taken into account.

Judge Myjer maintained that the NGOs with established reputations tried to be more objective. He concluded that

> we ... know that some NGOs are more one-sided than others. Most NGOs will realise that once they have a good name they should never spoil it and try to be as objective as possible, as once they make a clear mistake on purpose, their reputation is spoiled.[87]

The view of Judge 18 was quite representative of the opinion of the majority of the judges. He pointed out that the main source of comparative law should be the Research Division of the Court, while at the same time taking NGO reports into account:

> we are very happy to have a Research Division. It does a great job and it is a very important tool but we continue to use NGO reports. The Research Division is much more relevant however. We rely much more on our Research Division. We always need to be very careful, but if we compare what the Research Division does, and this is then confirmed by NGOs, then this is very important. I think that we rely increasingly on comparative reports because we have so many cases and if we find a new solution we want to be backed by what States do – States' practice.[88]

It seems that, in general, the judges praised the work of the Research Division of the Court. At the same time, however, this praise was not

---

[84] Dzehtsiarou, *Interview with Judge 4*. [85] Dzehtsiarou, *Interview with Judge Jaeger*.
[86] Dzehtsiarou, *Interview with Judge Malinverni*.
[87] Dzehtsiarou, *Interview with Judge Myjer*. [88] Dzehtsiarou, *Interview with Judge 18*.

blind. The judges clearly saw the limitations of what the Research Division could produce. Therefore, the judges believed that its work should be complemented by the third-party interventions which could contain more data capable of enriching and correcting the reports produced by the ECtHR.

7.6 Criticism from within the palace walls

This section deals with substantive criticism, which is understood as a criticism of the notion of consensus as such. The judges were not specifically asked to criticise the European consensus approach, but during the course of the discussions some of them revealed certain doubts over its applicability. There were two main areas of criticism expressed by the judges:

1. the anti-majoritarian argument, which was described by Judge 22 as the 'majority can always be wrong';[89]
2. some judges identified a specific challenge in relying on lack of consensus. While the presence of consensus was a clear sign of how the Convention should be interpreted, lack of consensus should not lead to the conclusion that the Convention did not have meaning in the particular situation. These arguments are considered in turn.

The anti-majoritarian difficulty as discussed in Chapter 5 has been not only recognised and analysed by academic commentators[90] but also acknowledged by some judges of the ECtHR. Judge 22 pointed out that

> [f]or me ... [European consensus] is not a priority. You look at the case and you have a sense of where it goes. And it matters little whether other countries have euthanasia or not. Consensus bases on a democratic majoritarian premise which says nothing – the majority can always be wrong. One reason why the majority here can be wrong is seen from the dissenting opinions. A single Judge dissenting in a particular case in the section or Grand Chamber can be correct. The best example is Justice Douglas of the US Supreme Court. He was such a minority of that court that he would write his dissent already on the bench. He knew where the majority was going to get and yet he had a better sense of justice, and in the long run his opinion proved to be good.[91]

---
[89] Dzehtsiarou, *Interview with Judge 22*.
[90] See, G. Letsas, *A Theory of Interpretation of the European Convention on Human Rights* (Oxford University Press, 2009); E. Benvenisti, 'Margin of Appreciation, Consensus, and Universal Standards', *Journal of International Law and Politics*, 31 (1999), 843.
[91] Dzehtsiarou, *Interview with Judge 22*.

Judge 1 expressed a similar idea by saying that

> I have some misgivings about this doctrine because historically and I do not mean necessarily in the last 50 years – I rather mean 70 or 100 years – the consensus of States has been the reason for grave injustices that have been committed. I find it difficult to always rely on this consensus.[92]

For some judges, the most concerning aspect of the anti-majoritarian argument was the fact that the majority could decide to weaken human rights protection and the Court would have to follow. Judge Myjer pointed out that

> imagine if there were to be a European consensus to diminish the content of protection in the context of terrorist threats. I wonder if the Court should also feel bound by that. By now the European consensus has always been widening the scope. It is interesting to see if you can also use [it] for narrowing the scope.[93]

Judge 8 concurred with Judge Myjer and added that 'it will also be risky if we were always following consensus. Consensus could go in the direction of things that we really do not like here, i.e., anti-human rights.'[94]

The majority of judges acknowledged these concerns but they pointed out that it was not detrimental to the value of consensus. The response to this criticism is that consensus can be disregarded if it is detrimental to human rights protections. However, many judges also pointed out that this was only a theoretical possibility and it had not yet happened. Judge 11 agreed that European consensus did have a link to majoritarian decision-making, but the fact that European consensus was not decisive and did not predetermine the outcome of the cases minimised the threat to human rights. She maintained that

> there we connect to the majority. That is true – on the one hand, we balance against the majority and, on the other hand, we look back to the majority. But we have to be critical of that ... Let's take the Middle Ages – if all the countries allowed witch-hunting and allowed torture – human rights ... would have to say 'no'. It is never an absolute model and it has always been ... [a chance] to say 'Yes, there is consensus' but there always should be a possibility to say 'but'. There should be some safeguards. The decisions of the democratic parliaments are not *per se* correct and they should be controlled. That is why we have constitutional courts and other systems, and the same time it is true in relation to consensus argument – you cannot use it just as a template.[95]

---

[92] Dzehtsiarou, *Interview with Judge 1*.
[93] Dzehtsiarou, *Interview with Judge Myjer*.
[94] Dzehtsiarou, *Interview with Judge 8*.
[95] Dzehtsiarou, *Interview with Judge 11*.

7.6 CRITICISM FROM WITHIN THE PALACE WALLS

The fact that the Court could avoid using consensus was seen as a response to the anti-majoritarian argument by a number of the judges interviewed. Judge 9 observed that

> I do not think that the Court should decide one way or another way simply on the basis of a headcount of national legislations in Europe. That is too crude. For me, although 'European' consensus is a kind of interpretative consideration that is inherent in the Convention (which is itself in origin a synthesis of shared human rights values in Europe), it goes to corroborate or confirm conclusions that have been arrived at by applying orthodox or classic methods of interpretation ... It is just an indicator; there is no definite rule that whenever you get a headcount going one way, this Court must apply the solution favoured by that headcount. That is an oversimplistic way of looking at consensus. Consensus is one strand of an interpretative process, and an inherent and important strand, but there are others ... You have to look at all various strands to see what the end-result in the particular case is.[96]

The rebuttable nature of consensus was also emphasised by a number of judges. Judge Tulkens observed that European consensus 'is an argument and when you use it as an argument it is important to rely on this argument in some cases and you can keep it aside in other cases. We should have a possibility to use it in a flexible way.'[97]

Judge Garlicki pointed out that the text of the Convention could be one of the limits of European consensus. According to Judge Garlicki, '[e]ven if there was a consensus among States that terrorists should be tortured ... we should still say no. There is something about torture in the text of the Convention and we must not accept any compromises.'[98]

The case law of the ECtHR has also been seen as another limit. Judge Malinverni pointed out that 'supposedly many European States would reintroduce the death penalty. In such a case, the European Court would not rely on the European consensus argument because this would be contrary to the Court's case law; contrary to the case law on article 2.'[99]

According to Judge 8, the national particularities of the respondent State could also justify a departure from European consensus:

> as it has been said in the number of recent cases, consensus, even if it is very clear in one direction yet because of very strong national particularities, may be the reason not to follow it. [To prove these strong national particularities] the State will try to establish that there is sort of uniqueness

---

[96] Dzehtsiarou, *Interview with Judge 9*.   [97] Dzehtsiarou, *Interview with Judge Tulkens*.
[98] Dzehtsiarou, *Interview with Judge Garlicki*.
[99] Dzehtsiarou, *Interview with Judge Malinverni*.

that distinguishes that State from most of the other States. And if that uniqueness is so embedded in the society or if it is about the tradition that is so generally accepted there is a strong reason to say – OK, let's give credit to that. Of course, I know and the Court knows that there are traditions and feelings that are not worthwhile being protected. For instance, the societies that are fundamentally racist or societies which are not willing to grant certain rights or advantages to minority groups – that would be a problem. But as long as you have a feeling that something is acceptable – that it would be better that this is still acceptable.[100]

Judge 9 gave the following opinion:

in certain areas, subject matters where the margin of appreciation is extremely wide – morals, when life begins and when it ends – it is really for each society [to decide through] an open debate with the elective representatives, civil society, philosophers, church leaders, NGOs – it is not for certain judges here to decide that this is the rule for everyone – no, I think that this Court can indicate what the values are and the principles are. But there are some areas where it is up to each society depending on whether they are a religious society or a lay society or a mixture ... Democracy is diversity as well, and there are some areas in which even if one State says that we want to do it this way – they can do it that way.[101]

Many judges of the ECtHR acknowledged the anti-majoritarian difficulty of European consensus in human rights adjudication. Having said that, they confirmed that a flexible and non-automatic approach of the Court to European consensus could offer a sufficient safeguard against abuse of majoritarian logic in the ECtHR case law. One of the main intentions of this book is to conceptualise European consensus as a rebuttable presumption that can be disregarded if there are valid reasons to do so. These reasons have to be clearly stated and explained by the ECtHR in its judgments.

Another area of criticism was that the lack of European consensus did not justify an abrogation of the Court's responsibility to interpret the Convention. It seems that this criticism was mostly directed at the margin of appreciation rather than European consensus. This is because if there is no consensus, the Court is then likely to leave the matter at hand in the State's margin of appreciation – in other words, transferring its role of the ultimate interpreter of the Convention to the Contracting Parties. The debate about margin of appreciation is well documented[102] and

---

[100] Dzehtsiarou, *Interview with Judge 8*.   [101] Dzehtsiarou, *Interview with Judge 9*.
[102] See Y. Arai-Takahashi, *The Margin of Appreciation Doctrine and the Principle of Proportionality in the Jurisprudence of the ECHR* (Intersentia, 2002); J.A. Brauch, 'The

7.6 CRITICISM FROM WITHIN THE PALACE WALLS

clearly beyond the scope of this book. Here it suffices only to mention some key concerns of the judges of the ECtHR. Judge 6 explained that

> [w]hen the Court finds that there is no European consensus on a particular issue, does this mean that the Convention itself is silent on that issue? Does this mean that the Convention, in order to obtain ability to express itself on a particular matter in the Court's case law, has to live until that meaning is provided by the consensus within Member States? To put it bluntly, does this mean that the Court, being faced with the complicated issue involving an 'essentially contested concept' or even a hotly debated issue, raises up hands and declares that it is not clear, or at least not yet clear, what the Convention says on that particular issue, and that this will become clear only when the European consensus is reached? But it may appear that it will not be reached in many years. Also, it may appear that with years a consensus reached on the national level may disperse or give way to a new consensus of a completely different content.[103]

He also observed that

> I do not find it very convincing to base the judgment, *inter alia*, on the fact that there is no European consensus on an issue which is covered by the Convention. True, as the Convention is not a constitution there are – and there have to be – a lot of issues not covered by the Convention such as, say, forms of government or systems of taxation. However, if an issue is covered by the Convention and European consensus is searched by the Court and its existence is not found, this normally leads to the assertion that Member States enjoy a wide margin of appreciation in the respective field. However, this means that the margin of appreciation is determined not by the Convention (or at least not only by the latter), but originates in the lack of European consensus on that issue.[104]

Judge 18 also thought that the lack of consensus was not detrimental to the Court's ability to interpret the Convention. According to Judge 18:

> We have to interpret the Convention in light of present day circumstances and therefore we look on those present days circumstances having regard to consensus. But we have in our case law judgments where there admittedly was no consensus. There was just a trend in the right direction... The mere

---

Margin of Appreciation and the Jurisprudence of the European Court of Human Rights: Threat to the Rule of Law', *Columbia Journal of European Law*, 11 (2004), 113; S. Greer, *The Margin of Appreciation: Interpretation and Discretion under the European Convention on Human Rights* (Council of Europe, 2000); J. Kratochvil, 'The Inflation of the Margin of Appreciation by the European Court of Human Rights', *Netherlands Quarterly of Human Rights*, 29 (2011), 324; A. Legg, *The Margin of Appreciation in International Human Rights Law* (Oxford University Press, 2012); G. Letsas, 'Two Concepts of the Margin of Appreciation', *Oxford Journal of Legal Studies*, 26 (2006), 705.

[103] Dzehtsiarou, Interview with Judge 6.   [104] Ibid.

fact that there is no consensus or not yet a consensus does not mean that we will not take the lead. As to new solutions we need a trend.[105]

This argument was not accepted by all judges. Judge 2 stated that 'if there is no consensus the Court should not put the cart before the horse and adopt solutions for which Europe is not ready yet'.[106] Overall, the judges agreed that a limited and flexible application of European consensus, which is based on a rigorous methodology of identification and clear application of consensus, was a legitimate practice of the Court, and it appears that the ECtHR will continue to use this argument in its case law.

7.7 Conclusion

While this chapter reveals that the judges of the ECtHR who were interviewed for this project were mostly in favour of the deployment of European consensus, it was not accepted unconditionally within the Court. The judges were mindful of the limitations of the argument and in their interviews often expressed views which coincided with the main tenets of this book, namely that European consensus is a rebuttable presumption that can enhance the legitimacy of the judgments of the ECtHR if it is properly identified and applied.

The majority of the judges were of the opinion that European consensus was persuasive, both for the judges on the bench and for the Contracting Parties, which were then more likely to execute judgments if their legal system diverted from a commonly accepted European standard.

The judges were mostly satisfied with the research reports produced by the Research Division of the Court and they were able to identify the presence or absence of European consensus on the basis of these materials. At the same time, most judges were in favour of these materials being complemented by third-party interventions.

Finally, the judges were aware of the anti-majoritarian argument that was often brought into the discussion of consensus by commentators of the Convention. However, at the same time, most of them thought that this argument was less pressing because of the non-absolute and non-automatic nature of European consensus.

---

[105] Dzehtsiarou, *Interview with Judge 18*.
[106] K. Dzehtsiarou, *Interview with Judge 2* (European Court of Human Rights, Strasbourg).

8

Conclusion

This book began by asserting that the ECtHR had not yet lost its legitimacy. What seems clear, however, is that the real issue it must face is whether its legitimacy is stable enough not to fade over time. After all, its legitimacy is constantly being questioned by the Contracting Parties, the media and civic society. There is nothing particularly unusual about this given that States do not like to lose court cases. Having said that, the Court needs to offer a counter-argument against accusations of arbitrariness and political decision-making which undermine its legitimacy. This book suggests that European consensus has the potential to enhance the legitimacy of the ECtHR by providing answers to some of its crucial legitimacy challenges.

How can European consensus enhance the legitimacy of the ECtHR if its own legitimacy and credibility are often questioned by the Convention commentators, politicians and even judges? For convenience, this criticism can be divided into procedural and substantive. Procedural criticism emphasises that European consensus is illegitimate because it has been deployed inconsistently by the Court. Procedural criticism mainly targets the method of consensus identification or application. In the past, the Court has not used a rigorous methodology for establishing the presence or absence of consensus. The commentators have pointed out that the comparative research which was used as the basis of European consensus was not comprehensive, that the methodology of assessment of comparative data was not consistent and that consensus often acted as a smokescreen for the solutions arbitrarily picked by the judges. This criticism, however, is not entirely fair. During the last decade, the Court has invested a lot of resources in enhancing the credibility of its deployment of consensus. This is especially evident at the stage of preparation of comparative law reports, which has developed from an *ad hoc*, loose exercise to a well-structured and relatively comprehensive study conducted by a special department of the ECtHR – the Research Division. The Court usually quotes some parts of comparative law reports prepared by the Research Division in its judgment, and this clearly shows that the decisions that are made by the Court are informed and credible.

This does not mean that all challenges associated with procedural criticism have been resolved. Despite the fact that the Court has deployed European consensus in many cases, it has never been defined. Moreover, the ECtHR has used various terms to indicate European consensus. Clarification of the meaning of European consensus may enhance the consistency of its application.

This book has argued that European consensus can be conceptualised as a rebuttable presumption in favour of the rule or practice adopted by the majority of the Contracting Parties to the ECHR. This means that the Court will find a violation of the Convention and request the diverging State to adopt a legal provision in line with European consensus. However, this presumption can be rebutted if the State has a justification for remaining outside European consensus. In this case, the Court has to describe the reasons for non-application of consensus clearly and consistently. The Court should explain why it uses one type of consensus but not another. It should also clearly explain what level of abstraction of consensus is required to influence the outcome in a particular case. These are the challenges that the Court will have to deal with in its case law. If they are resolved, then those commentators who represent procedural criticism might perhaps agree that European consensus is a legitimate tool of interpretation of the Convention.

Unlike procedural criticism, substantive criticism does not target the method of identification of consensus but focuses on the value and appropriateness of consensus in human rights adjudication. The core point of substantive criticism has been termed the 'anti-majoritarian' argument. The proponents of this argument claim that human rights are naturally anti-majoritarian and it is illegitimate to adjudicate human rights cases on the basis of majoritarian logic. Human rights are anti-majoritarian because often they are called to protect 'unpopular' minorities, that is those who cannot be protected through normal democratic instruments. European consensus is majoritarian because it links the meaning of the ECHR with the meaning that is adopted by the majority of the Contracting Parties. However, substantive criticism is far-fetched for a number of reasons. The ECtHR does not apply European consensus automatically, which means that if there is a concern about minority rights being infringed, the Court can disregard European consensus. Moreover, on a number of occasions, the Court's case law has demonstrated that deployment of European consensus has enhanced the protection of minorities by justifying evolutive interpretation in this area. Another reason is the nature of European consensus, which operates on a supra-national level. There is a crucial difference between majoritarian decision-making within the Contracting Party, for example, through referendums or opinion polls, and decision-making of the ECtHR by counting the Contracting Parties which are under an obligation to comply with the Convention. People in a particular State do not bear such obligations. Many States have a mechanism for checking the compliance of laws and practice with human rights provisions. Therefore, it seems safe to suggest that majoritarian decision-making on the inter-State level is more legitimate than within a particular country.

A lot of criticism by commentators is directed at the margin of appreciation or evolutive interpretation, and European consensus bears the collateral damage of this criticism because consensus is associated with both of them. This book has argued that this criticism should be separated, and, in fact, European consensus is the most objective determinant of the scope of the margin of appreciation and the moment when it is appropriate for the Court to deploy evolutive interpretation.

This book has argued that European consensus is a legitimate tool of interpretation of the Convention if it is deployed consistently and if its identification is based on rigorous methodology. Another question worth asking is whether European consensus can enhance the legitimacy of the ECtHR and its judgments. This book has argued that European consensus is capable of providing a counter-argument to the core legitimacy challenges that the ECtHR faces.

These challenges are divided into international constitutional challenges and national constitutional challenges. The former stem from the nature of the Court as an international tribunal. These challenges are closely connected to the widely discussed issue of what makes international law valid. It seems that State consent is the most straightforward legitimising tool: namely if some reading of the Convention was anticipated by the Contracting Parties at the moment of ratification of the Convention, then this reading is legitimate. However, the Court's case law cannot be endlessly legitimised through State consent for at least two reasons. First, the Court's deployment of evolutive interpretation cuts against the original consent of the Contracting Parties. Moreover, it is absolutely unreasonable to expect the drafters of the Convention to have anticipated the crucial developments that have happened during the last 60 years in terms of technological and societal progress. Second, it is impossible to request a specific formal consent in every case that the Court adjudicates. Therefore, the Court should look for some updated consent which does not require formal approval. This book has argued that European consensus can be conceptualised as such an implicit consent. The majority of the Contracting Parties agrees to accept a particular meaning of the ECHR.

Interaction between the ECtHR and the Contracting Parties is crucial for the effectiveness of the former. Due to the mostly voluntary nature of the Strasbourg system, the Parties decide whether they wish to execute the judgments of the Court. In this situation, the Court should talk to the Parties and persuade them to execute judgments as a means of ensuring that their voice is heard in Strasbourg. European consensus is an avenue for the Contracting Parties to be heard because in its judgments the Court integrates the solutions that have been reached at the national level. Through this mechanism, the Court can respond to those commentators who think that the ECtHR imposes its own political judgments on the Contracting Parties. Another way to respond to this critique is to create an impression that the Court does not do anything but interpret legal texts using legal, as opposed to 'political', tools.

European consensus can be connected to the sources of international law. This book has argued that a legal rule or principle which is supported by European consensus is akin to a customary international norm or a general principle of law. This conceptualisation of consensus adds extra weight to the judgment as it is derived from legal norms, not from some arbitrary decision of seven or seventeen international judges.

Finally, the Contracting Parties often criticise the Court because it oversteps its subsidiary role. This is another international constitutional challenge. The ECtHR is indeed a subsidiary structure that should complement human rights protection mechanisms created at the national level. The ECtHR should take its subsidiary role seriously; European consensus is a tool of substantive subsidiarity. Substantive subsidiarity, as opposed to procedural subsidiarity, not only suggests that the ECtHR should adjudicate the cases only after they have been dealt with by the Contracting Parties but also implies that national decisions and hard choices should be respected by the ECtHR. By means of European consensus, the Court shows that it takes national choices seriously.

The ECtHR is increasingly portrayed as a constitutional court, which means that some national constitutional challenges of legitimacy are also applicable in the case of the ECtHR. The core national constitutional challenge has been termed the counter-majoritarian difficulty. This means that unelected judges of constitutional courts are capable of striking down pieces of legislation that were adopted by democratically elected parliaments. This challenge is less pressing in the case of the ECtHR as it can only declare laws or practices incompatible with the Convention; it cannot directly invalidate them. Having said that, some softer form of 'counter-majoritarian difficulty' is applicable to the ECtHR. In this connection, European consensus can be seen as a tool that offers some democratic legitimation to the choices made by the ECtHR. A decision supported by European consensus cannot claim the same level of democratic legitimacy as the decision of a directly elected parliament but, as explained above, it brings the ECtHR closer to people without undermining the Court's anti-majoritarian nature.

European consensus is perceived as a legitimate tool of interpretation by the ECtHR judges. There is a very small minority of judges which is critical of European consensus and does not see any legitimising potential in it. That said, even those judges who support further deployment of European consensus in the case law of the ECtHR can see its limitations. None of the judges has suggested that European consensus should be applied automatically and be decisive in a case. It seems that there is consensus about consensus in the Strasbourg Human Rights Palace where the ECtHR is located.

This book does not exhaust the topic of European consensus, and I hope that it will be a reason for more discussions on consensus. For years, in legal scholarship, European consensus was in the shadows of the margin of appreciation and evolutive interpretation. I hope that this book will generate some interest in the area. There will be some changes in the structure and attitude to European consensus in the future, especially in the context of the European Union (EU) accession to the ECHR. European consensus based on comparative research should take into account the laws of all Contracting Parties. The EU will be one of those. Moreover, there are 28 Member States of the EU which are at the same time Contracting Parties to the Convention. One can suggest that for that reason, the law of the European Union will have a serious impact on the process of consensus identification if the matter at issue falls within the EU jurisdiction. In particular, such impacts should be examined in relation to those Contracting Parties which are not EU Member States. This accession will create new challenges and opportunities for the Court in the area of application of the European consensus argument.

APPENDIX 1   LIST OF INTERVIEWEES

No	Name	Position	Date of the interview	Length of the interview
1	Corneliu Bîrsan	Judge elected in respect of Romania	30 April 2010	23:54
2	Lucius Caflisch	Judge elected in respect of Liechtenstein	17 June 2008	9:20
3	Vincent De Gaetano	Judge elected in respect of Malta	22 September 2012	50:32
4	Dmitry Dedov	Judge elected in respect of Russia	27 March 2014	48:39
5	Montserrat Enrich-Mas	Head of the Research and Library Division of the Court	24 March 2014	51:30
6	Lech Garlicki	Judge elected in respect of Poland	1 July 2009	31:21
7	Valeriu Griţco	Judge elected in respect of Moldova	26 February 2013	12:17
8	Khanlar Hajiyev	Judge elected in respect of Azerbaijan	24 March 2014	25:30
9	Päivi Hirvelä	Judge elected in respect of Finland	22 September 2012	21:18
10	Renate Jaeger	Judge elected in respect of Germany	12 June 2010	31:06

(cont.)

No	Name	Position	Date of the interview	Length of the interview
11	Zdravka Kalaydjieva	Judge elected in respect of Bulgaria	22 September 2012	33:30
12	Işıl Karakaş	Judge elected in respect of Turkey	4 October 2013	34:01
13	Anatoly Kovler	Judge elected in respect of Russia	1 July 2009	54:53
14	Egidijus Kūris	Judge elected in respect of Lithuania	20 March 2014	57:20
15	Julia Laffranque	Judge elected in respect of Estonia	4 July 2012	41:16
16	Paul Lemmens	Judge elected in respect of Belgium	26 February 2013	25:46
17	Paul Mahoney	Judge elected in respect of the United Kingdom	4 October 2013	48:03
18	Egbert Myjer	Judge elected in respect of the Netherlands	2 June 2009	52:28
19	Giorgio Malinverni	Judge elected in respect of Switzerland	1 July 2009	30:52
20	Erik Møse	Judge elected in respect of Norway	22 September 2012	48:07
21	Angelika Nußberger	Judge elected in respect of Germany	22 September 2012	36:23
22	Michael O'Boyle	Deputy Registrar of the Court	2 June 2009	33:07
23	Mihai Poalelungi	Judge elected in respect of Moldova	6 August 2012	33:32
24	Dragoljub Popović	Judge elected in respect of Serbia	26 February 2013	25:19
25	Guido Raimondi	Judge elected in respect of Italy	4 July 2013	26:31

APPENDIX 1

(cont.)

No	Name	Position	Date of the interview	Length of the interview
26	Christos Rozakis	Judge elected in respect of Greece	12 June 2010	35:45
27	András Sajó	Judge elected in respect of Hungary	21 April 2010	17:20
28	Ján Šikuta	Judge elected in respect of Slovakia	20 June 2010	26:37
29	Johannes Silvis	Judge elected in respect of the Netherlands	24 March 2014	28:49
30	Dean Spielmann	Judge elected in respect of Luxemburg	11 May 2010	20:29
31	Mirjana Lazarova Trajkovska	Judge elected in respect of Macedonia	26 February 2013	43:01
32	Françoise Tulkens	Judge elected in respect of Belgium	11 May 2010	31:12
33	Ganna Yudkivska	Judge elected in respect of Ukraine	22 March 2014	13:02
34	Ineta Ziemele	Judge elected in respect of Latvia	4 July 2012	48:59
35	Boštjan Zupančič	Judge elected in respect of Slovenia	30 April 2010	23:59

APPENDIX 2 LIST OF THE GRAND CHAMBER JUDGMENTS WITH INTERNATIONAL OR COMPARATIVE LAW

Year	Judgments in which the ECtHR has mentioned European or comparative law	Total number of judgments
1998	1. *Guerra and others* v. *Italy*, Application No 116/1996/735/932, Judgment of 19 February 1998 2. *Sheffield and Horsham* v. *the United Kingdom*, Application No 22985/93 and 23390/94, Judgment of 30 July 1998	11
1999	1. *Beer and Regan* v. *Germany*, Application No 28934/95, Judgment of 18 February 1999 2. *Matthews* v. *the United Kingdom*, Application No 24833/94, Judgment of 18 February 1999 3. *Pellegrin* v. *France*, Application No 28541/95, Judgment of 8 December 1999 4. *T.* v. *the United Kingdom*, Application No 24724/94, Judgment of 16 December 1999 5. *V.* v. *the United Kingdom*, Application No 24888/94, Judgment of 16 December 1999 6. *Waite and Kennedy* v. *Germany*, Application No 26083/94, Judgment of 18 February 1999	62
2000	1. *Beyeler* v. *Italy*, Application No 33202/96, Judgment of 5 January 2000 2. *Cha'are Shalom Ve Tsedek* v. *France*, Application No 27417/95, Judgment of 27 June 2000 3. *Frydlender* v. *France*, Application No 30979/96, Judgment of 27 June 2000 4. *Salman* v. *Turkey*, Application No 21986/93, Judgment of 27 June 2000	22
2001	1. *Al-Adsani* v. *the United Kingdom*, Application No 35763/97, Judgment of 21 November 2001	18

(cont.)

Year	Judgments in which the ECtHR has mentioned European or comparative law	Total number of judgments
	2. *Beard* v. *the United Kingdom*, Application No 24882/94, Judgment of 18 January 2001	
	3. *Chapman* v. *the United Kingdom*, Application No 27238/95, Judgment of 18 January 2001	
	4. *Coster* v. *the United Kingdom*, Application No 24876/94, Judgment of 18 January 2001	
	5. *Fogarty* v. *the United Kingdom*, Application No 37112/97, Judgment of 21 November 2001	
	6. *Jane Smith* v. *the United Kingdom*, Application No 25154/94, Judgment of 18 January 2001	
	7. *K.-H. W.* v. *Germany*, Application No 37201/97, Judgment of 22 March 2001	
	8. *Lee* v. *the United Kingdom*, Application No 25289/94, Judgment of 18 January 2001	
	9. *McElhinney* v. *Ireland*, Application No 31253/96, Judgment of 21 November 2001	
	10. *Prince Hans-Adam II of Liechtenstein* v. *Germany*, Application No 42527/98, Judgment of 12 July 2001	
	11. *Streletz, Kessler and Krenz* v. *Germany*, Application No 34044/96, 35532/97 and 44801/98, Judgment of 22 March 2001	
2002	1. *Calvelli and Ciglio* v. *Italy*, Application No 32967/96, Judgment of 17 January 2002	10
	2. *Christine Goodwin* v. *the United Kingdom*, Application No 28957/95, Judgment of 11 July 2002	
	3. *I.* v. *the United Kingdom*, Application No 25680/94, Judgment of 11 July 2002	
	4. *Stafford* v. *the United Kingdom*, Application No 46295/99, Judgment of 28 May 2002	
2003	1. *Sahin* v. *Germany*, Application No 30943/96, Judgment of 8 July 2003	12
	2. *Slivenko* v. *Latvia*, Application No 48321/99, Judgment of 9 October 2003	
	3. *Sommerfeld* v. *Germany*, Application No 31871/96, Judgment of 8 July 2003	
2004	1. *Gorzelik and others* v. *Poland*, Application No 44158/98, Judgment of 17 February 2004	15

APPENDIX 2   217

(cont.)

Year	Judgments in which the ECtHR has mentioned European or comparative law	Total number of judgments
	2. *Ilaşcu and others* v. *Moldova and Russia*, Application No 48787/99, Judgment of 8 July 2004	
	3. *Makaratzis* v. *Greece*, Application No 50385/99, Judgment of 20 December 2004	
	4. *Öneryıldız* v. *Turkey*, Application No 48939/99, Judgment of 30 November 2004	
	5. *Perez* v. *France*, Application No 47287/99, Judgment of 12 February 2004	
	6. *Vo* v. *France*, Application No 53924/00, Judgment of 8 July 2004	
2005	1. *Bosphorus Hava Yolları Turizm ve Ticaret Anonim Şirketi* v. *Ireland*, Application No 45036/98, Judgment of 30 June 2005	11
	2. *Hirst* v. *the United Kingdom (No 2)*, Application No 74025/01, Judgment of 6 October 2005	
	3. *Jahn and others* v. *Germany*, Application No 46720/99, 72203/01 and 72552/01, Judgment of 30 June 2005	
	4. *Kyprianou* v. *Cyprus*, Application No 73797/01, Judgment of 15 December 2005	
	5. *Leyla Şahin* v. *Turkey*, Application No 44774/98, Judgment of 10 November 2005	
	6. *Mamatkulov and Askarov* v. *Turkey*, Application No 46827/99 and 46951/99, Judgment of 4 February 2005	
	7. *Nachova and others* v. *Bulgaria*, Application No 43577/98 and 43579/98, Judgment of 6 July 2005	
	8. *Öcalan* v. *Turkey*, Application No 46221/99, Judgment of 12 May 2005	
2006	1. *Apicella* v. *Italy*, Application No 64890/01, Judgment of 29 March 2006	25
	2. *Blečić* v. *Croatia*, Application No 59532/00, Judgment of 8 March 2006	
	3. *Cocchiarella* v. *Italy*, Application No 64886/01, Judgment of 29 March 2006	
	4. *Jalloh* v. *Germany*, Application No 46410/99, Judgment of 11 July 2006	
	5. *Markovic and others* v. *Italy*, Application No 1398/03, Judgment of 14 December 2006	

(*cont.*)

Year	Judgments in which the ECtHR has mentioned European or comparative law	Total number of judgments
	6. *Mostacciuolo Giuseppe* v. *Italy (No 1)*, Application No 64705/01, Judgment of 29 March 2006	
	7. *Mostacciuolo Giuseppe* v. *Italy (No 2)*, Application No 65102/01, Judgment of 29 March 2006	
	8. *Musci* v. *Italy*, Application No 64699/01, Judgment of 29 March 2006	
	9. *Procaccini Giuseppina and Orestina* v. *Italy*, Application No 65075/01, Judgment of 29 March 2006	
	10. *Ramirez Sanchez* v. *France*, Application No 59450/00, Judgment of 4 July 2006	
	11. *Riccardi Pizzati* v. *Italy*, Application No 62361/00, Judgment of 29 March 2006	
	12. *Scordino* v. *Italy (No 1)*, Application No 36813/97, Judgment of 29 March 2006	
	13. *Sorensen and Rasmussen* v. *Denmark*, Application No 52562/99 and 52620/99, Judgment of 11 January 2006	
	14. *Stec and others* v. *the United Kingdom*, Application No 65731/01 and 65900/01, Judgment of 12 April 2006	
	15. *Üner* v. *the Netherlands*, Application No 59450/00, Judgment of 18 October 2006	
	16. *Zullo Ernestina* v. *Italy*, Application No 64897/01, Judgment of 29 March 2006	
2007	1. *Anheuser-Busch Inc.* v. *Portugal*, Application No 73049/01, Judgment of 11 January 2007	12
	2. *D. H. and others* v. *the Czech Republic*, Application No 57325/00, Judgment of 13 November 2007	
	3. *Dickson* v. *the United Kingdom*, Application No 44362/04, Judgment of 4 December 2007	
	4. *Evans* v. *the United Kingdom*, Application No 6339/05, Judgment of 10 April 2007	
	5. *Stoll* v. *Switzerland*, Application No 69698/01, Judgment of 10 December 2007	
	6. *Vilho Eskelinen and others* v. *Finland*, Application No 63235/00, Judgment of 19 April 2007	

(*cont.*)

Year	Judgments in which the ECtHR has mentioned European or comparative law	Total number of judgments
2008	1. *Burden* v. *United Kingdom*, Application No 13378/05, Judgment of 29 April 2008 2. *Demir and Baykara* v. *Turkey*, Application No 34503/97, Judgment of 12 November 2008 3. *E. B.* v. *France*, Application No 43546/02, Judgment of 22 January 2008 4. *Guja* v. *Moldova*, Application No 14277/04, Judgment of 12 February 2008 5. *Kafkaris* v. *Cyprus*, Application No 21906/04, Judgment of 12 February 2008 6. *Korbely* v. *Hungary*, Application No 9174/02, Judgment of 19 September 2008 7. *Kovačić and others* v. *Slovenia*, Application No 44574/98, 45133/98 and 48316/99, Judgment of 3 October 2008 8. *Maslov* v. *Austria*, Application No 1638/03, Judgment of 23 June 2008 9. *Ramanauskas* v. *Lithuania*, Application No 74420/01, Judgment of 5 February 2008 10. *S. and Marper* v. *the United Kingdom*, Application No 30562/04 and 30566/04, Judgment of 4 December 2008 11. *Saadi* v. *Italy*, Application No 37201/06, Judgment of 12 February 2008 12. *Saadi* v. *the United Kingdom*, Application No 13229/03, Judgment of 29 January 2008 13. *Salduz* v. *Turkey*, Application No 36391/02, Judgment of 27 November 2008 14. *Yumak and Sadak* v. *Turkey*, Application No 10226/03, Judgment of 8 July 2008	17
2009	1. *A.* v. *the United Kingdom*, Application No 3455/05, Judgment of 19 February 2009 2. *Andrejeva* v. *Latvia*, Application No 55707/00, Judgment of 18 February 2009 3. *Enea* v. *Italy*, Application No 74912/01, Judgment of 17 September 2009	18

(cont.)

Year	Judgments in which the ECtHR has mentioned European or comparative law	Total number of judgments
	4. *Guiso-Gallisay* v. *Italy*, Application No 58858/00, Judgment of 22 December 2009	
	5. *Kart* v. *Turkey*, Application No 8917/05, Judgment of 3 December 2009	
	6. *Kozacıoğlu* v. *Turkey*, Application No 2334/03, Judgment of 19 February 2009	
	7. *Micallef* v. *Malta*, Application No 17056/06, Judgment of 15 October 2009	
	8. *Paladi* v. *Moldova*, Application No 39806/05, Judgment of 10 March 2009	
	9. *Scoppola* v. *Italy (No 2)*, Application No 10249/03, Judgment of 17 September 2009	
	10. *Sejdić and Finci* v. *Bosnia and Herzegovina*, Application No 27996/06 and 34836/06, Judgment of 22 December 2009	
	11. *Sergey Zolotukhin* v. *Russia*, Application No 14939/03, Judgment of 10 February 2003	
	12. *Šilih* v. *Slovenia*, Application No 71463/01, Judgment of 9 April 2009	
	13. *Varnava and others* v. *Turkey*, Application No 16064/90, Judgment of 18 September 2009	
	14. *Verein Gegen Tierfabriken Schweiz (VgT)* v. *Switzerland (No 2)*, Application No 32772/02, Judgment of 30 June 2009	
2010	1. *A., B. and C.* v. *Ireland*, Application No 25579/05, Judgment of 16 December 2010	18
	2. *Brosset-Triboulet and others* v. *France*, Application No 34078/02, Judgment of 29 March 2010	
	3. *Carson and others* v. *the United Kingdom*, Application No 42184/05, Judgment of 16 March 2010	
	4. *Cudak* v. *Lithuania*, Application No 15869/02, Judgment of 23 March 2010	
	5. *Depalle* v. *France*, Application No 34044/02, Judgment of 29 March 2010	
	6. *Gäfgen* v. *Germany*, Application No 22978/05, Judgment of 1 June 2010	

(cont.)

Year	Judgments in which the ECtHR has mentioned European or comparative law	Total number of judgments
	7. *Kononov* v. *Latvia*, Application No 36376/04, Judgment of 17 May 2010	
	8. *Mangouras* v. *Spain*, Application No 12050/04, Judgment of 28 September 2010	
	9. *Medvedyev and others* v. *France*, Application No 3394/03, Judgment of 29 March 2010	
	10. *Neulinger and Shuruk* v. *Switzerland*, Application No 41615/07, Judgment of 6 July 2010	
	11. *Oršuš and others* v. *Croatia*, Application No 15766/03, Judgment of 16 March 2010	
	12. *Perdigão* v. *Portugal*, Application No 24768/06, Judgment of 16 November 2010	
	13. *Sanoma Uitgevers BV* v. *the Netherlands*, Application No 38224/03, Judgment of 14 September 2010	
	14. *Şerife Yiğit* v. *Turkey*, Application No 3976/05, Judgment of 2 November 2011	
	15. *Tănase* v. *Moldova*, Application No 7/08, Judgment of 27 April 2010	
	16. *Taxquet* v. *Belgium*, Application No 926/05, Judgment of 16 November 2010	
2011	1. *Al-Jedda* v. *the United Kingdom*, Application No 27021/08, Judgment of 7 July 2011	13
	2. *Al-Khawaja and Tahery* v. *the United Kingdom*, Application No 26766/05 and 22228/06, Judgment of 15 December 2011	
	3. *Al-Skeini and others* v. *the United Kingdom*, Application No 55721/07, Judgment of 7 July 2011	
	4. *Bayatyan* v. *Armenia*, Application No 23459/03, Judgment of 7 July 2011	
	5. *Giuliani and Gaggio* v. *Italy*, Application No 23458/02, Judgment of 24 March 2011	
	6. *Lautsi and others* v. *Italy*, Application No 30814/06, Judgment of 18 March 2011	
	7. *M.S.S.* v. *Belgium and Greece*, Application No 30696/09, Judgment of 21 January 2011	

(cont.)

Year	Judgments in which the ECtHR has mentioned European or comparative law	Total number of judgments
	8. *Nejdet Şahin and Perihan Şahin* v. *Turkey*, Application No 13279/05, Judgment of 20 October 2011 9. *Paksas* v. *Lithuania*, Application No 34932/04, Judgment of 6 January 2011 10. *Palomo Sánchez and others* v. *Spain*, Application No 28955/06, 28957/06, 28959/06 and 28964/06, Judgment of 12 September 2011 11. *S.H. and others* v. *Austria*, Application No 57813/00, Judgment of 3 November 2011 12. *Sabeh El Leil* v. *France*, Application No 34869/05, Judgment of 29 June 2011 13. *Stummer* v. *Austria*, Application No 37452/02, Judgment of 7 July 2011	
2012	1. *Aksu* v. *Turkey*, Application No 4149/04 and 41029/04, Judgment of 15 March 2012 2. *Axel Springer AG* v. *Germany*, Application No 39954/08, Judgment of 7 February 2012 3. *Boulois* v. *Luxembourg*, Application No 37575/04, Judgment of 3 April 2012 4. *Catan and others* v. *Moldova and Russia*, Application No 43370/04, 18454/06 and 8252/05, Judgment of 19 October 2012 5. *Centro Europa 7 S.r.l. and Di Stefano* v. *Italy*, Application No 38433/09, Judgment of 7 June 2012 6. *Chabauty* v. *France*, Application No 57412/08, Judgment of 4 October 2012 7. *El-Masri* v. *the former Yugoslav Republic of Macedonia*, Application No 39630/09, Judgment of 13 December 2012 8. *Gillberg* v. *Sweden*, Application No 41723/06, Judgment of 3 April 2012 9. *Herrmann* v. *Germany*, Application No 9300/07, Judgment of 26 June 2012 10. *Hirsi Jamaa and others* v. *Italy*, Application No 27765/09, Judgment of 23 February 2012	26

(cont.)

Year	Judgments in which the ECtHR has mentioned European or comparative law	Total number of judgments
	11. *Konstantin Markin* v. *Russia*, Application No 30078/06, Judgment of 22 March 2012	
	12. *Kotov* v. *Russia*, Application No 54522/00, Judgment of 3 April 2012	
	13. *Kurić and others* v. *Slovenia*, Application No 26828/06, Judgment of 12 March 2012	
	14. *Mouvement raëlien suisse* v. *Switzerland*, Application No 16354/06, Judgment of 13 July 2012	
	15. *Nada* v. *Switzerland*, Application No 10593/08, Judgment of 12 September 2012	
	16. *Sabri Güneş* v. *Turkey*, Application No 27396/06, Judgment of 29 June 2012	
	17. *Scoppola* v. *Italy (No 3)*, Application No 126/05, Judgment of 22 May 2012	
	18. *Sitaropoulos and Giakoumopoulos* v. *Greece*, Application No 42202/07, Judgment of 15 March 2012	
	19. *Souza Ribeiro* v. *France*, Application No 22689/07, Judgment of 13 December 2012	
	20. *Stanev* v. *Bulgaria*, Application No 36760/06, Judgment of 17 January 2012	
	21. *Van der Heijden* v. *the Netherlands*, Application No 42857/05, Judgment of 3 April 2012	
	22. *Von Hannover* v. *Germany (No 2)*, Application No 40660/08 and 60641/08, Judgment of 7 February 2012	
2013	1. *Allen* v. *the United Kingdom*, Application No 25424/09, Judgment of 12 July 2013	12
	2. *Animal Defenders International* v. *the United Kingdom*, Application No 48876/08, Judgment of 22 April 2013	
	3. *Del Río Prada* v. *Spain*, Application No 42750/09, Judgment of 21 October 2013	
	4. *Fabris* v. *France*, Application No 16574/08, Judgment of 7 February 2013	
	5. *Janowiec and others* v. *Russia*, Application No 55508/07 and 29520/09, Judgment of 21 October 2013	

(cont.)

Year	Judgments in which the ECtHR has mentioned European or comparative law	Total number of judgments
	6. *Maktouf and Damjanović* v. *Bosnia and Herzegovina*, Application No 2312/08 and 34179/08, Judgment of 18 July 2013
7. *Sindicatul 'Păstorul cel Bun'* v. *Romania*, Application No 2330/09, Judgment of 9 July 2013
8. *Söderman* v. *Sweden*, Application No 5786/08, Judgment of 12 November 2013
9. *Vallianatos and others* v. *Greece*, Application No 29381/09 and 32684/09, Judgment of 7 November 2013
10. *Vinter and others* v. *the United Kingdom*, Application No 66069/09, 130/10 and 3896/10, Judgment of 9 July 2013
11. *X. and others* v. *Austria*, Application No 19010/07, Judgment of 19 February 2013
12. *X.* v. *Latvia*, Application No 27853/09, Judgment of 26 November 2013	

INDEX

abstraction of consensus, 14
ad hoc argument, 10, 17, 73, 79, 140
African Commission on Human Rights, 128
Ahern, S., 76–77
Ambrus, M., 14
amicus curiae briefs, 108
anti-majoritarian argument, 2, 4–6, 116–122
  against consensus, 116–122
  human rights, 5
  proponents of, 5
Arai-Takahashi, Y., 79
Article 38, International Court of Justice (ICJ) Statute, 161
assessment stage (European consensus), 3, 24–27
  comparative law and international treaties, 60–65
  consensus among experts and, 55–56
  consensus interactions, 56–65
  consensus types, 39, 71
  convention and protocols text, 30–32
  evolutive interpretation, margin of appreciation, 129–142, 150–152
  historical and political justification, 32–34
  and internal consensus, 57–59
  internal consensus, respondent State, 49–55
  international treaties and, 45–49
  international trends and, 65–71
  judges' perceptions, 7
  laws and practice of Contracting Parties, comparative analysis, 40–45
  limited deployment reasons, 21–23
  limits, moral sensitivity, 34–36
  Mahoney-Kondack approach to, 29–30

Austrian law, same-sex marriages in, 126

Bailey, K. D., 181
Bakircioglu, O.r, 133–134
Barak, A., 76
Bayatyan v. Armenia, 15
Benvenisti, E., 122–123, 127, 149–150
Bîrsan, C., 103, 190
Brauch, J., 70
Brems, E., 45–46, 120
Brighton Declaration, 157
British law, 26, 64
Brun, N., 164
Buchanan, A., 151

Caflisch, L., 76
Çalı, B., 164
Carozza, P. G., 72
Cassese. S., 162
cherry-picking criticism, comparative law, 103
comparative law, ECtHR, 109
  benefits of outsourcing, 93–94
  challenges in, 111, 197
  cherry-picking criticism, 103
  complexity of, 95
  Court's deployment of, 94, 95
  European consensus based on, 57–59
  importance of, 80
  Judgments of Grand Chamber in, 97
  level of, 7, 14–15
  materials, ECtHR, 24
  purposes of, 74–78, 101
  research prepared by ECtHR, 86–92
  statistical approach to, 44
  transparent outline of, 105
comparative legal analysis, ECtHR
  comparative law purposes, 74–78

INDEX

comparative legal research,
  evolution, 78–81
  comprehensive comparative
    research and, 102–105
  Contracting Parties laws and
    practice, 40–45
  ECtHR law research, 86–97
  factual justification, criticism, 82–84
  fit, vision, 74–77
  information, persuasion, 77–78
  key challenges, 101–114
  legal provisions in context and,
    105–109
  legitimising solutions, 73
  recourse to previous findings,
    criticism, 84–86
  subject matter of comparison and,
    109–110
  third-party comparative research,
    97–101
  translation of legal terms and,
    111–113
comparative legal research, 78–81
  conducted by third parties, 97–101
  criticism of, 78–81
  evolution of, 82
  prepared by the ECtHR, 86–92
comprehensive comparative research,
  102–105
consensus typology, 38–55, 71
continuing international trend, 66–71
Contracting Parties
  analysis of national laws of, 71
  comparative legal analysis, 40–45
  comprehensive and transparent
    analysis of, 27
  domestic legal provisions
    of, 94
  implicit consent of, 67
  individual laws of, 124
  and international law, 2
  and legitimacy, 145–146, 155–158
  margin of appreciation of, 78
  national authorities of, 100
  national laws of, 32
  positive obligations of, 17–18
  sovereign consent of, 130
  trend in laws of, 12
variety and complexity of legal
  systems of, 83
warning mechanism for, 121
corporal punishment, 51, 60
counter-majoritarian, 144, 168
criticism anti-majoritarian argument,
  2, 4–6, 116–122
  evolutive interpretation, margin of
    appreciation, 129–142, 150–152
  and factual justification, 82–84
  minority rights challenge, 122–129
  procedural vs. substantive, 115
  and recourse to previous findings,
    84–86

Dahl, R. A., 159
Davis, D., 64
De Cruz, P., 106
de Londras, F., 60–63, 145–146, 158
deployment stage of consensus, 3, 27–29
  comparative law, 114
  of European consensus, 115, 116
  of international law, 46
  reasons for limited, 21–23
Drzemczewski, A., 47
Dudgeon v. the United Kingdom, 34
Dworkin, R., 159

ECtHR, *see* European Court of Human
  Rights
English law, 50
Epstein, L., 179–180
European consensus
  application in action, 23–30
  assessment stage, *see* assessment
    stage, European consensus
  based on international treaties, 45–49
  concept of, 9
  consensus levels, 14–17
  criticism anti-majoritarian
    argument, 2, 4–6, 116–122
  definition of, 10
  ECtHR judges perceptions, *see*
    judges perceptions, ECtHR
  identification of, 2, 4
  judges use of, 182–189
  persuasive effect of, 189–196
  presence/absence of, 26

INDEX 227

principles level, 16–17
reason for application of, 1–2
rules level, 15–16
substantive criticism of, 122
terminology, 10–13
European consensus, spread of consensus importance, 17–20
  freedom of association (Article 11), 19
  freedom of expression (Article 10), 19
  freedom of religion (Article 9), 19
  prohibition of slavery, and forced labour (Article 4), 18
  prohibition of torture (Article 3), 18
  property rights (Article 1, Protocol 1), 20
  right to education (Article 2, Protocol 1), 20
  right to fair trial (Article 6), 18
  right to liberty and security (Article 5), 18
  right to life (Article 2), 17
  right to marry (Article 12), 20
  right to privacy (Article 8), 18–19
  voting rights (Article 3, Protocol 1), 20
European Court of Human Rights (ECtHR)
  clarity and foreseeability of, 38
  comparative law reports, *see* comparative law, ECtHR
  comparative legal analysis, *see* comparative legal analysis, ECtHR
  consensus identification, selection by, 4
  credibility of, 72
  European consensus, *see* judges perceptions, ECtHR
  European public order, 77
  human rights disputes, 74
  internal consensus, 50, 62
  judges perceptions, *see* judges perceptions, ECtHR
  legitimacy, *see* legitimacy, ECtHR
  prima facie legitimacy of, 1
  Research Division, 41, 86–97
  structural deficiencies, 1

types of consensus, 39
U.S. Supreme Court and, 174
European public order, 95, 154
  Court's role in shaping, 74
  principles of, 77
evolutive interpretation, margin of appreciation, 129–142, 150–152
experts, consensus among, 55–56

Fallon, R., 171
Flanagan, B., 76–77
freedom of association (Article 11), 19
freedom of expression (Article 10), 19
freedom of religion (Article 9), 19

Garlicki, L., 82, 187, 190–191, 203
Gross, O., 134

Habermas, J., 159
Helfer, L. R., 121
Higgins, R., 134
Hoffman, L., 75–76
Hollobone, P., 64
human rights
  adjudication, 4
  collective protection of, 120
  complex and sensitive, 7
  conduct investigations of, 90
  counter-majoritarian nature of, 54
  development of, 121
  disputes, 74
  domestic safeguards against, 5
  European, 55
  moral foundations of, 117
  moral prevalence of, 6
  moral value of, 118
  national legal systems, domestic safeguards, 5–6
  norms, 119
  protection, 74, 88
  regional, 73, 74
  restrictive/conservative approaches to, 128
  standards for Europe, 90

Inter-American Court of Human Rights (IACtHR), 80, 127
intermediary sex, 68

internal consensus, 50, 62
  analysis of, 64–65
  argument, 51, 52
  European consensus and, 38, 60
  and expert consensus, 40
  methodology of identification of, 53, 54
  within respondent State, 49–55
  trumping, 62–63
International Court of Justice (ICJ) Statute Article 38, 161
international law
  classical legitimising factor in, 155
  comparative and, 114
  consensus as source of, 158–165
  Contracting Parties and, 2
  development in, 124
  European and, 58
  materials, 48
  recognised sources of, 161
  voluntarism of, 151
  voluntary nature of, 149
international treaties, 4, 39, 45–49
  analysis of, 45
  European consensus based on, 45–49, 57–59
international trends, 65–71
  among democratic nations, 67
  concept of, 67
  reliance on, 66, 70
interpretation
  methods of, 20, 27, 66, 72, 117
  primary principles of, 118
Islamic law, 67

Jaeger, R., 107, 182–183, 191–192
Johnson, P., 132
judges perceptions, ECtHR, 7
  comparative research, procedural criticism, 196–201
  judges use of European consensus, 182–189
  persuasive effect of European consensus, 189–196
  research design, methodology, 178–182

Kamba, W. J., 111
Kavanaugh. A., 170–171
Kelsen, H., 159
King, G., 179–180
Koch, A., 164
Krisch, N., 155, 156

laws and practice of Contracting Parties, comparative analysis, 40–45
legal provisions in comparative legal analysis, 105–109
legal terms translation, comparative legal analysis, 111–113
Legg, A., 80–81
legitimacy, ECtHR, 6–7
  challenges to, 143–144
  comparative legal analysis, legitimising solutions, 73
  consensus as source of international law and, 158–165
  Contracting Parties and, 145–146, 155–158
  counter-majoritarian view and, 143–144, 167–175
  evolutive interpretation and, 150–152
  human rights moral value and, 143
  international constitutional challenges, State consent, 149–155
  national constitutional challenges, 167–175
  original consent and, 144–145
  subsidiarity and, 165–167
legitimacy wall, 155
Letsas, G., 116–117, 119–120, 122, 153
level of consensus, 14–15
level of principles, consensus at, 16–17
level of rules, consensus at, 15–16
Lever, A., 171
limited deployment of consensus, reasons for, 21–23
Lukashevich, V., 77

MacDonald, R. St J., 134
Malinverni, G., 187, 191, 200, 203
margin of appreciation, 150–152
  breadth of, 135–136
  clarity in application of, 133–134

definition of, 134–135
interpretation and, 130–142
principal objection to, 134
scope of, 136
marriages, same-sex, *see* same-sex marriages
Martens, P., 122
McCrudden, C., 82–83
methods of interpretation, 20, 27, 66, 72, 117
minority rights
    challenges of, 122–129
    protection of, 126
moral sensitivity, 34–36
Morawa, A., 23–24
Mowbray, A., 31
municipal law, European consensus, 25
Murray, J. L., 39, 122
Myjer, E., 148, 186, 200

national constitutional courts, 167
national law, developments in, 50
Ní Aoláin, F., 134
non-governmental organisation (NGO)
    amicus curiae briefs, 108
    comparative data submitted by, 93
    human rights, 66
    practice of, 99
    ready-made comparative law reports submitted by, 100
    third-party interventions from, 98

O'Donnell, T. A., 134
Ostrovsky, A. A., 134

political morality, abstract values of, 117

Rozakis, C., 138, 186, 189

same-sex marriages
    in Austrian law, prohibition of, 126
    consensus in relation to, 25
    rights, 127

same-sex relationship, 26, *see also* same-sex marriages
Schmidt, B., 14–15
Shany, Y., 123
Slaughter, A.-M., 121
Strasbourg Court, 63, 152, 194
Strasbourg mechanism, 121
Straw, J., 64
subsidiarity, 165–167
substantive criticism, European consensus, 201–206
Sunstein, C. R., 174

transsexuals, 68
    legal recognition of, 55–56
    in Muslim world, 68
'trumping consensus' phenomenon, 60
Tulkens, F., 76, 79, 91–92, 107, 110, 190, 193
Tzevelekos, V., 162

Ünal Tekeli v. Turkey, 15
United Nations Convention Against Torture and Other Cruel, Inhuman or Degrading Inhuman or Degrading Treatment or Punishment, 16
United Nations Human Rights Committee (UNHRC), 80, 128
U.S. Supreme Court, 172–174

van der Meersch, G., 120
Vienna Convention on the Law of Treaties (VCLT), 47–48

Waldron, J., 154, 169–170
Weber, M., 159
Wildhaber, L., 138, 167

Yourow, H. C., 134–135

Ziemele, I., 161
Zwart, T., 81

For EU product safety concerns, contact us at Calle de José Abascal, 56–1°,
28003 Madrid, Spain or eugpsr@cambridge.org.